Books by Russell Stetler

The Battle of Bogside

The Military Art of People's War:
Selected Writings of General Vo Nguyen Giap

Palestine

The Arab-Israeli Conflict

A Ramparts Press Reader

Edited by Russell Stetler

Photographs by Jeffrey Blankfort

Ramparts Press
San Francisco, California

Acknowledgments

In the summer of 1971 all of us who were then working at Ramparts Press spent a weekend assessing the books we had worked on and collectively brainstorming about books which might be of value in the future. In the course of a general discussion on the need to extend the Press's international coverage, someone suggested that no area had been more neglected than the Middle East, despite the appearance of highly incisive analysis and reportage in scattered periodicals. We decided then to put together a Reader on Palestine, and I took responsibility for editing the volume. The book was a collective effort from the outset, and its strengths reflect the contributions of many individuals. Naturally, I accept sole responsibility not only for its shortcomings but also for the editorial opinions and judgments expressed herein.

I wish to thank Jim Mellen for reading my original selections and pinpointing the areas which required most development. Steve Halbrook and Robert Shanab also took an early interest in the project, and I appreciate their advice and help in selecting and obtaining materials. Most of all, I am indebted to Sheila Ryan, George Cavalletto, and Jeffrey Blankfort for sharing with me their personal experience of the Palestinian resistance. Part 3 of this book would not exist were it not for the important work of George and Sheila in

Amman in 1970 which uncovered several of the documents used here. As the book went to press, they helped generously to insure that the texts used were the most authentic. Jeff's photos deepen the book's impact enormously, but I am equally grateful for his friendship and for the many nights of discussions which added much to my understanding of the problems of the Middle East. I am of course very grateful to all the authors and original publishers of the selections for their cooperation and permission to reprint.

To my coworkers at Archetype and Ramparts Press, who shared the burden of rushing the Reader to completion and bearing with my belated revisions, I express my warmest thanks and love.

Contents

Introduction   11

Part One: The Setting
   1. The Six-Day War 25
   Isaac Deutscher

   2. The Class Nature of Israeli Society   53
   Haim Hanegbi, Moshe Machover and Akiva Orr

   3. Israel's Mission in Africa   91
   Africa Research Group

Part Two: The Palestinian Resistance Movement
   1. Origins of the Armed Resistance   117
   Leila S. Kadi

   2. Inside Fateh   146
   Gerard Chaliand

   3. Strategy for Revolution   168
   Popular Front for the Liberation of Palestine

   4. The August Program   190
   Democratic Popular Front for the Liberation of Palestine

   5. Jews and Arabs: One Future   201
   Naef Hawatmeh

   6. Towards a Democratic State in Palestine   205
   Fateh

Part Three: Black September
    1. Skyjack   223
    Interview with Leila Khaled
    2. Diary of a Resistance Fighter   241
    3. Black September: An Organized Retreat   259
    Interview with Yasser Arafat
    4. PFLP and the September Attack   267
    Interview with Ghassan Kannafani
    5. The Resistance After September: An Appraisal   281
    Robert Elias Abu Shanab
    6. An End   289
    Khalil al Hindi

Maps   28–31
Photo Captions   299

Introduction

Shortly before eight o'clock on the morning of June 5, 1967, Premier Kosygin was trying urgently to reach Lyndon Johnson on his direct space-age teletype circuit. The much-vaunted "hot line" was in use for the first time, so the Soviet leader had no way of knowing that the U.S. military had never bothered to connect it all the way to the White House. Like a macabre joke out of *Fail-Safe* or *Dr. Strangelove*, the hot line stopped at the Pentagon. Defense Secretary McNamara took the call and phoned LBJ at home to relay the message.* War had broken out in the Middle East. For the next six days the two superpowers would keep in close touch, working towards a cease-fire, as Israel destroyed the combined military might of Egypt, Jordan and Syria.

An hour or two before Kosygin's call, Israel had wiped out the entire Egyptian air force—demolished it on the ground in a blitzkrieg attack. Day by day, the Israeli tanks moved westward into the Sinai Peninsula, eastward into Jordan, and finally northward into the Golan Heights in Syria. Napalm

---

* See Lyndon Baines Johnson, *The Vantage Point: Perspective of the Presidency, 1963-1969* (New York: Holt, Rinehart & Winston, 1971). The excerpt "Crisis and War in the Mideast in 1967" appeared in the *New York Times*, October 23, 1971.

and similar implements of counterinsurgency, observed by
General Dayan in his inspection tour of South Vietnam a
year before, saw their first use in the Middle East; as always,
indiscriminate technology displayed its built-in capacity to
exact its heaviest toll on noncombatants. On the last day of
the war, the U.S. Sixth Fleet cruised closer to the Syrian
shore, as symbolic guarantor of the Israeli mission. The whole
episode was brief and stunning.

I was in England when the war erupted. For the past four
years I had spent most of my energy writing, speaking, and
campaigning against the war in Vietnam. This activity had
taken me to London, where I was working for the International War Crimes Tribunal initiated by Bertrand Russell
and presided over by Jean-Paul Sartre. For the tribunal's
whole staff of full-time political activists (drawn from many
different countries), the six-day war came as a rude shock.
Even the tribunal's most esteemed members—specialists in
ethics and politics—found themselves politically and intellec-
tually unprepared for the dramatic turn of events in the
Middle East. More than that, no one in the ranks of the
mounting antiwar movement would have expected the out-
burst of divisive irrationality which soon surrounded us.

In a sense, the very simplicity of Vietnam had deceived us
and fostered a rebirth of political naiveté. The unity of
Russell and Sartre in the tribunal was an emblem, in intellectual terms, of the breadth of the global opposition to the
Vietnam war. Contemporary philosophy's irreconcilables
were joined. The radical aristocrat, lifelong anticommunist,
followed cold and emotionless logic to a total condemnation
of American barbarism in Vietnam. The existential Marxist
rooted his same political conclusion in "the dialectical totality of reason and emotion." Vietnam had produced a
moral revulsion in what we might simply call thinking and
feeling people. The Arab-Israeli war seemed to be fought on
an altogether different terrain. Its complexity was paralyzing.

One of the most striking features of the controversy surrounding the war was the cynicism which appeared as the
private counterpart to public pomposity. I felt this on both
sides. Russell, for example, released statements which condemned Israel's aggression but pleaded that the state's right
to exist should not be confused with its unjustifiable expan-
sionism. In private, he was given to the anti-Semitism characteristic of the class of Victorian society into which he was
born. One of his associates happened, in fact, to be strongly
pro-Arab and anti-Zionist, but because the man was a Jew,
Russell didn't wait to hear his views. "We know which side
he'll take," Russell snapped, hours after the war began.
Russell's public stance of moderation (accepting Zionism and
merely deploring its excesses) was retribution for his private
prejudice.

A month later I was talking to an old friend, an attorney
from New York. His schizophrenia on the issue showed the
mirror image of Russell's. Publicly, he stood with Fidel
Castro and the revolutionary New Left in denouncing Israel;
more confidentially he confessed, "I just can't help feeling a
great pride, as a Jew, in the way we smashed them. We finally
showed 'em!" The cynics were as confused as everyone else.

In the aftermath of the June war there was an opportunity
for people to delve into their prejudices and re-think their
reactions to the Israeli victory. My own education on the
Middle East was intense in the period immediately following
the war, and it came most directly from two Israelis-in-exile,
the cartoonist Shimon Tzabar and the poet Dan Omer.
Tzabar, a native-born Palestinian Jew, lost his job as a cartoonist on Israel's "liberal" daily newspaper because of his
unpopular call for withdrawal from the territories occupied
in the June war. Blacklisted, he came to England and published a brilliant satirical paper called the *Israel Imperial
News,* which was a graphic expression of his "theory of
debacles." His thesis was that throughout history, the victors

inevitably lose the peace, and he marshaled scores of in-
stances where victory so deformed nations that they perished
of their own decay. As a theory of history, the "theory of
debacles" was rather whimsical, and I argued daily with him
about the implications of victory and defeat among the
Greek city states or the modern-day parties to the world
wars. But in the case which truly inspired his bizarre histori-
ography, the thesis was indisputable.

The *Imperial News* documented the story of Israel's transformation into a total military state: the demolition of some
seven thousand Arab homes between 1967 and 1969, render-
ing fifty thousand Arabs homeless (in addition to the new
refugees); tens of thousands of Arabs imprisoned; the extension of compulsory military service from thirty to thirty-six
months and increasing the age limit for service in the reserves
from forty-nine to fifty-five (thereby withdrawing 10 percent
more of the labor force from industry); and, perhaps dearest
to Tzabar as a veteran journalist, the suppression of civil
liberty and muzzling of the press. The debacle of victory was
to destroy the hope of peace with Israel's Arab neighbors. In
the name of secure borders, Israel had proceeded to encircle
tens of thousands of its enemy within its new frontiers. An
internal fifth column was thus created, and it would only be
a matter of time until the Arab population would naturally
increase to majority status in the new, "secure" state. The
myopic, gloating propaganda which came from Israel's equivalent of Madison Avenue, faithfully translated and reproduced in the *Imperial News,* provided ominous confirmation
of the debacle: "Visit the Pyramids in Israel," said an ad for
the local Kodak outlet.

Dan Omer, who shared my home in the summer of 1968,
had brought the poetry of America's beat generation to
Israel. Now parallel foreign policies in Washington and Tel
Aviv had begun to turn Israel's beats into a fledgling New
Left—drug busts gave way to political repression, as the kids

from Jerusalem's polytechnic found themselves in prison for painting "Out of the Occupied Territories" and "Fed Up with Imperialism" on walls. In another parallel, reminding me of the last epidemic of wedlock in the summer of 1965 when married men were still exempt from the Vietnam draft, Dan married in August 1968 so that his bride of eighteen could escape the universal Israeli conscription which did not discriminate between the sexes.

Dan Omer returned to Israel. It is his home, and one day he will hopefully be part of a new society shared by Arabs and Jews. Since the June war, a movement of Palestinian Arabs has appeared which is dedicated to building that society. Technically, the Palestinian national liberation movement predates the six-day war; but the war altered it so drastically as to make it effectively a new movement. The politics of 1967 was still rooted in a conflict of state powers: Israel pitted against the Arab triumvirate of Egypt, Syria, and Jordan. The Palestinians were a forgotten people, the anonymous refugees in UN camps. Their "official" spokesman, Ahmed Shukeiri (placeman of the "sympathetic" Arab states), disgraced his people during June 1967 with his racist bravado from Cairo radio, vowing to "drive the Jews into the sea." After 1967, Fateh, as well as the smaller Palestinian resistance groups, not only disavowed this racism but made a magnificent effort to overcome anti-Semitic feelings among camp dwellers who have known Israelis only as invading soldiers.

Unfortunately, Fateh's allies abroad have sometimes done the Palestinian movement a disservice in failing to be as subtle in their own understanding. In Algiers in early 1970, Fateh spokesmen at a Palestinian solidarity conference painstakingly clarified their attitude toward the future of the Jews in the Middle East. That same week, Eldridge Cleaver told Josie Fanon in an interview in *El Moujahid* that the Panthers and the Palestinians had one struggle: witness the pack of "Zionist" judges (Hoffman, Friedman, etc.) who were trying to railroad the Black Panther party to the electric chair!

One Jewish friend of mine returned from a couple of months of reporting on the Palestinian movement and said with amazement that he couldn't understand why the Palestinians didn't hate all Jews. From the outset, Zionism was insensitive to the fact that the land they colonized was already inhabited. Martin Buber related the incredible story of the early discovery of the Palestinian Arabs as follows: "When Max Nordau, Herzl's second-in-command, first received details on the existence of the Arab population in Palestine, he came shocked to Herzl, exclaiming, 'I never realized this—we are committing an injustice.' " Many decades later, Golda Meir suffered historical amnesia; she told *The Times* of London (June 15, 1969), "There was no such thing as Palestinians . . . It was not as though there was a Palestinian people and we came and threw them out and took their country away from them. They did not exist." It is true that the Palestinians didn't have a country, in the sense that they were always victim to one imperial ruler or another, whether the Ottoman Empire of the Turks, or Great Britain. Up to 1967, Palestine remained a pawn in the chess match of Arab diplomacy. Since then, the guerrilla movement has established the existence of the Palestinian nation, and no future settlement of the conflict will be possible without the accord of the Palestinian population.

The literature on the area has not kept abreast of this fact, and this Reader has been prepared as an elementary contribution toward filling this gap. I have tried to set the conflict in its new context, that of the confrontation between Israel and the Palestinian resistance. Part 1 of the book sketches in the background and offers a critique of contemporary Israel, exposing its entanglements in Africa and analyzing the mechanisms of social integration which make imminent change in Israel unlikely. On the other hand, I have avoided reiterating the standard leftist attack on Israel as the guarantor of the oil-rich Middle East for the Western imperial powers. The fact is that the main oil-producing countries in the Arab world (such as Saudi Arabia) are in themselves firm allies of imperialism. Western support of Israel is based on farther-reaching political considerations—such as indirect penetration of the new African nations—as our selections bear out.

Part 2 attempts to unveil the Palestinian resistance movement, through reportage and primary documents from the major groups who struggle for leadership of the resistance. None of this material has appeared in book form before, though it provides the essential backdrop for understanding the bare news reports that occasionally filter through to us concerning commandos in the Middle East. Ignorance about the Palestinian struggle has hardly been the monopoly of its opponents; much good will and sincere solidarity were summed up in the onetime SDS slogan, "Yes sir, Yasser; no sir, Nasser." The June war and subsequent discovery of the Palestinian movement coincided with a high point of Third World–oriented internationalism: the expansion of the Vietnam war into Laos, Che Guevara's mission in Bolivia, the OLAS conference in Havana calling for a continental revolution in Latin America. In this context, it was easy to expect that Fateh was a straightforward equivalent of the National Liberation Front of South Vietnam. What a shock it was, then, to see the divisions in the Palestinian movement which were apparent in the summer of 1970.

The hijackings demonstrated the visible split in the movement, but the relation of this tactic to politics was obscure. The PFLP hijackers argue that only a Marxist-Leninist party can lead the Palestinian struggle to victory. Fateh replies that leadership is generated in the guerrilla *foco*. But without the understanding that comes from reading these debates in the original documents, the events of September 1970 are a mystery.

Part 3 delves into this mystery; it seeks to shed some light on the causes and effects of the September events, as seen from a number of Palestinian viewpoints. "Black September" was King Hussein's Tet offensive in reverse: a bloodbath in which the resistance movements and their supporters were dealt hard blows. The documents included here contain the hijackers' self-defense, Yasser Arafat's contention that the events were a victory for the revolution, as well as more critical appraisals.

Needless to say, this collection is intended only to fill an existing need, not to offer a definitive perspective on rapidly changing events and situations. We can look forward in the coming months to more complete works (by Abdullah Schleifer later this year and by George Cavalletto and Sheila Ryan early next year) which I am convinced will help answer many of the questions which this book can only hope to raise in the reader's mind. Hopefully, new works will illuminate areas which we are unable even to touch on in this collection simply because there is a lack of written (not to say published) material on the subjects. For example, the divisions in Israeli society between European and Oriental Jews has given rise to a movement calling itself the "Israeli Black Panthers"—a name perhaps sensationally chosen but nonetheless indicative of the Sephardim's sense of racial discrimination. Traditional Israeli Marxists tend to dismiss this force in their analysis of Israel's class structure; but their large numbers (60 percent of the population) will compel further attention if a large block begins to move in a radical direction. The non-European Jews (or Jewish Arabs, as some call them) have always lived in peace with the Moslem Arabs. Indeed, one of the points that the Palestinians make is that it was Christian Europe's inability to get along with its Jews that drove the

European Jews to the Near East—where the non-European Jews had no problems. It seems that the Zionists may be destined to follow the path of the Crusaders, who benefited from the disunity among the Arabs to gain control of Palestine. Once there was unity among the Arabs, the conditions were balanced. What tipped the balance away from the Europeans were the non-European Christians (Greek, Armenian, Syrian), who were exploited and mistreated by the European Christians and ultimately sided with the Arabs to gain some liberation from the European Christians.

The most serious omission in this work is the lack of any treatment of the situation of women in the Middle East. Anyone unfamiliar with the debate concerning the relation of women's liberation to national liberation would do well to read the "Fourth World Manifesto,"* with its excellent discussion of the unfulfilled promise to the women who were so vital to the Algerian revolution. The traditional oppression of women in Moslem culture is too often refracted in the resistance movement. In Gerard Chaliand's inside description of Fateh, note how simply sex-determined roles are reproduced (women as nurses and teachers, men as doctors and fighters). Recently returned correspondents have been impressed with developments in, for example, the Democratic Popular Front for the Liberation of Palestine, encouraging the growth of women's organizations, careful attempts to "integrate" the formerly segregated political domain, and of course the organization of women's militias. But it would be an injustice to attempt to treat this subject at all in the absence of primary documents and firsthand accounts emanating from women. We will leave it to our Arab sisters to write that book.

* *See* Barbara Burris, "The Fourth World Manifesto," in Anne Koedt and Shulamith Firestone, editors, *Notes from the Third Year: Women's Liberation* (New York, 1971), pp. 102–119.

I believe this book does fill a need—that of informing ourselves on a conflict which may be of decisive importance to the seventies. At least, it removes from the Palestinians the stigma of a forgotten people and from us the shame of having forgotten them.

RUSSELL STETLER
Oakland, California
March 1972

The Setting

1. The Six-Day War

Isaac Deutscher

This article is based on an interview which Isaac Deutscher granted to the New Left Review *on June 23, 1967, just a few weeks before his death. Originally published that year in the journal's July-August issue, it was later revised by Deutscher's widow, Tamara, for inclusion in* The Non-Jewish Jew *(New York: Oxford University Press, 1968).*

The war and the "miracle" of Israel's victory have solved none of the problems that confront Israel and the Arab states. They have, on the contrary, aggravated all the old issues and created new, more dangerous ones. They have not increased Israel's security, but have rendered it more vulnerable than it had been before June 5, 1967. This "six-day wonder," this latest, all-too-easy triumph of Israeli arms will be seen one day, in a not very remote future, to have been a disaster in the first instance for Israel itself.

Let us consider the international background. We have to relate this war to the great power struggle and ideological conflicts in the world which form its context. In these last years, American imperialism and the forces associated with it and supported by it have been engaged in a tremendous political, ideological, economic, and military offensive over a vast area of Asia and Africa; while the forces opposed to the American penetration, the Soviet Union in the first instance, have barely held their ground or have been in retreat. This trend emerges from a long series of events: the Ghanaian upheaval, in which Nkrumah's government was overthrown; the growth of reaction in various Afro-Asian countries; the bloody triumph of anticommunism in Indonesia, which was a huge victory for counter-revolution in Asia; the escalation of the American war in Vietnam; and the "marginal" right-wing military coup in Greece. The Arab-Israeli war was not an isolated affair; it belongs to this category of events. The counter-trend has manifested itself in revolutionary ferment in various parts of India, the radicalization of the political mood in Arab countries, the effective struggle of the National Liberation Front in Vietnam; and the worldwide growth of opposition to American intervention. The advance of American imperialism and of Afro-Asian counter-revolution has not gone unopposed, but its success everywhere outside Vietnam has been evident.

In the Middle East the American forward push has been of relatively recent date. During the Suez war, the United States still adopted an "anticolonialist" stance. It acted, in seeming accord with the Soviet Union, to bring about the British and French withdrawal. The logic of American policy was still the same as in the late 1940s, when the state of Israel was in the making. As long as the American ruling class was interested primarily in squeezing out the old colonial powers from Africa and Asia, the White House was a mainstay of "anticolonialism." But having contributed to the debacle of the old empires, the United States took fright at the "power vacuum" that might be filled by native revolutionary forces or the Soviet Union or a combination of both. Yankee anticolonialism faded out, and America stepped in. In the Middle East this happened during the period between the Suez crisis and the last Israeli war. The American military landings in

Lebanon in 1958 were designed to stem a high tide of revolution in that area, especially in Iraq. Since then the United States, no doubt relying to some extent on Soviet "moderation," has avoided open and direct military involvement in the Middle East and maintained a posture of detachment. This posture does not make the American presence there any less real.

The Israelis have, of course, acted on their own motives, and not merely to suit the convenience of American policy. That their leaders and the great mass of Israelis believe themselves to be menaced by Arab hostility need not be doubted. That some "bloodthirsty" Arab declarations about "wiping Israel off the map" made Israeli flesh creep is evident. The Israelis are haunted by the memories of the Jewish tragedy in Europe and now feel isolated and encircled by the teeming millions of a hostile Arab world. Nothing was easier for their own propagandists, aided by Arab verbal excesses, than to play up the fear of another "final solution" threatening the Jews, this time in Asia. Conjuring up biblical myths and all the ancient religious-national symbols of Jewish history, the propagandists whipped up that frenzy of belligerence, arrogance, and fanaticism of which the Israelis gave such startling displays as they rushed to Sinai and the Wailing Wall and to Jordan and the walls of Jericho. Behind the frenzy and arrogance there lay Israel's suppressed sense of guilt towards the Arabs, the feeling that the Arabs would never forget or forgive the blows Israel had inflicted on them: the seizure of their land, the fate of a million or more refugees, and repeated military defeats and humiliations. Driven half-mad by fear of Arab revenge, the Israelis have, in their overwhelming majority, accepted the "doctrine" inspiring their government's policy, the "doctrine" that holds that Israel's security lies in periodic warfare which every few years must reduce the Arab states to impotence.

PARTITION OF PALESTINE

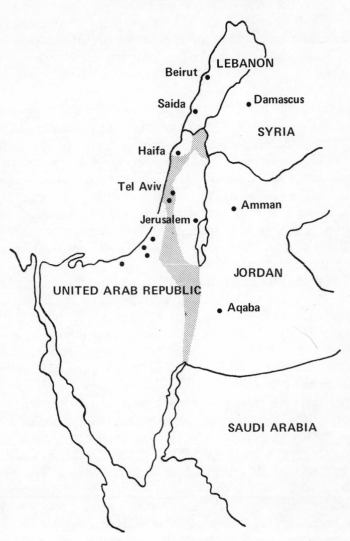

TERRITORY CONQUERED BY ISRAEL IN 1949

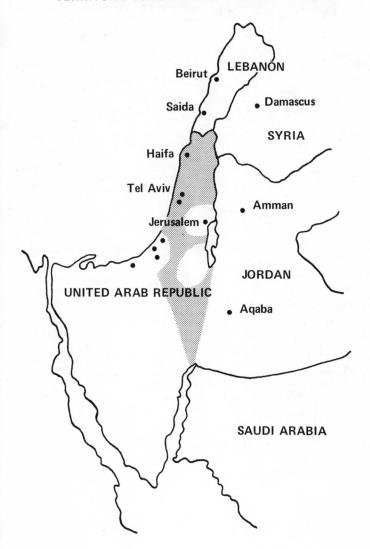

TERRITORY OCCUPIED BY ISRAEL IN 1956

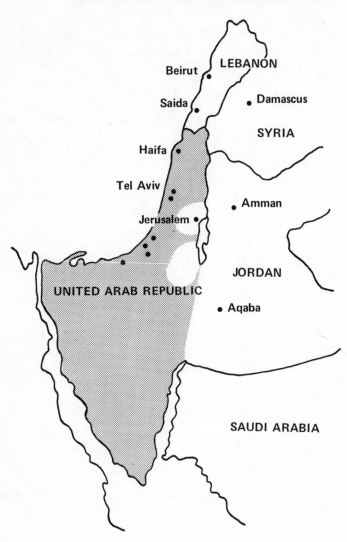

TERRITORY OCCUPIED BY ISRAEL IN 1967

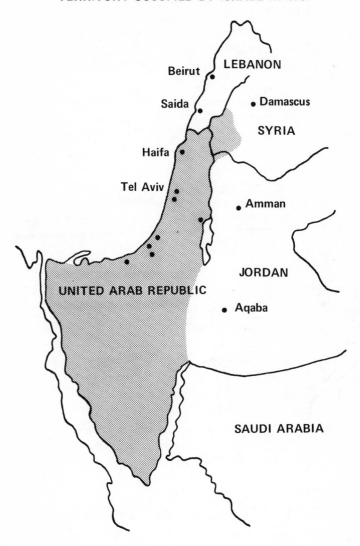

Yet, whatever their own motives and fears, the Israelis are not and cannot be independent agents. The factors of Israel's dependence were to some extent "built in" in its history over the last two decades. All Israeli governments have staked Israel's existence on its Western orientation. This alone would have sufficed to turn Israel into a Western outpost in the Middle East, and so to involve it in the great conflict between imperialism (or neocolonialism) and the Arab peoples struggling for their emancipation. Other factors have been in play as well. Israel's economy has depended for its tenuous balance and growth on foreign Zionist financial aid, especially on American donations. These donations have been a curse in disguise for the new state. They have enabled the government to manage its balance of payments in a way in which no country in the world can do it, without engaging in any trade with its neighbors. The influx of foreign funds has distorted Israel's economic structure by encouraging the growth of a large, unproductive sector and a standard of living which is not related to the country's own productivity and earnings. This has, of course, unfailingly kept Israel well within the Western sphere of influence. Israel has in effect lived far above its means. Over many years nearly half of Israel's food was imported from the West. As the American administration exempts from taxation earnings and profits earmarked as donations for Israel, the Treasury in Washington has held its hand on the purses on which Israel's economy depends. Washington could at any time hit Israel by refusing the tax exemption (even though this would lose it the Jewish vote in elections). The threat of such a sanction, never uttered but always present, and occasionally hinted at, has been enough to align Israeli policy firmly with the U.S.

Years ago, when I visited Israel, a high Israeli official listed to me the factories that they could not build because of American objections—among them steel mills and plants producing agricultural machinery. On the other hand, there was a list of virtually useless factories turning out fantastic amounts of plastic kitchen utensils, toys, etc. Nor could any Israeli administration ever feel free to consider seriously Israel's vital, long-term need for trade and close economic ties with its Arab neighbors or for improving economic relations with the U.S.S.R. and Eastern Europe.

Economic dependence has affected Israel's domestic policy and cultural atmosphere in other ways as well. The American donor is also the most important foreign investor operating in the Holy·Land. A wealthy American Jew, a worldly business-man among his gentile associates and friends in New York, Philadelphia or Detroit, is at heart proud to be a member of the Chosen People, and in Israel he exercises his influence in favor of religious obscurantism and reaction. A fervent be-liever in free enterprise, he views with a hostile eye even the mild "socialism" of the Histadruth and kibbutzim, and has done his bit in taming it. Above all, he has helped the rabbis to maintain their stranglehold on legislation and much of the education and so to keep alive the spirit of racial-talmudic exclusiveness and superiority. All this has fed and inflamed the antagonism towards the Arabs.

The cold war imparted great momentum to the reactionary trends in Israel and exacerbated the Arab-Jewish conflict. Israel was firmly committed to anticommunism. True, Stalin's policy in his last years, outbreaks of anti-semitism in the U.S.S.R., anti-Jewish motifs in the trials of Slansky, Rajk, and Kostov, and Soviet encouragement of even the most irra-tional forms of Arab nationalism, all bear their share of responsibility for Israel's attitude. Yet it should not be for-gotten that Stalin had been Israel's godfather; that it was with Czechoslovak munitions, supplied on Stalin's orders, that the Jews had fought the British occupation army—and the Arabs—in 1947–48; and that the Soviet envoy was the first to vote for the recognition of the state of Israel by the

United Nations. It may be argued that Stalin's change of attitude towards Israel was itself a reaction to Israel's alignment with the West. And in the post-Stalin era the Israeli governments have persisted in this alignment.

Irreconcilable hostility to Arab aspirations to unity and national emancipation from the West thus became *the* axiom of Israeli policy. Hence Israel's role in 1956, in the Suez war. Israel's Social Democratic ministers, no less than Western colonialists, have embraced a *raison d'état* which sees its highest wisdom in keeping the Arabs divided and backward and in playing their reactionary Hashemite and other feudal elements against the republican, national-revolutionary forces. Early in 1967, when it seemed that a republican uprising or coup might overthrow King Hussein, Mr. Eshkol's government made no bones about it that, in case of a "Nasserite coup" in Amman, Israeli troops would march into Jordan. And the prelude to the events of June 1967 was provided by Israel's adoption of a menacing attitude towards Syria's new regime which it denounced as "Nasserite" or even "ultra-Nasserite" (for Syria's government appeared to be a shade more anti-imperialist and radical than Egypt's).

Did Israel, in fact, plan to attack Syria some time in May, as Soviet intelligence services believed and as Moscow warned Nasser? We do not know. It was as a result of this warning, and with Soviet encouragement, that Nasser ordered mobilization and concentration of troops on the Sinai frontier. If Israel had such a plan, Nasser's move may have delayed the attack on Syria by a few weeks. If Israel had no such plan, its behavior gave to its anti-Syrian threats the kind of plausibility that Arab threats had in Israeli eyes. In any case, Israel's rulers were quite confident that their aggressiveness vis-à-vis either Syria or Egypt would meet with Western sympathy and bring them reward. This calculation underlay their decision to strike the pre-emptive blow on June 5. They were absolutely sure of American—and to some extent

British—moral, political, and economic support. They knew that no matter how far they went in attacking the Arabs, they could count on American diplomatic protection or, at the very least, on American official indulgence. And they were not mistaken. The White House and the Pentagon could not fail to appreciate men who, for their own reasons, were determined to put down the Arab enemies of American neo-colonialism. General Dayan acted as a kind of Marshal Ky for the Middle East and appeared to be doing his job with startling speed, efficiency, and ruthlessness. He was, and is, a much cheaper and far less embarrassing ally than Ky.

The Arab behavior, especially Nasser's divided mind and hesitation on the eve of the hostilities, presents a striking contrast to Israel's determination and uninhibited aggressiveness. Having, with Soviet encouragement, moved his troops to the Sinai frontier, and even put his Russian-made missiles in position, Nasser then, without consulting Moscow, proclaimed the blockade of the Straits of Tiran. This was a provocative move, though practically of very limited significance. The Western powers did not consider it important enough to try and "test" the blockade. It provided Nasser with a prestige gain and enabled him to claim that he had wrested from Israel the last fruit of their 1956 victory. (Before the Suez war Israeli ships could not pass these straits.) The Israelis played up the blockade as a mortal danger to their economy, which it was not; and they replied by mobilizing their forces and moving them to the frontiers.

Soviet propaganda continued to encourage the Arabs in public. However, a conference of Middle Eastern Communist parties held in May (its resolutions were summarized in *Pravda*) was strangely reticent about the crisis and allusively critical of Nasser. More important were the curious diplomatic maneuvers behind the scenes. On May 26, in the dead of night (at 2:30 A.M.), the Soviet ambassador woke up

Nasser to give him a grave warning that the Egyptian army must not be the first to open fire. Nasser complied. The compliance was so thorough that he not only refrained from starting hostilities, but took no precautions whatsoever against the possibility of an Israeli attack: he left his airfields undefended and his planes grounded and uncamouflaged. He did not even bother to mine the Tiran Straits or to place a few guns on their shores (as the Israelis found to their surprise when they got there).

All this suggests hopeless bungling on Nasser's part and on the part of the Egyptian command. But the real bunglers sat in the Kremlin. Brezhnev's and Kosygin's behavior during these events was reminiscent of Khrushchev's during the Cuban crisis, though it was even more muddle-headed. The pattern was the same. In the first phase there was needless provocation of the other side and a reckless move towards the brink; in the next, sudden panic and a hasty retreat; and then followed frantic attempts to save face and cover up the traces. Having excited Arab fears, encouraged them to risky moves, promised to stand by them, and having brought out their own naval units into the Mediterranean to counter the moves of the American Sixth Fleet, the Russians then tied Nasser hand and foot.

Why did they do it? As the tension was mounting, the "hot line" between the Kremlin and the White House went into action. The two super-powers agreed to avoid direct intervention and to curb the parties to the conflict. If the Americans went through the motions of curbing the Israelis, they must have done it so perfunctorily, or with so many winks, that the Israelis felt, in fact, encouraged to go ahead with their plan for the pre-emptive blow. (We have, at any rate, not heard of the American ambassador waking up the Israeli prime minister to warn him that the Israelis must not be the first to open fire.) The Soviet curb on Nasser was heavy, rude, and effective. Even so, Nasser's failure to take elementary military precautions remains something of a puzzle. Did the Soviet ambassador in the course of his nocturnal visit tell Nasser that Moscow was sure that the Israelis would not strike first? Had Washington given Moscow such an assurance? And was Moscow so gullible as to take it at face value and act on it? It seems almost incredible that this should have been so. But only some such version of the events can account for Nasser's inactivity and for Moscow's stunned surprise at the outbreak of hostilities.

Behind all this bungling there loomed the central contradiction of Soviet policy. On the one hand the Soviet leaders see in the preservation of the international status quo, including the social status quo, the essential condition of their national security and of "peaceful co-existence." They are therefore anxious to keep at a safe distance from storm centers of class conflict in the world and to avoid dangerous foreign entanglements. On the other hand, they cannot, for ideological and power-political reasons, avoid altogether dangerous entanglements. They cannot quite keep at a safe distance when American neocolonialism clashes directly or indirectly with its Afro-Asian and Latin American enemies, who look to Moscow as their friend and protector. In normal times this contradiction is only latent, Moscow works for détente and rapprochement with the U.S.A., and it cautiously aids and arms its Afro-Asian or Cuban friends. But sooner or later the moment of crisis comes and the contradiction explodes in Moscow's face. Soviet policy must then choose between its allies and protégés working against the status quo, and its own commitment to the status quo. When the choice is pressing and ineluctable, it opts for the status quo.

The dilemma is real and in the nuclear age dangerous enough. But it confronts the U.S.A. as well, for the U.S.A. is just as much interested as is the U.S.S.R. in avoiding world war and nuclear conflict. This, however, limits its freedom of action and of political-ideological offensive far less than it restricts Soviet freedom. Washington is far less afraid of the possibility that some move by one of its protégés, or its own military intervention, might lead to a direct confrontation of the super powers. After the Cuban crisis and the war in Vietnam, the Arab-Israeli war has once again sharply illuminated the difference.

To some extent the present situation has been determined by the whole course of Arab-Israeli relations since the Second World War and even since the First. Yet I believe that some options were open to the Israelis. There is a parable with the help of which I once tried to present this problem to an Israeli audience.

A man once jumped from the top floor of a burning house in which many members of his family had already perished. He managed to save his life; but as he was falling he hit a person standing down below and broke that person's legs and arms. The jumping man had no choice; yet to the man with the broken limbs he was the cause of his misfortune. If both behaved rationally, they would not become enemies. The man who escaped from the blazing house, having recovered, would have tried to help and console the other sufferer; and the latter might have realized that he was the victim of circumstances over which neither of them had control. But look what happens when these people behave irrationally. The injured man blames the other for his misery and swears to make him pay for it. The other, afraid of the crippled man's revenge, insults him, kicks him, and beats him up whenever they meet. The kicked man again swears revenge and is again punched and punished. The bitter enmity, so fortuitous at first, hardens and comes to overshadow the whole existence of both men and to poison their minds.

You will, I am sure, recognize yourselves (I said to my Israeli audience), the remnants of European Jewry in Israel, in the man who jumped from the blazing house. The other character represents, of course, the Palestinian Arabs, more than a million of them, who have lost their lands and their homes. They are resentful; they gaze from across the frontiers on their old native places; they raid you stealthily, and swear revenge. You punch and kick them mercilessly; you have shown that you know how to do it. But what is the sense of it? And what is the prospect?

The responsibility for the tragedy of European Jews, for Auschwitz, Majdanek, and the slaughters in the ghetto, rests entirely on our Western bourgeois "civilization," of which Nazism was the legitimate, even though degenerate, offspring. Yet it was the Arabs who were made to pay the price for the crimes the West committed towards the Jews. They are still made to pay it, for the "guilty conscience" of the West is, of course, pro-Israeli and anti-Arab. And how easily Israel has allowed itself to be bribed and fooled by the false "conscience money."

A rational relationship between Israelis and Arabs might have been possible if Israel had at least attempted to establish it, if the man who threw himself down from the burning house had tried to make friends with the innocent victim of his jump and to compensate him. This did not happen. Israel never even recognized the Arab grievance. From the outset Zionism worked towards the creation of a purely Jewish state and was glad to rid the country of its Arab inhabitants. No Israeli government has ever seriously looked for any opportunity to remove or assuage the grievance. They refused even to consider the fate of the huge mass of refugees unless the Arab states first recognized Israel—unless, that is, the Arabs surrendered politically before starting negotiations. Perhaps this might still be excused as bargaining tactics. The disastrous aggravation of Arab-Israeli relations was brought about by the Suez war, when Israel unashamedly acted as the spearhead of the old bankrupt European imperialisms in their last common stand in the Middle East, in their last attempt to maintain their grip on Egypt. The Israelis did not have to align themselves with the shareholders of the Suez Canal Company. The pros and cons were clear; there was no question of any mixture of rights and wrongs on either side. The Israelis put themselves totally in the wrong, morally and politically.

On the face of it, the Arab-Israeli conflict is only a clash of two rival nationalisms, each moving within the vicious circle of its self-righteous and inflated ambitions. From the viewpoint of an abstract internationalism nothing would be easier than to dismiss both as equally worthless and reactionary. However, such a view would ignore the social and political realities of the situation. The nationalism of the people in semicolonial or colonial countries, fighting for their independence, must not be put on the same moral-political level as the nationalism of conquerors and oppressors. The former has its historic justification and progressive aspect, which the latter has not. Clearly, Arab nationalism, unlike Israeli, still belongs to the former category.

Yet even the nationalism of the exploited and oppressed should not be viewed uncritically, for there are various phases in its development. In one phase progressive aspirations prevail; in another reactionary tendencies come to the surface. From the moment independence is won or nearly won, nationalism tends to shed its revolutionary aspect altogether and turns into a retrograde ideology. We have seen this happening in India, Indonesia, Israel, and to some extent even in China. And even in the revolutionary phase each nationalism has its streak of irrationality, an inclination to exclusiveness, national egoism and racism. Arab nationalism, despite all its historic merits and progressive functions, has also carried within itself these reactionary ingredients.

The June crisis has revealed some of the basic weaknesses of Arab political thought and action: the lack of political strategy; a proneness to emotional self-intoxication; and an excessive reliance on nationalist demagogy. These weaknesses were among the decisive causes of the Arab defeat. By indulging in threats of the destruction of Israel and even of "extermination"—and how empty these threats were has been amply demonstrated by the Arabs' utter military unpreparedness—some of Egypt's and Jordan's propagandists provided plenty of grist to Israeli chauvinism, and enabled Israel's government to work up the mass of its people into the paroxysm of fear and ferocious aggressiveness which then burst upon Arab heads.

It is a truism that war is a continuation of policy. The six-days' war has shown up the relative immaturity of the present Arab regimes. The Israelis owe their triumph not merely to the pre-emptive blow, but also to a more modern economic, political, and military organization. To some extent the war drew a balance on the decade of Arab development since the Suez war and has revealed its grave inadequacies. The modernization of the socio-economic structures of Egypt and the other Arab states and of Arab political thinking has proceeded far more slowly than people, inclined to idealize the present Arab regimes, have assumed.

The persisting backwardness is, of course, rooted in socio-economic conditions. But Arab ideology and methods of organization are in themselves factors of weakness. I have in mind the single-party system, the cult of Nasserism, and the absence of free discussion. All this has greatly hampered the political education of the masses and the work of socialist enlightenment. The negative results have made themselves felt on various levels. When major decisions of policy depend on a more or less autocratic leader, there is in normal times no popular participation in the political processes, no vigilant and active consciousness, no initiative from below. This has had many consequences, even military ones. The Israeli pre-emptive blow, delivered with conventional weapons, would not have had such devastating impact if Egypt's armed forces had been accustomed to rely on the initiative of individual officers and soldiers. Local commanders would then have taken the elementary defensive precautions without waiting for orders from above. Military inefficiency reflected here a wider and deeper social-political weakness. The military-bureaucratic methods of Nasserism also hamper the political integration of the Arab movement of liberation. Nationalist demagogy flourishes all too easily; but it is no substitute for a real impulse to national unity and for a real mobilization of popular forces against the divisive, feudal and reactionary elements. We have seen how, during the emergency, excessive reliance on a single leader made the fate of the Arab states dependent in fact on Great Power intervention and accidents of diplomatic maneuver.

Paradoxically and grotesquely, the Israelis appear now in the role of the Prussians of the Middle East. They have now won three wars against their Arab neighbors. Just so did the Prussians a century ago defeat all their neighbors within a few years, the Danes, the Austrians, and the French. The succession of victories bred in them an absolute confidence in their own efficiency, a blind reliance on the force of their arms, chauvinistic arrogance, and contempt for other peoples. I fear that a similar degeneration—for degeneration it is—may be taking place in the political character of Israel. Yet as the Prussia of the Middle East, Israel can be only a feeble parody of the original. The Prussians were at least able to use their victories for uniting in their Reich all German-speaking peoples living outside the Austro-Hungarian Empire. Germany's neighbors were divided among themselves by interest, history, religion, and language. Bismarck, Wilhelm II, and Hitler could play them off against one another. The Israelis are surrounded by Arabs only. Attempts to play off the Arab states against one another are bound to fail in the end. The

Arabs were at loggerheads with one another in 1948, when Israel waged its first war; they were far less divided in 1956, during Israel's second war; and they formed a common front in 1967. They may prove far more firmly united in any future confrontation with Israel.

The Germans have summed up their own experience in the bitter phrase: *"Man kann sich totsiegen!"* "You can drive yourself victoriously into your grave." This is what the Israelis have been doing. They have bitten off much more than they can swallow. In the conquered territories and in Israel there are now nearly a million and a half Arabs, well over 40 percent of the total population. Will the Israelis expel this mass of Arabs in order to hold "securely" the conquered lands? This would create a new refugee problem, more dangerous and larger than the old one. Will they give up the conquered territories? No, say most of their leaders. Ben-Gurion, the evil spirit of Israeli chauvinism, urges the creation of an "Arab Palestinian state" on the Jordan that would be an Israeli protectorate. Can Israel expect that the Arabs will accept such a protectorate? That they will not fight it tooth and nail? None of the Israeli parties is prepared even to contemplate a bi-national Arab-Israeli state. Meanwhile great numbers of Arabs have been "induced" to leave their homes on the Jordan, and the treatment of those who have stayed behind is far worse than that of the Arab minority in Israel that was kept under martial law for nineteen years. Yes, this victory is worse for Israel than a defeat. Far from giving Israel a higher degree of security, it has rendered it much more insecure. If Arab revenge and extermination is what the Israelis feared, they have behaved as if they were bent on turning a bogey into an actual menace.

There was a moment, at the cease-fire, when it looked as if Egypt's defeat had led to Nasser's downfall and to the undoing of the policy associated with his name. If that had happened, the Middle East would have almost certainly been brought back into the Western sphere of influence. Egypt might have become another Ghana or Indonesia. This did not happen, however. The Arab masses who came out in the streets and squares of Cairo, Damascus, and Beirut to demand that Nasser stay in office, prevented it from happening. This was one of those rare historic popular impulses that redress or upset a political balance within a few moments. This time, in the hour of defeat, the initiative from below worked with immediate impact. There are only very few cases in history when a people have stood by a defeated leader in this way. The situation is, of course, still fluid. Reactionary influences will go on working within the Arab states to achieve something like a Ghanaian or Indonesian coup. But for the time being, neocolonialism had been denied the fruit of Israel's "victory."

"The Russians have let us down!" was the bitter cry that came from Cairo, Damascus, and Beirut in June. And when the Arabs saw the Soviet delegate at the United Nations voting, in unison with the Americans, for a cease-fire to which no condition for a withdrawal of the Israeli troops was attached, they felt utterly betrayed. "The Soviet Union will now sink to the rank of a second- or fourth-rate power," Nasser was reported to have told the Soviet ambassador. The events appeared to justify the Chinese accusation of Soviet collusion with the United States. The debacle aroused an alarm in Eastern Europe as well. "If the Soviet Union could let Egypt down like this, may it not also let us down when we are once again confronted by German aggression?" the Poles and the Czechs wondered. The Yugoslavs, too, were outraged. Tito, Gomulka, and other leaders rushed to Moscow to demand an explanation and a rescue operation for the Arabs. This was all the more remarkable as the demand came from the "moderates" and the "revisionists" who normally stand for "peaceful coexistence" and rapprochement with the U.S.A. It was they who now spoke of Soviet "collusion with American imperialism."

The Soviet leaders had to do something. The fact that the intervention of the Arab masses had saved the Nasser regime unexpectedly provided Moscow with fresh scope for maneuver. After the great let-down, the Soviet leaders again came to the fore as the friends and protectors of the Arab states. A few spectacular gestures, breaking off diplomatic relations with Israel, and speeches at the United Nations, cost them little. Even the White House showed "understanding" for Moscow's "predicament" and for the "tactical necessity" which presently brought Kosygin to the United Nations Assembly.

However, something more than gestures was required to restore the Soviet position. The Arabs demanded that the Soviet Union should at once help them rebuild their military strength, the strength they had lost through compliance with Soviet advice. They asked for new planes, new tanks, new guns, new stocks of munitions. But apart from the cost this involved—the value of the military equipment lost by Egypt alone is put at a billion pounds—the reconstitution of the Arab armed forces carries, from Moscow's viewpoint, major political risks. The Arabs refuse to negotiate with Israel; they may well afford to leave Israel choke on its victory. Rearmament is Cairo's top priority. Israel has taught the Egyptians a lesson: next time the Egyptian air force may strike the pre-emptive blow. And Moscow has had to decide whether it will supply the weapons for that blow.

Moscow cannot favor the idea of such an Arab retaliation, but neither can it refuse to rearm Egypt. Yet Arab rearmament will almost certainly tempt Israel to interrupt the process and strike another pre-emptive blow—in which case the Soviet Union would once again be faced with the dilemma which worsted it in May and June. If Egypt were to strike first, the United States would almost certainly intervene. Its Sixth Fleet would not look on from the Mediterranean if the Israeli air forces were knocked out and the Arabs were about to march into Jerusalem or Tel Aviv. If the U.S.S.R. again kept out of the conflict, it would irretrievably destroy its international power position.

A week after the cease-fire the Soviet chief of staff was in Cairo; and Soviet advisers and experts crowded the hotels there, beginning to work on the reconstitution of Egypt's armed forces. Yet Moscow cannot face with equanimity the prospect of an Arab-Israeli competition in pre-emptive blows and its wider implications. Probably the Soviet experts in Cairo were making haste slowly, while Soviet diplomacy tried to "win the peace" for the Arabs after it had lost them the war. But even the most clever playing for time cannot solve the central issue of Soviet policy. How much longer can the Soviet Union adapt itself to the American forward push? How far can it retreat before the American economic-political and military offensives across the Afro-Asian area? Not for nothing did *Krasnaya Zvezda* already in June suggest that the current Soviet conception of peaceful coexistence might be in need of some revision. The military—and not they alone—fear that Soviet retreats are increasing the dynamic of the American forward push; and that if this goes on a direct Soviet-American clash may become inevitable. If Brezhnev and Kosygin do not manage to cope with this issue, changes in leadership are quite possible. The Cuban and Vietnamese crises contributed to Khrushchev's downfall. The full consequences of the Middle Eastern crisis have yet to unfold.

I do not believe that the conflict between Arabs and Israelis can be resolved by military means. To be sure, no one can deny the Arab states the right to reconstitute their armed forces to some extent. But what they need far more urgently is a social and political strategy and new methods in their struggle for emancipation. This cannot be a purely negative strategy dominated by the anti-Israeli obsession. They may refuse to parley with Israel as long as Israel has not given up its conquests. They will necessarily resist the occupation regime on the Jordan and in the Gaza strip. But this need not mean a renewal of war.

The strategy that can yield the Arabs far greater gain than those that can be obtained in any Holy War or through a pre-emptive blow, a strategy that would bring them real victory, a civilized victory, must be centered on the imperative and urgent need for an intensive modernization of the structure of the Arab economy and of Arab politics and on the need for a genuine integration of Arab national life, which is still broken up by the old, inherited and imperialist-sponsored frontiers and divisions. These aims can be promoted only if the revolutionary and socialist tendencies in Arab politics are strengthened and developed.

Finally, Arab nationalism will be incomparably more effective as a liberating force if it is disciplined and rationalized by an element of internationalism that will enable the Arabs to approach the problem of Israel more realistically than hitherto. They cannot go on denying Israel's right to exist and indulging in bloodthirsty rhetoric. Economic growth, industrialization, education, more efficient organization and more sober policies are bound to give the Arabs what sheer numbers and anti-Israeli fury have not been able to give them, namely, an actual preponderance which should almost automatically reduce Israel to its modest proportions and its proper role in the Middle East.

This is not, of course, a short-term program. Yet its realization need not take too much time; and there is no shorter way to emancipation. The short cuts of demagogy, revenge, and war have proved disastrous enough. Meanwhile, Arab policy should be based on a direct appeal to the Israeli people over the heads of the Israeli government, on an appeal to the workers and the kibbutzim. The latter should be freed from their fears by clear assurances and pledges that Israel's legitimate interests are respected and that Israel may even be welcome as a member of a future Middle Eastern Federation. This would cause the orgy of Israeli chauvinism to subside and would stimulate opposition to Eshkol's and Dayan's policy of conquest and domination. The capacity of Israeli workers to respond to such an appeal should not be underrated.

More independence from the Great Power game is also necessary. That game has distorted the social-political development of the Middle East. I have shown how much American influence has done to give Israel's policy its present repulsive and reactionary character. But Russian influence has also done something to warp Arab minds by feeding them with arid slogans, by encouraging demagogy, while Moscow's egoism and opportunism have fostered disillusionment and cynicism. If Middle East policy continues to be merely a plaything of the Great Powers, the prospect will be bleak indeed. Neither Jews nor Arabs will be able to break out of their vicious spirals. This is what we, of the left, should be telling both the Arabs and the Jews as clearly and bluntly as we can.

The confusion of the international left has been undeniable and widespread. I shall not speak here of such "friends of Israel" as Guy Mollet and his company, who, like Lord Avon and Selwyn Lloyd, saw in this war a continuation of the Suez campaign and their revenge for their discomfiture in 1956. Nor shall I waste words on the right-wing Zionist lobby in the British Labour party.But even on the "extreme left" of that party men like Sidney Silverman behaved in a way that might have been designed to illustrate someone's saying: "Scratch a Jewish left-winger and you find only a Zionist." But the confusion showed itself even further on the left and affected people with an otherwise unimpeachable record of struggle against imperialism. A French writer known for his courageous stand against the wars in Algeria and Vietnam this time called for solidarity with Israel, declaring that, if Israel's survival demanded American intervention, he would favor it and even raise the cry *"Vive le President Johnson."* Didn't it occur to him how incongruous it was to cry *"A bas Johnson!"* in Vietnam and *"Vive!"* in Israel? Jean-Paul Sartre also called, though with reservations, for solidarity with Israel, but then spoke frankly of the confusion in his own mind and its reasons. During the Second World War, he said, as a member of the Resistance he learned to look upon the Jew as a brother to be defended in all circumstances. During the Algerian war the Arabs were his brothers, and he stood by them. The present conflict was therefore for him a fratricidal struggle in which he was unable to exercise cool judgment and was overwhelmed by conflicting emotions.

Still, we must exercise our judgment and must not allow it to be clouded by emotions and memories, however deep or haunting. We should not allow even invocations of Auschwitz to blackmail us into supporting the wrong cause. I am speaking as a Marxist of Jewish origin, whose next-of-kin perished in Auschwitz and whose relatives live in Israel. To justify or condone Israel's wars against the Arabs is to render Israel a very bad service indeed and to harm its own long-term interest. Israel's security, let me repeat, was not enhanced by the wars of 1956 and 1967; it was undermined and compromised by them. The "friends of Israel" have in fact abetted Israel in a ruinous course.

They have also, willy-nilly, abetted the reactionary mood that took hold of Israel during the crisis. It was only with disgust that I could watch on television the scenes from Israel in those days: the displays of the conquerors' pride and brutality; the outbursts of chauvinism; and the wild celebrations of the inglorious triumph, all contrasting sharply with the pictures of Arab suffering and desolation, the treks of Jordanian refugees and the bodies of Egyptian soldiers killed by thirst in the desert. I looked at the medieval figures of the rabbis and *hassidim* jumping with joy at the Wailing Wall; and I felt how the ghosts of Talmudic obscurantism—and I know these only too well—crowded in on the country, and how the reactionary atmosphere in Israel had grown dense and stifling. Then came the many interviews with General Dayan, the hero and savior, with the political mind of a regimental sergeant-major, ranting about annexations and venting a raucous callousness about the fate of the Arabs in the conquered areas. ("What do they matter to me?" "As far as I am concerned, they may stay or they may go.") Already wrapped in a phony military legend—the legend is phony for Dayan neither planned nor conducted the six days' campaign —he cut a rather sinister figure, suggesting a candidate for the dictator's post: the hint was conveyed that if the civilian parties get too "soft" on the Arabs, this new Joshua, this mini De Gaulle, will teach them a lesson, himself take power, and raise Israel's "glory" even higher. And behind Dayan there was Begin, cabinet minister and leader of the extreme right-wing Zionists, who had long claimed even Trans-Jordan as part of "historic" Israel. A reactionary war inevitably breeds the heroes, the moods, and the consequences in which its character and aims are faithfully mirrored.

On a deeper historical level the Jewish tragedy finds in Israel a dismal sequel. Israel's leaders exploit in self-justification, and over-exploit Auschwitz and Treblinka; but their actions mock the real meaning of the Jewish tragedy.

European Jews paid a horrible price for the role they had played in past ages, and not of their own choosing, as representatives of a market economy, of "money," among peoples living in a natural, moneyless, agricultural economy. They were the conspicuous carriers of early capitalism, traders and money lenders, in precapitalist society. The image of the rich

Jewish merchant and usurer lived on in gentile folklore and remained engraved on the popular mind, stirring distrust and fear. The Nazis seized this image, magnified it to colossal dimensions, and constantly held it before the eyes of the masses.

August Bebel once said that antisemitism is the "socialism of the fools." There was plenty of that kind of "socialism" about, and all too little of the genuine socialism, in the era of the Great Slump, and of the mass unemployment and mass despair of the 1930s. The European working classes were unable to overthrow the bourgeois order; but the hatred of capitalism was intense and widespread enough to force an outlet for itself and focus on a scapegoat. Among the lower middle classes, the lumpenbourgeoisie and the lumpen-proletariat, a frustrated anticapitalism merged with fear of communism and neurotic xenophobia. The impact of Nazi Jew-baiting was so powerful in part because the image of the Jew as the alien and vicious "bloodsucker" was to all too many people still an actuality. This accounted also for the relative indifference and passivity with which so many non-Germans viewed the slaughter of Jews. The socialism of the fools gleefully watched Shylock led to the gas chamber.

Israel promised not merely to give the survivors of the European-Jewish communities a "national home" but also to free them from the fatal stigma. This was the message of the kibbutzim, the Histadruth, and even of Zionism at large. The Jews were to cease to be unproductive elements, shop-keepers, economic and cultural interlopers, carriers of capitalism. They were to settle in "their own land" as "productive workers."

Yet they now appear in the Middle East once again in the invidious role of agents not so much of their own, relatively feeble, capitalism, but of powerful Western vested interests and as protégés of neocolonialism. This is how the Arab world sees them, not without reason. Once again they arouse bitter emotions and hatreds in their neighbors, in all who have ever been or still are victims of imperialism. What a fate it is for the Jewish people to be made to appear in this role! As agents of early capitalism of our days, their role is altogether lamentable; and they are placed once again in the position of potential scapegoats. Is Jewish history to come full circle in such a way? This may well be the outcome of Israel's "victories"; and of this Israel's real friends must warn it.

The Arabs, on the other hand, need to be put on guard against the socialism or the anti-imperialism of the fools. We trust that they will not succumb to it; and that they will learn from their defeat and recover to lay the foundations of a truly progressive, a socialist, Middle East.

2. The Class Nature of Israeli Society

Haim Hanegbi, Moshe Machover, and Akiva Orr

In the preceding selection Deutscher calls on the Arab left to appeal directly to the Israeli "workers and kibbutzim," over the heads of the reactionary government. Now, five years later, this hope of union between Arabs and Israelis seems more distant than ever. Only one militant anti-Zionist group inside Israel has grown in this time: the Israeli Socialist Organization (often known by the name of its journal, Matzpen). *In the next essay, published originally in the* New Left Review *(January-February 1971), three leading theoreticians of the Israeli Socialist Organization analyze Zionism's working-class base in Israel and offer new insights into the society's class structure.*

Israeli society, like all other class societies, contains conflicting social interests—class interests which give rise to an internal class struggle. Yet Israeli society as a whole has been engaged, for the last fifty years, in a continuous external conflict: the conflict between Zionism and the Arab world, particularly the Palestinians. Which of these two conflicts is dominant and which is subordinate? What is the nature of this subordination and what is its dynamic? These are questions that everyone involved with Israeli society and politics must answer.

For revolutionaries inside Israel these questions are not academic. The answers given determine the strategy of the revolutionary struggle. Those who consider the internal class conflict to be the dominant one concentrate their efforts on the Israeli working class and attach secondary importance to the struggle against the colonizatory, nationalistic and discriminatory character of the Zionist state. This position sees the external conflict as a derivative of the internal one. Moreover, in this perspective, the internal dynamics of Israeli society will lead to a revolution in Israel, without this necessarily depending on a social revolution in the Arab world.

The experience of classical capitalist countries has often demonstrated that internal class conflicts and interests dominate external conflicts and interests. However, this theory fails to hold in certain specific cases. For example, in a colonized country under the direct rule of a foreign power, the dynamics of the colonized society cannot be deduced simply from the internal conflicts of that society, since the conflict with the colonizing power is dominant. Israel is neither a classic capitalist country nor is it a classic colony. Its economic, social and political features are so unique that any attempt to analyze it through the application of theories or analogies evolved for different societies will be a caricature. An analysis must rather be based on the specific characteristics and specific history of Israeli society.

A Society of Immigrants

The first crucial characteristic of Israeli society is that the majority of the population are either immigrants or the children of immigrants. In 1968 the adult (i.e., over fifteen) Jewish population of Israel numbered 1,689,286, of whom only 24 percent were Israeli-born and only 4 percent of Israeli-born parents.* Israeli society today is still an immi-

* Statistical Yearbook of the Israeli Government, 1969.

grant community and has many features typical of such a community. In such a society classes themselves, not to mention class consciousness, are still in a formative stage. Immigration produces an experience, and a mentality, of having "turned over a new page in life." As a rule the immigrant has changed his occupation, social role and class. In the case of Israel the majority of the immigrants come from the petty bourgeoisie, whether they are from urban areas in Central and Eastern Europe or from towns and cities in the Arab world. The new immigrant looks forward to changing his place in society. Moreover, he sees that all the advantageous positions in the new society are filled by earlier immigrants and this enhances his ambition to climb the social scale through long, hard work. The immigrant considers the actual social role he occupies as transitional. This applies to Israeli workers as well. His father was rarely a worker, and he himself lives in the hope that he too will one day become independent, or at least that his son will be able to do so. The class consciousness and pride which exist among the British and French proletariats do not exist in Israel, and appear odd to many Israeli workers. An English worker, if asked about his origins, will almost automatically reply in class terms ("I'm working-class"), and will define his attitudes to other people in terms of similar class concepts; an Israeli worker, however, will use ethnic categories and consider himself and others in terms of being "Polish," "Oriental," and so on. Most people in Israel still consider their social position in terms of their ethnic and geographic origins, and such a social consciousness is obviously a barrier hindering the working class from playing an independent role, let alone a revolutionary one aiming at a total transformation of society.

No working class can play a revolutionary role in society while the majority of its members desire to improve their situation individually, within the framework of the existing society, by leaving the ranks of their class. This truth is reinforced when the proletariat does not recognize itself as a stable social class with its own group interests and its own value system in conflict with those of the existing social order. The impulse towards a total transformation of society does not arise easily in a community of immigrants who have just changed their social and political status and who are still living in conditions of high social mobility. This does not mean that the Israeli working class cannot become a revolutionary force in the future; it merely implies that today political activity inside this class cannot proceed from the same assumptions and expectations as apply in a classic capitalist country.

A Society of Settlers

If the uniqueness of the Israeli working class consisted only in the fact that it was composed mainly of immigrants, then it could still be assumed that through time and patient socialist propaganda it would start to play an independent, possibly revolutionary, role. In such a situation patient educational work would not differ much from similar work elsewhere. However, Israeli society is not merely a society of immigrants; it is one of settlers. This society, including its working class, was shaped through a process of colonization. This process, which has been going on for eighty years, was not carried out in a vacuum but in a country populated by another people. The permanent conflict between the settlers' society and the indigenous, displaced Palestinian Arabs has never stopped and it has shaped the very structure of Israeli sociology, politics and economics. The second generation of Israeli leaders is fully aware of this. In a famous speech at the burial of Roy Rutberg, a kibbutz member killed by Palestinian guerrillas in 1956, General Dayan declared: "We are a settler generation, and without the steel helmet and the cannon we cannot plant a tree or build a house. Let us not flinch from the hatred inflaming hundreds of thousands of Arabs around us. Let us not turn our head away lest our hand tremble. It is our generation's destiny, our life's alternative, to be prepared and armed, strong and harsh, lest the sword drop from our fist and our life cease."* This clear evaluation stands in sharp contrast to official Zionist mythology about "making the desert bloom," and Dayan brought this out by going on to say that the Palestinians had a very good case since "their fields are cultivated by us in front of their very eyes."

When Marx made the famous statement that "a people oppressing another cannot itself be free" he did not mean this merely as a moral judgment. He also meant that in a society whose rulers oppress another people the exploited class which does not actively oppose this oppression inevitably becomes an accomplice in it. Even when this class does not directly gain anything from this oppression it becomes susceptible to the illusion that it shares a common interest with its own rulers in perpetuating this oppression. Such a class tends to trail behind its rulers rather than to challenge their rule. This, furthermore, is even truer when the oppression takes place not in a far-away country, but "at home," and when national oppression and expropriation form the very conditions for the emergence and existence of the oppressing society. Revolutionary organizations have operated within the Jewish community in Palestine since the 1920s and have accumulated considerable experience from such practical activity; this experience provides clear proof of the dictum that "a people oppressing another cannot itself be free." In the context of Israeli society it means that as long as Zionism is politically and ideologically dominant within that society, and forms the accepted framework of politics, there is no chance whatsoever of the Israeli working class becoming

* Moshe Dayan, in *Davar*, May 2, 1956.

a revolutionary class. The experience of fifty years does not contain a single example of Israeli workers being mobilized on material or trade-union issues to challenge the Israeli regime itself; it is impossible to mobilize even a minority of the proletariat in this way. On the contrary, Israeli workers nearly always put their national loyalties before their class loyalties. Although this may change in the future, this does not remove the need for us to analyze why it has been so for the last fifty years.

Ethnic Diversity

A third crucial factor is the ethnic character of the Israeli proletariat. The majority of the most exploited strata within the Israeli working class are immigrants from Asia and Africa.* At first sight it might appear as if the reduplication of class divisions by ethnic divisions might sharpen internal class conflicts within Israeli society. There has been a certain tendency in this direction. Yet the ethnic factor has worked mainly in the opposite direction over the past twenty years. There are a number of reasons for this. First, many of the immigrants from Asia and Africa improved their standard of living by becoming proletarians in a modern capitalist society. Their discontent was not directed against their condition as proletarians but against their condition as "Orientals," i.e., against the fact that they were looked down upon, and sometimes even discriminated against, by those of European origin. The Zionist rulers have taken measures to try to fuse the two groups together. But, in spite of these, the differences remained clear: in the mid-sixties, two-thirds of

* The vast majority of those who immigrated before 1948 were of European origin; between 1948 and 1951 the proportions were about equal; and since then the majority of immigrants have come from outside Europe. By 1966 only half of the Israeli population were of European origin.

those doing unskilled work were Orientals; 38 percent of
Orientals lived three or more people to a room, whereas only
7 percent of those from Europe did so; and in the Knesset
only sixteen of the one hundred twenty members were
Orientals before 1965 and only twenty-one after it. However,
such social differences are interpreted by the Orientals in
ethnic terms; they do not say, "I am exploited and discriminated against because I am a worker," but "I am exploited
and discriminated against because I am an Oriental." Secondly, in the present context of colonial Israeli society the
Oriental workers are a group whose equivalent would be the
"poor whites" of the U.S.A. or the Algerian *pieds noirs.* Such
groups resent being identified with Arabs, blacks and natives
of any kind, who are considered as "inferior" by these settlers. Their response is to side with the most chauvinist, racist
and discriminatory elements in the establishment; most
supporters of the semi-fascist Herut party are Jewish immigrants from Asia and Africa, and this must be borne in mind
by those whose revolutionary strategy for Israeli society is
based upon a future alliance of Arab Palestinians and Oriental
Jews, whether on the basis of their common exploited condition or on the basis of a putative cultural affinity they
might have as a result of the Oriental Jews having come from
Arab countries. This does not mean that these strata of the
Israeli proletariat are reactionary by "their very nature";
their reactionary character is merely a product of rule by
political Zionism. These strata could become the agents of
socially revolutionary processes in Israeli society if the Zionist establishment itself shattered. It is doubtful, however,
whether they will spearhead the movement to shatter it.

A Privileged Society: Capital Inflow

Israeli society is not only a settlers' society shaped by a
process of colonizing an already populated country, it is also

a society which benefits from unique privileges. It enjoys an influx of material resources from the outside of unparalleled quantity and quality; indeed it has been calculated that in 1968 Israel received 10 percent of all aid given to under-developed countries.* *Israel is a unique case in the Middle East; it is financed by imperialism without being economically exploited by it.* This has always been the case in the past: imperialism used Israel for its political purposes and paid for this by economic support. Oscar Gass, an American economist who at one time acted as an economic adviser to the Israeli government, recently wrote:†

> What is unique in this development process . . . is the factor of capital inflow. . . . During the seventeen years 1949–65 Israel received $6 billion more of imports of goods and services than she exported. For the twenty-one years 1948–68, the import surplus would be in excess of $7.5 billion. This means an excess of some $2650 per person during the twenty-one years for every person who lived in Israel (within the pre-June 1967 borders) at the end of 1968. And of this supply from abroad . . . only about 30 percent came to Israel under conditions which call for a return outflow of dividends, interest or capital. This is a circumstance without parallel elsewhere, and it severely limits the significance of Israel's economic development as an example to other countries.

Seventy percent of this $6 billion deficit was covered by "net unilateral capital transfers," which were not subject to conditions governing returns on capital or payment of dividends. They consisted of donations raised by the United

* *Le Monde,* July 2, 1969.
† *Journal of Economic Literature,* December 1969, p. 1177.

Jewish Appeal, reparations from the German government and grants by the U.S. government. Thirty percent came from "long-term capital transfers"—Israeli government bonds, loans by foreign governments, and capitalist investment. The latter benefits in Israel from tax exemptions and guaranteed profits by virtue of a "Law for the Encouragement of Capital Investments"*; nevertheless, this quasi-capitalist source of investment came far behind the unilateral donations and long-term loans. In the entire period from 1949 to 1965, capital transfers (both forms taken together) came from the following sources: 60 percent from world Jewry, 28 percent from the German government and 12 percent from the U.S. government. Of the "unilateral capital transfers," 51.5 percent came from world Jewry, 41 percent from the German government, and 7.2 percent from the U.S. government. Of the "long-term capital transfers," 68.7 percent came from world Jewry, 20.5 percent from the U.S. government and 11 percent from other sources. During the 1949–65 period the net saving of the Israeli economy averaged zero, being sometimes +1 percent and sometimes -1 percent. Yet the rate of investment over the same period was around 20 percent of the GNP. This could not have come from within because there was no internal saving within the Israeli economy; it came entirely from abroad in the form of unilateral and long-term capital investments. In other words, the growth of the Israeli economy was based entirely on the inflow of capital from outside.†

---

* This law was passed in 1959.
† These figures are taken from *The Economic Development of Israel,* by N. Halevi and R. Klinov-Malul, published by the Bank of Israel and Frederick A. Praeger, 1968. The category "other sources," included under "long-term capital transfers," has been omitted from the figures for both long-term and unilateral transfers taken together.

Since 1967 this dependence on foreign capital has increased. As a result of the changed Middle Eastern situation, military expenditure has risen. According to the Israeli Minister of the Treasury, in January 1970 military expenditure was estimated as 24 percent of GNP for 1970, which was twice the U.S. ratio in 1966, three times the British ratio and four times that of France.* This has placed an additional strain both on internal sources of investment money and on the balance of payments, and has had to be met by a commensurate rise in capital inflow. In 1967–68 three "millionaires' conferences" were called in Israel; foreign capitalists were invited to join in increasing the inflow of capital and foreign participation in industrial and agricultural projects. In September 1970, the Israeli Minister of the Treasury, Pinhas Sapir, returned from a three-week money-raising tour in the U.S.A. and summed up the situation at that time: "We set ourselves the aim of raising $1 billion from world Jewry in the coming year, by means of the United Jewish Appeal and the Israel Development Bonds campaign sponsored by the Jewish Agency. This sum is $400 million higher than that raised in the record year of 1967 . . . During the recent visit to Israel of the U.S. financial research team we explained to them that even if we succeed in raising all that we expect from the United Jewish Appeal and the Israel Development Bonds campaign we shall still be millions of dollars short of our requirements. After summing up our requirements in arms we informed the U.S. that we shall need $400–500 million per year."† It thus appears that the dependence of Israel on the United States has changed significantly since the 1967 war. Fund-raising among Jews all over the world (by

* Professor D. Patienkin in *Ma'ariv*, January 30, 1970.
† *Yediot Aharanot*, September 30, 1970. Out of a total of $1034 million U.S. military aid to foreign countries excluding Vietnam during 1970, Israel received $500 million.

cashing in on their sentiments and fears) no longer suffices to support the enormously increased military budget. The rough average of $500 million from fund raising has now to be doubled, and on top of this the U.S. government has been asked to provide directly an additional $500 million. It is obvious that the readiness of the U.S. government to forward these sums depends on what it gets in return. In the particular case of Israel this return is not economic profit.*

British capital has also been developing close ties with Israel.† Twenty percent of Israel's imports come from Britain, and trade has nearly doubled since the June war. British Leyland participate with the Histadruth (who have a 34 percent holding) in bus production, and with private Israeli capital in car and jeep production. Marks and Spencers buy £2–3 million a year of goods from Israel, one-third being textiles and the rest oranges, vegetables and fruit juices. British financial interests, led by Sir Isaac Wolfson and Charles Clore, are also major participants. Wolfson is the chairman of Great Universal Stores in Britain, which has a 30 percent share of GUS Industries (Israel). Wolfson and Clore cooperate with Israel's largest domestic capitalist group, the Mayer brothers, in real estate in Israel and Africa, and built the only skyscraper in the country, the Shalom tower in Tel Aviv. Wolfson also controls 30 percent of the major petroleum chain, Paz, which was sold off by Shell under Arab pressure in 1959. Wolfson is also one of the backers of the Israel Corporation, a $30 million company with a minimum subscription of $100,000, which was set up after the June war to finance industrial development in Israel.

* Early in December 1970 Sapir presented the budget for the period 1970–71; 40 percent was devoted to military purposes. This included: the purchase of arms, partly covered by the $500 million promised by Nixon; the development of the arms industry and of military research; and the everyday costs of national security operations.
† *See* "Why This Nation *Does* Buy British," *The Times*, March 28, 1969.

The increased participation of foreign capital in Israel has led to certain changes within the economy itself, which have also been carried out under the increased pressures set off directly by the level of military expenditure. The economy has been made more "efficient" by American capitalist standards: taxes have been reformed, investment conditions "liberalized," and army generals sent to U.S. business schools and then put in charge of industrial enterprises. In the period 1968–69 there was a compulsory wage freeze, and some public enterprises were even sold off to private capital—for instance, the 26 percent state share in the Haifa oil refinery.

This influx of resources from abroad does not include the property which the Zionist establishment in Israel took over from refugee Palestinians as "abandoned property." This includes land, both cultivated and uncultivated; only 10 percent of the land held by Zionist bodies in pre-1967 Israel had been bought before 1948. It also includes many houses, and completely deserted cities like Jaffa, Lydda and Ramleh, where much property was confiscated after the 1948 war.

The Distribution of Foreign Funds

The enormous influx of capital did not come into the hands of the small Israeli bourgeoisie, but into the hands of the state, of the Zionist establishment,* and this establishment has been under the control of the bureaucracies of the Labor parties since the 1920s. This has determined the way in which all inflowing capital, as well as conquered property, has been put to use. Funds collected abroad are channeled through the Jewish Agency, which, with the Histadruth and the government, forms part of the triangle of governing insti-

---

* The term "Zionist establishment" is that conventionally used in Israel to denote the ruling group present in the interlocking set of Zionist institutions.

tutions. All the Zionist parties, from Mapam to Herut, are represented in the Jewish Agency. It finances sections of the Israeli economy, in particular the non-profitable parts of agriculture like the kibbutzim, and it also distributes funds to the Zionist parties, enabling them to run their newspapers and economic enterprises. The funds are divided according to the votes cast for the parties at the previous election, and this system of subsidies enables the Zionist parties to survive long after the social forces that created them have disappeared.*

Historically the purpose of this system was the strengthening of the colonization process, in accordance with the ideas of the Zionist Labor parties, and the strengthening of the grip which the bureaucracy itself had over Israeli society. This has proved successful, since not only is the Israeli working class organizationally and economically under the complete control of the Labor bureaucracy but so too is the Israeli bourgeoisie. Historically the bureaucracy has shaped most of the institutions, values and practices of Israeli society without any successful opposition from within, and subject only to the external constraints imposed by imperialism and the resistance of the Arabs. Most of this enormous inflow of resources went into immigration projects and the housing and employment necessary to cope with the inflow that raised the Jewish population from 0.6 million in 1948 to 2.4 million in 1968.

This process was accompanied by relatively little personal corruption, but by a lot of political and social corruption. The influx of resources had a decisive effect on the dynamics

---

* In January 1970 there were ten daily Hebrew papers in Israel, of which seven were subsidized party papers; these included the Labor papers *Davar* and *Lamerhav,* and the MAPAM paper *al-Hamishmar.* The three private papers were *Ma'ariv* and *Yediot Ahanarot,* both evening papers with expanionist policies, and *Ha'aretz,* a more liberal morning paper run by Gershom Shoken. Military censorship operates in Israel.

of Israeli society, for the Israeli working class shared, directly and indirectly, in this transfusion of capital. Israel is not a country where foreign aid flows entirely into private pockets; it is a country where this aid subsidizes the whole of society. The Jewish worker in Israel does not get his share in cash, but he gets it in terms of new and relatively inexpensive housing, which could not have been started or kept going without external subsidies; and he gets it in terms of a general standard of living which does not correspond to the output of that society. The same obviously applies to the profits of the Israeli bourgeoisie, whose economic activity and profit-making is regulated by the bureaucracy through subsidies, import licenses and tax exemptions. In this way the struggle between the Israeli working class and its employers, both bureaucrats and capitalists, is fought not only over the surplus value produced by the worker, but also over the share each group receives from this external source of subsidies.

Israel and Imperialism

What political circumstances enabled Israel to receive external aid in such quantities and under such unparalleled conditions? This question was answered as early as 1951 by the editor of the daily paper *Ha' aretz*: "Israel has been given a role not unlike that of a watchdog. One need not fear that it will exercise an aggressive policy towards the Arab states if this will contradict the interests of the U.S.A. and Britain. But should the West prefer for one reason or another to close its eyes one can rely on Israel to punish severely those of the neighboring states whose lack of manners towards the West has exceeded the proper limits."* This evaluation of Israel's role in the Middle East has been verified many times, and it is

---

* Shoken in *Ha'aretz*, "The prostitute of the sea ports and ourselves. Meditations on the eve of new year," September 30, 1951.

clear that Israel's foreign and military policies cannot be deduced from the dynamics of the internal social conflicts alone. The entire Israeli economy is founded on the special political and military role which Zionism, and the settlers' society, fulfill in the Middle East as a whole. If Israel is viewed in isolation from the rest of the Middle East there is no explanation for the fact that 70 percent of the capital inflow is not intended for economic gain and is not subject to considerations of profitability. But the problem is immediately solved when Israel is considered as a component of the Middle East. The fact that a considerable part of this money comes from donations raised by Zionists among Jews all over the world does not alter its being a subsidy by imperialism. What matters is rather the fact that the U.S. Treasury is willing to consider these funds, raised in the United States for transferring to another country, as "charity donations" qualifying for income tax exemptions. These donations depend on the goodwill of the U.S. Treasury and it is only reasonable to assume that this goodwill would not continue were Israel to conduct a principled anti-imperialist policy.

This means that although class conflicts do exist in Israeli society they are constrained by the fact that the society as a whole is subsidized from the outside. This privileged status is related to Israel's role in the region, and as long as this role continues there is little prospect of the internal social conflicts acquiring a revolutionary character. On the other hand, a revolutionary breakthrough in the Arab world would change this situation. By releasing the activity of the masses throughout the Arab world it could change the balance of power; this would make Israel's traditional politico-military role obsolete, and would thus reduce its usefulness for imperialism. At first Israel would probably be used in an attempt to crush such a revolutionary breakthrough in the Arab world; yet once this attempt had failed, Israel's politico-military role vis-à-vis the Arab world would be finished. Once this role and its associated privileges had been ended, the Zionist regime, depending as it does on these privileges, would be open to mass challenge from within Israel itself.

This does not mean that there is nothing for revolution- aries inside Israel to do except sit and wait for the emergence of objective external conditions on which they have no influence. It only means that they must base their activity on a strategy that acknowledges the unique features of Israeli society, rather than on one that reproduces the generaliza- tions of analysis of classic capitalism. The main task for revolutionaries who accept this assessment is to direct their work towards those strata of the Israeli population who are immediately affected by the political results of Zionism and who have to pay for it. These strata include Israeli youth, who are called on to wage "an eternal war imposed by des- tiny," and the Palestinian Arabs who live under Israeli rule. These strata share an anti-Zionist tendency which makes them potential allies in the revolutionary struggle inside Israel and the revolutionary struggle throughout the Middle East. Anyone who follows closely the revolutionary struggles within the Arab world becomes aware of the dialectical rela- tionship between the struggle against Zionism within Israel and the struggle for social revolution within the Arab world. Such a strategy does not imply that activity within the Israeli working class should be neglected; it only implies that this activity too must be subordinated to the general strategy of the struggle against Zionism.

Which Is the Ruling Class?

The subordination of the entire economy to political con- siderations has characterized Zionist colonization from the very beginning, and is the key to decoding the unique nature of the Israeli ruling class. Zionist colonization did not pro- ceed as an ordinary, capitalist, colonizatory process motivated by considerations of profitability. The bourgeois elements in this colonization always preferred to employ Arab labor, but the Zionist Labor bureaucracy struggled against this and demanded a policy of "Jewish labor only." It was a bitter struggle that was waged throughout the 1920s and 1930s and formed the main conflict within the Zionist community in Palestine. It was finally won by the Labor bureaucracy, to a considerable extent due to the support it received from the world Zionist movement. That support was based on political considerations, for the aim of political Zionism was, from the very beginning, to establish a purely Jewish nation-state in Palestine and to displace the indigenous population. As early as June 1895 Theodor Herzl wrote in his diary: "The private lands in the territories granted us we must gradually take out of the hands of the owners. The poorer amongst the population we try to transfer quietly outside our borders by providing them with work in the transit countries, but in our country we deny them all work. Those with property will join us. The transfer of land and the displacement of the poor must be done gently and carefully. Let the landowners believe they are exploiting us by getting overvalued prices. But no lands shall be sold back to their owners."*

It was this consideration embodied by the world Zionist movement that tipped the scales in favor of the Zionist Labor bureaucracy in Palestine and its policy of "Jewish labor only." The defeat of the bourgeois elements established a pattern of joint rule in which the Labor bureaucracy played the senior role and the bourgeoisie the junior one, combining to form a new embryonic ruling class. This specific combination within the ruling establishment has remained unchanged from the 1940s to this day and constitutes a unique feature

* Herzl, *Selected Works*, Newman Edition, Tel Aviv, vol. 7, book 1, p. 86.

of Israeli society. If the dominant ideology in any given society is the ideology of the dominant class, then if the identity of the dominant class is rather blurred one can try to analyze the dominant ideology itself and deduce from it the identity of the ruling class. In Israel the dominant ideology was never a capitalist one; it was a blend of bourgeois elements combined with dominant themes and ideas typical of the Zionist Labor movement, ideas derived from the socialist movement in Eastern Europe but transformed to express the aims of political Zionism.

This balance between the different sections of the ruling class is not static, and recently the balance has been shifting in favor of the bourgeois partner. One of the symptoms of this is the division between Golda Meir and Ben-Gurion on the one hand and their disciple Dayan on the other. The issue was the old one of whether to employ Palestinians from the occupied territories for work within the Israeli economy. Meir was strongly opposed to this policy, whereas Dayan supported it and the bourgeois paper *Ha'aretz* supported Dayan. But whatever the different tendencies at any one moment the Labor bureaucracy still dominates through its three centers: government, Jewish Agency and Histadruth. Wielding the tremendous apparatus of the state and the unions, it dominates Israeli society and most of the economy. In 1960 the privately owned sector produced only 58.5 percent of the total net product of the Israeli economy,* and it is doubtful if this proportion has changed much in the subsequent decade.

But the economic power of the Zionist Labor bureaucracy is far greater than this figure suggests. Apart from its direct control of the state and the Histadruth it has indirect bureaucratic control over the private sector. This control goes far

* Falk Institute Report, 1961–63. The remainder was owned in approximately equal proportions by the state and by the Histadruth.

beyond the ordinary intervention of the state in the economy of the kind that occurs in most capitalist countries. The entire Israeli economy, including the private sector, depends on subsidies from abroad which flow mostly through state-controlled channels. By controlling the flow of subsidies through the policies of the Treasury and the Jewish Agency, the Labor bureaucracy directs and regulates this flow. This also gives it a useful grip on its capitalist partner. Israel is a unique form of capitalism, ruled by a unique class partnership. The control of the bureaucracy over the flow of funds from abroad enables it to exercise a far-reaching control over the broad masses of the population, not only in political and economic matters, but even in aspects of everyday life. The majority of the Israeli population depend directly, and daily, on the good will of this bureaucracy for their jobs, housing and health insurance. Some of the workers who have rebelled against the bureaucracy, like the seamen in the great strike of December 1951, were denied employment, and some who refused to surrender were forced in the end to emigrate. At the same time there is no national health service in Israel, only that of the Histadruth, so those who refuse to join or who fight it are deprived of health insurance. Indeed the key to the hold of the bureaucracy over the proletariat is the trade union federation, the Histadruth.

The Histadruth: National Interest Before Class Interest

Israeli workers might seem to be in an enviable situation, since the Trade Union Federation, known simply as the "Federation" (Histadruth), gives the impression of being an advanced and powerful workers' union. From a certain viewpoint the Histadruth and its facilities are indeed quite exceptional: it has 1.1 million members out of a total population of nearly 3 million; a quarter of Israeli wage-earners work in concerns belonging to the Histadruth; and the Histadruth has for years accounted for around 22–25 percent of the Israeli Net National Product.

The Histadruth was founded in 1920 during a general congress of Jewish workers and until 1966 it was known as the "General Confederation of Hebrew Workers in the Land of Israel." The number of Jewish workers in Palestine in 1920 was some five thousand, while there were around fifty thousand Arab workers, according to the estimate of a Zionist historian.*

The founders of this "General" Federation, who were all inspired by Zionist ideology, and most of whom were members of Jewish petty-bourgeois parties, limited membership of the Histadruth exclusively to Jews, and to Jews "living on the fruits of their labor"—workers, artisans, tradesmen, and self-employed workers. When the basic principles of the Histadruth were being laid down, the founders made it clear that "national interest" took priority over "economic interest" and "cultural interests." The internationalist approach to the class nature of society was never brought up at the Histadruth's founding congress, not even by a minority group. A year after its foundation, the Histadruth created its first enterprises. These were a large company dealing with Public Works—"Solel Boneh"—and the "Workers' Bank," the latter in association with the World Zionist Organization. "Solel Boneh" has been engaged on a variety of construction work over the past few years, in several parts of the world; for example, it has built luxury hotels in certain African countries, and has constructed roads and various military installations in several Asian countries, including U.S. air bases in Turkey. The fact that from the start, the Histadruth made Zionist interests its primary concern, at the expense of its trade-union role, has led to an extremely hierarchized organizational structure. A bureaucratic machinery was set up such

* *The Arabs in Palestine* (in Hebrew), by Joseph Washitz, p. 151.

that the entire organization of the trade union was subordinated to the management and to the political "bosses"— who were always from Zionist parties. There has never been the least trade-union independence in the Histadruth.*

The Histadruth was not merely concerned with its role of maintaining Jews in national isolation while they were living in an essentially Arab milieu. Since its creation it has been at the spearhead of Zionist colonization in Palestine. Its choice position amongst the country's Zionist colonizers, and its extremely strong organization, made it a pioneer in the process of agricultural colonization and in winning places of work for Jewish workers, by evicting Arab peasants and workers. The Zionist slogans of the twenties and thirties— "the conquest of work" and "the conquest of the soil"— found their principal realizers in the Histadruth. Its leader, Berl Katznelson, explained: "Our Histadruth is unique among trade unions, for it is a union which both plans and executes. This is not due to our wisdom or perspicacity. This was always our vision, in all our actions. From the moment that the young immigrant reaches the shores of Palestine and looks for work in the plantations, he finds himself up against hard reality, and, at the same time, in our world of vision."† More recently, the then general secretary of the Histadruth, Pinhas Lavon, summed up the historical role of the Federation: "The General Federation of Workers was founded forty years ago by several thousand young people wanting to work in an underdeveloped country where labor was cheap, a country which rejected its inhabitants and which was inhos-

---

* Union dues are collected by special collection offices which the Histadruth has set up throughout Israel, and local branches receive their funds from the center, not from their local membership. This severely limits their independence. The Histadruth employs a permanent staff of thirty thousand and its bureaucracy has a very tight hold on its members; indeed the Histadruth building in Tel-Aviv is known as "the Kremlin."

† International Supplement on the Jubilee of the Histadruth, 1920-70.

pitable to newcomers. Under these conditions, the foundation of the Histadruth was a central event in the process of
the rebirth of the Hebrew people in its fatherland. Our
Histadruth is a general organization to its core. It is not a
workers' trade union, although it copes perfectly well with
the real needs of the workers."* Being "general to its core,"
the Histadruth has effectively become the central force of the
Jewish community in its many aspects. It organized the
Zionist armed forces, sometimes in collusion with the British
occupation, and sometimes secretly against its wishes; it
created a system of social security, the only one in existence
in Israel, which has become an important weapon in the
domination of the Jewish masses and the organization of the
workers under the authority of the Histadruth; it has opened
recruitment offices everywhere, thus reinforcing its domination, while at the same time regulating the right to work; it
possesses its own school network, its own promotion societies, and its own production and service cooperatives; as an
organization it completely dominates all the kibbutzim and
collective farms of the whole country. It is not for nothing
that the Histadruth was considered as the central pillar of the
Zionist enterprise from its beginning, or as the Zionists say,
"the state in embryo."

The Histadruth leadership decided the political line of the
Jewish community, both in matters of "Jewish interest" and
in its relations with the British occupiers and the Arab
masses. The political leaders of the state of Israel—David Ben-
Gurion, Levi Eshkol, Golda Meir—have all come from the
ranks of the Histadruth.

It was only at the end of the period of the British mandate, in 1943, that the Histadruth created a special department for Arab laborers; its aim was to organize them within a

* *Moed*, published by the Department of Culture and Education of the
Histadruth (in Hebrew), 1960, p. 3.

paternalistic and puppet framework, so as to divert them from the political struggle—i.e., from the anti-imperialist and anti-Zionist struggle. The experiment was summed up at the time by a Zionist historian—a specialist in Arab questions and a Histadruth member: "As a national feeling develops among the workers (Arabs) their opposition to those who want to organize them from the outside is becoming stronger. The most intelligent and dynamic among them never have an opportunity to show their talent and initiative. A pamphlet in Arabic (published by the Histadruth) explains that one should only be concerned with the economic interests of the Arab workers, and that one should exclude all political activity. This condition is difficult for people who are aware and close to public life to accept. The conception of work and the conquest of work held by the majority of the Histadruth is equally an obstacle, since it is difficult to explain things convincingly to an Arab worker. The discrimination in salaries between Jewish workers and Arab workers exasperates the Arabs, particularly since work conditions and price-levels tend to be equal. In these circumstances it was easy for Arab organizations to send us their members to ask 'naive questions' at the time of the May Day demonstration—'Is proletarian solidarity compatible with a call for the conquest of labor, and for the creation of the Jewish State?' "* No Zionist has ever been able to answer that question; they cannot answer it today, any more than they could yesterday.

A Crisis of Confidence in the Histadruth

With the creation of the state of Israel in 1948, the integration of the Histadruth into the ruling Zionist system became more evident. The economic sector of the Histadruth, with its business concerns and its immense wealth, forms part of

---

* Washitz, *op. cit.,* p. 173.

the public sector, whose development had to accelerate with the arrival of new immigrants, at the same time as capital was flowing into the new State. The Histadruth made it possible to form a nationalized economy. The theory propagated for years by Histadruth leaders, according to which the economic sector of the Histadruth constitutes the basis for the construction of socialism, collapsed with independence. Another often-stated argument, that the economic sector of the Histadruth belongs to the workers, was also invalidated. The Minister of Agriculture, Haim Gvati, who is one of the principal leaders of the Histadruth, had to admit during the Histadruth conference in 1964: "We have not succeeded in transforming this immense richness into socialist economic cells. We have not succeeded in maintaining the working-class nature of our economic sector. Actually there are *no* characteristics to differentiate it from the rest of the public sector, and sometimes even from the private sector. The atmosphere, work relations and human relations of our economic sector are in no way different from any other industrial enterprise."*

A complement and illustration to these remarks is to be found in the attitude of the Israeli workers towards the Histadruth. Among all the evidence on this point it is most interesting to quote some from the Histadruth itself, published in its 1966 Yearbook. "A very considerable number of workers hardly notice the Histadruth's trade-union activities, and they consider that their situation would not have been modified if there had been no trade union." According to an inquiry undertaken for the Histadruth, the results of which are in the

* The general secretary of Histadruth Enterprises, the industrial wing that controls 25 percent of the economy, told a group of Zionist businessmen in Los Angeles in early 1969 that Histadruth Enterprises was no different from any other capitalist organization, despite its trade union links; it was expected to make a profit and show a decent return on capital just like any private firm (*Sunday Times*, July 27, 1969).

Yearbook, a growing number of workers believe that the local trade-union branches in their places of work (called "workers' committees" in Israel) should be independent of the Histadruth. Twenty percent of all wage-earners indicated that strikes have broken out in their enterprises against the advice of the Histadruth; 47 percent thought that in certain cases it was desirable for the workers to embark on a strike without Histadruth authorization. The Yearbook continues: "The conclusions of the inquiry into the action committees are even more serious." (These are committees formed against the authorization of the Histadruth and aimed at, or on the occasion of, wildcat strikes or wildcat action.) "Against 8 percent of wage-earners who stated that strikes which had broken out were contrary to the advice of the local trade-union branch, 29 percent were of the opinion that such strikes are justified in certain cases. *In short, the tendency to break with the established order is getting stronger,* in so far as work relations go . . ." (our italics). The same publication shows that a majority of Histadruth members consider that the trade-union conference has no influence on the functioning of the central body. Among the minority who do believe that ordinary members can exercise some influence, there is still a major number who estimate this influence to be insufficient. In reply to the question "Why are you a member of the Histadruth?" the official source says that about 70 percent replied that it was an "automatic thing," or "because they made us" or "because it was the done thing" or "because of the social security." A minority (16 percent) stated that they belonged for ideological reasons, whereas 15 percent said they were members because the Histadruth defended the interest of the workers.

The Yearbook concludes that "a majority of Histadruth members, i.e., 55 percent, joined of their own free will, a third (24 percent) joined automatically on immigrating to Israel, and a fifth (20 percent) found they had become members automatically because they had been registered as such in their employment." Histadruth leaders, industrial circles and government members are now openly expressing their concern at what they call the workers' "crisis of confidence" towards the Histadruth. This crisis is getting worse from year to year. It is, in fact, the reason for the change in the Histadruth top leadership in 1969, when the former general secretary, Aharon Becker, was replaced by Itzhak Ben-Aharon, known for his vigorous rhetorical style and working-class phraseology. The former general secretary and the new one are both members of the ruling Labor party.

Wildcat Strikes and Action Committees

Certain important strikes have occurred in the short history of the workers' struggle in Israel. The first took place in 1951, relatively soon after the creation of the state of Israel, with the famous seamen's strike; next came a series of wildcat strikes in 1962, after the devaluation of the Israeli pound; the third wave took place in 1969, with the postal workers' and the Ashdod port workers' strike.

The seamen's strike was the most violent in the history of strikes in Israel. The battlefield was the port of Haifa, and Israeli ships there and in foreign ports. It was special, because it was a strike led by young seamen without a trade-union tradition, and because the conflict was about the means of electing trade-union delegates by the mass of seamen. For those who know the nature of the Histadruth it is not surprising that it immediately mobilized all the forces at its disposal against the strikers. The strike leaders were dragged before an "internal tribunal" of the Histadruth and mobilized into the army. Vast police forces engaged in violent battles against the strikers. The 1962 wave of strikes for the first time gave rise extensively to a kind of organization now known as an "action committee." The two fronts were once more clearly defined: the Histadruth on one side of the barricade, the workers on the other. It was during this period that the first steps to group the action committees on a national, or at least a regional, basis, were taken—but this attempt was not successful. The 1969 strikes were a warning to the government and to the employers that strikes were possible despite the situation of war and of "national unity." The postal workers' strike saw the Israeli government once again issue mobilization orders, with the Histadruth's agreement, against the strikers, to force them back to work, as the existing laws allow. The strikers broke state laws and were brought before the courts, but the trial was never concluded. Another factor characterized the Ashdod port-workers' struggle. The Histadruth threatened to bring the local trade-union militants before an "internal tribunal," but the local militants, with the support of the workers, held their ground. The trial opened in the presence of television cameras and had a wide coverage in the country. The workers were denounced as Fateh agents and as "saboteurs." The threats of the Histadruth leadership were: "If you are found guilty the maximum sanctions will be applied, which means you will be excluded from the Histadruth, thus losing all the advantages of social security for you and your families." The workers continued their struggle and passed from accused to accusers. The Histadruth leadership received bad publicity, and hastened to end the spectacle without pronouncing a verdict.

Strikes in Israel Year	No. of Strikes	Strikers in 1,000s	Strike days in 1,000s
1949	53	5	57
1950	72	9	55
1951	76	10	114
1952	94	14	58
1953	84	9	35
1954	82	12	72
1955	87	10	54
1956	74	11	114
1957	59	4	116
1958	48	6	83
1959	51	6	31
1960	135	14	49
1961	128	27	141
1962	146	38	243
1963	127	87	129
1964	138	48	102
1965	288	90	208
1966	282	87	156
1967	142	25	58
1968	100	42	72

Sources: Statistical Books, 1965, 1967 and 1968. Annual Report from the Bank of Israel.

Note: Until 1959, only strikes lasting more than one day were included. Since 1960, strikes lasting more than two hours were also included. The figures also include lock-outs, but these are rare and do not affect the yearly comparisons.

The Parties of the Zionist Right

If the Histadruth is controlled by the parties of the Zionist left, the other two main centers of power, government and Jewish Agency, reflect a wider spectrum of Zionist opinion. The electoral system is a proportional one, with each party presenting a nationwide list at the elections and the one hundred twenty seats in the Knesset being allocated accordingly, to parties obtaining over 1 percent of the votes.

From the 1930s to the 1960s the Zionist right consisted of two parties, the "General Zionists" and Herut (Freedom). The General Zionists represented Zionist private capital in Palestine—the citrus grove owners, other landowners, and the industrialists. It was a typical capitalist party with the same slogans as in the West, except that it called for limiting Histadruth powers, rather than for turning the economy into a fully private one. Herut was not based on economic interests in the way the General Zionists were, but rather on militant and extremist Zionism. Its mottoes were (from the 1930s onwards): "Two banks has the Jordan; one is ours, the other is ours too," and "In blood and fire Judaea fell, in blood and fire Judaea will rise." They demanded a policy of military conquest, rather than one of colonizatory settlement, which was the policy of the Zionist left. Herut employed fascist tactics in the 1930s, including brown shirts and armed terror, and it draws most of its adherents from the Oriental Jews who are attracted by its crude nationalistic slogans. In the mid-1960s these two parties merged under the leadership of Herut's leader, Begin, and formed the Herut-Liberal Block—"Gahal." (In Israel "Liberal" means "Conservative.") For the first time in Israeli history Herut was accepted into the cabinet on the eve of the June war to form part of the so-called "National Unity cabinet"; but they left Golda Meir's cabinet in August 1970 because of her acceptance of the Rogers plan, which called for an Israeli withdrawal from the 1967 cease-fire lines. Like the Zionist left, Gahal receives most of its financial support from the Jewish Agency.

The Dilemmas of the Zionist Left

From the early 1900s to this very day the backbone of the Zionist enterprise in Palestine has been the Zionist left, and in particular those émigrés who came from Eastern Europe in the years between 1904 and 1914. This left has always been reformist and nationalist, but even as such it has split again and again as a result of the inherent conflicts between its Zionism and its socialism. The conflicts it has experienced can be grouped under three headings:

1. *Foreign policy:* What position to adopt on imperialism in the Middle East and elsewhere, and on the socialist movement throughout the world, especially when the struggle against imperialism or cooperation with socialist movements conflicts with Zionist aspirations.

2. *Class struggle:* What policy to have towards Jewish employers in Palestine and towards the capitalist sector within Zionism.

3. *Socialist internationalism:* Whether to have a joint or separate struggle with the Palestinian peasants and workers against capitalism in Palestine, and whether to support other revolutionary movements.

All those who differed on these issues were still Zionists, i.e., they considered their main goal to be the establishment and maintaining of an exclusively Jewish nation-state and of Jewish immigration from all over the world. Outside the Zionist left there were always a few groups making up the anti-Zionist left; they did not face the political dilemmas outlined here; their differences with each other were on issues of the strategy and tactics of the struggle against Zionism and for socialism in Palestine. They will be examined later. Of the Zionist parties by far the most important is MAPAI (Israeli Labor party), founded in 1930 through the merger of two smaller parties, and the dominant party in all coalition governments in Israel since 1948. Originally the two components of MAPAI agreed that Jewish exclusiveness must take precedence over cooperation with Arab workers and peasants in Palestine. However, they differed on the degree of class collaboration with Zionist employers, and only when agreement was reached did they decide to merge. The policy they agreed on was one of subordinating class interests to Zionist interests within the Jewish community itself, and MAPAI became the main protagonist of the "Jewish labor only" policy. This policy meant that Jewish employers were pressured to employ only Jewish workers, and both Arab workers and Jewish employers were terrorized, often by violence, into enforcing this policy. This was the main internal issue within the Jewish community in the 1930s and it was finally won by MAPAI, thus ensuring its dominant role.

Leaders like Ben-Gurion, Eshkol and Golda Meir have remained dedicated to this policy to this day and are still dominant within Israel. MAPAI has never considered itself Marxist or revolutionary, but socialist and reformist; yet although Golda Meir spoke in 1950 of "socialism in our time" the party no longer claims any allegiance to socialism. In all the conflicts between imperialist and anti-imperialist forces in the Middle East this party had consciously collaborated and even plotted secretly (as in the Suez war) with imperialism. It has a clear stake in the continuation of imperialist influence in the area and considers any victory for anti-imperialist forces as a threat to Israel itself.

After twenty-two years in power certain changes have occurred in the party, the most important of which has been the emergence of a technocracy consisting of army officers who have entered the economy as administrators and as specialists;* this group is in conflict with the old guard and represents the growing influence of the army on Israeli politics, both because of the technical skills it contains and because of the increased weight of the military in the period after the June war. When Ben-Gurion was ousted from power in 1965 many of this group joined him to form RAFI (List of Israel's Workers), but when these technocrats realized that Ben-Gurion could no longer return to power they hastened to rejoin the ruling party. The newly reunited party is now called Ha'avoda (The Labor), and it can be expected that when the old guard disappears over the next few years it will be this new group that will be the dominant force in Israeli politics.

The second largest Zionist left party is MAPAM (United Workers' Party), formed in the late 1940s; its main component is Hashomer Hatz'air (The Young Guard). MAPAM originally considered itself to be both Marxist and revolutionary and proposed a binational state in Palestine; however, there had to be a Jewish majority guaranteed by the constitution, and until such a majority was achieved—through immigration—Palestine was to remain under "international trusteeship." The idea of a binational state was dropped in 1947 when the U.N. and the U.S.S.R. accepted the partition of Palestine. MAPAM was always a little to the left of MAPAI on many trade-union issues in Israel, and—at least verbally—in matters of foreign policy as well. But it has always remained loyal to Zionism and this had led it into collaboration with imperialism, as over Suez. In Israeli politics MAPAM always trails, under protest, behind MAPAI, but it is the main instrument for defending Zionism against criticism by socialists, Marxists and revolutionaries at home and abroad, and it still

---

* *See* Eli Lobel, "L'escalade à l'intérieur de la société israélienne," *Partisans* no. 52, March/April 1970.

plays this role, although somewhat less so since 1967. MAPAM always points to its kibbutzim as a new mode of communal life; but it never mentions that many of them are on lands from which the Arab peasants were driven off, that there is not a single Jewish-Arab kibbutz, and that all are subsidized by Zionist funds.* MAPAM talks of the "right of the Jews to self-determination in Palestine," but by this it does not mean the rights of the Jewish population now living in Israel, but the political rights of world Jewry in Palestine. Like all Zionists MAPAM insists on maintaining the Israeli immigration law, which grants automatic immigration rights to Jews while denying them to anyone else. Like all other Zionist parties MAPAM is financed by the Jewish Agency, and this enables it to maintain a party apparatus, daily papers and a publicity network abroad.

The permanent conflict with the Arab world, and with anti-imperialist trends within it, forces Zionism to depend increasingly on imperialism, and this creates a permanent pressure shifting the Zionist left to the right. On its long road from its origins in the Russia of 1905 the Zionist left has one by one shed its slogans of revolution, socialism and anti-imperialism. Each shift to the right leaves behind it a splinter group loyal to the abandoned slogan.

The latest offspring of this kind is SIAH (Israeli New Left). It was formed after the 1967 war by members of MAPAM who were opposed to their party's collaboration with the Dayan-Eshkol-Begin bloc, and their main emphasis is on the lack of a peace initiative in Israeli policy. Yet although they consider themselves Marxists and revolutionaries they pledge allegiance to Zionism. The editor of one of their publications

* The kibbutzim never contained more than 5 percent of the Jewish population of Palestine or Israel. Hence, whatever their other limitations, they cannot be said to constitute Israeli society or to be evidence for Israel being a socialist country.

recently stated: "Our struggle to change the image of Israeli
society and to consolidate a peace policy must be based,
whatever happens, on principled and consistent affirmation
of the State of Israel and of the Zionist principles on which it
is founded. Any departure from this will lead SIAH astray
from the aims it set itself when it was founded."* At the
same time SIAH has been able to attract support from young
Israelis hostile to the official line; its second congress, held in
Tel Aviv in November 1970, was attended by three hundred
fifty people—mainly ex-MAPAM and ex-MAKI—and passed
resolutions calling for peace without annexations of Arab
territory, recognition of the right of the Palestinian people to
self-determination, unconditional talks with the Arabs and
Palestinians, and Israeli acceptance of the Jarring mission.

The Non-Zionist Left

Outside the Zionist camp there exist two forces: the Israeli
Communist party—RAKAH—and the Matzpen group. The
Israeli CP was founded in the late 1920s and was, almost
from the beginning, a Stalinist party. It has remained so to
this day. In its history the party has undergone many splits,
most of them over the question of what policy to adopt
towards Arab nationalism; and in general the party has
always followed the foreign policy of the U.S.S.R. The most
recent of the many absurd positions which such a policy
leads to is the support of the party for the Rogers peace plan.
The aim of this plan is to stabilize the political setup in the
region and to consolidate both the Zionist regime and the
reactionary Arab regimes. RAKAH originally defined this
plan as an attempt by the United States "to save its tottering
influence in the Arab world"†; it subsequently called for a

* J. Amitain, editor, in *SIAH* no. 5, August 1970.
† *Zo Haderekh*, September 2, 1970.

joint struggle of all peace-loving forces in Israel to implement it. The key to this absurd position is the policy of the U.S.S.R., since the Rogers plan is the result of an agreement between the United States and the U.S.S.R.

In 1965 there was a split in the party, when the Mikunis-Sneh leadership, which had always leaned towards Zionism, demanded a "more constructive" policy towards Zionism. This group supported the June 1967 war and applied for membership in the Zionist Congress. Although it has usurped the official daily paper of the party and its name, MAKI, it has hardly any influence in Israel. The other faction, led by Vilner and Tuby, is the same old Stalinist party; it has an equal number of Jewish and Arab members, and appears under the name of New Communist List, RAKAH. Actually, there is nothing new about it. The CP has always defended the rights of the Palestinian Arabs, and not only their right to self-determination, but many of their daily rights in Israel. It has waged a courageous, trade-union, day-to-day struggle to defend the rights of the Palestinians, but it abandoned the theory and practice of revolution a long time ago. It is now dedicated to the slogan of "the peaceful road to socialism," and considers its main goal to be "peace and democracy."

It was this absence of revolutionary politics that compelled a group of members to leave MAKI in 1962 and to form the Israeli Socialist Organization, better known by the name of its magazine, *Matzpen* (Compass). The Matzpen group accepted the MAKI positions on the right of the Palestinian people as well as the Israeli people to self-determination. It gives primacy to the anti-Zionist struggle and subordinates all other issues, such as the economic struggle of the working class, to this struggle. It considers the overthrow of Zionism as the first task confronting revolutionaries in Israel. At the same time it believes that Israeli society, unlike white society in South Africa, can be revolutionized from within, provided that such a development is subordinated to revolutionary developments in the Arab world. Despite its small size Matzpen has gained influence among the youth in Israel, especially after the 1967 June war, which it opposed. Matzpen has carried out an open dialogue with left tendencies within the Palestinian resistance movement and throughout the Arab world. It supports anti-imperialist struggles and the Palestinian struggle against Israeli domination. However, it does not support Arab nationalism or Nasserism. Recently two tendencies split off from Matzpen on these issues. One considers the struggle against Zionism irrelevant, and is calling for ordinary "working-class struggle against bourgeois policies." The other regards Arab nationalism as a revolutionary force. Such a split was expected, but the majority of Matzpen members have chosen to reject these two lines. Matzpen believes that revolutionaries in Israel have a significant role to play in contributing to the overthrow of Zionism within Israeli society; and in this Matzpen differs not only from SIAH and the Communist party, but also from the groups which have split off.

This analysis has illustrated the specific class structure of Israeli society, and the particular structure of the ruling class. It is a society formed through immigration and the colonization of an already populated land, a society whose internal unity is maintained through conflict with an external enemy. In this society the ruling class is allied to imperialism and depends on it, but does not itself serve imperialism by economic exploitation of the Israeli people. This class rules through a set of bureaucratic institutions that were developed during the colonization process (Histadruth, Jewish Agency), and only a subordinate section of it operates through private ownership of the means of production. These features cannot be explained as products of the internal dynamic of Israeli society; yet they are easily understood as products of the dynamic of the Zionist enterprise as a whole.

The Class Nature of Israel

Both the experience of political activity in Israel and the theoretical conclusions presented here lead to a conclusion about the strategy of the revolutionary struggle in Israel: in the immediate future, political struggle against the Zionist nature of the regime must take precedence over everything else. This struggle must be directed to win the support of all those who directly suffer from Zionism. This includes all those who, like Israeli youth or Israeli Arabs, are brought in their daily experience into conflict with the regime itself. It is a strategy which points to the shattering of the Zionist character of the regime.

3. Israel's Mission in Africa

Africa Research Group

The preceding article demonstrates, among other things, Israel's total economic dependence on the West. The following essay explores the other side of the equation: what the Western powers exact from Israel in return. While much Marxist argument about Israel's importance to the West has rested on the obvious value of a stable and loyal ally in the oil-rich Middle East, the present study (undertaken by the Africa Research Group) investigates the more strategic question of Israel's expanding role in sub-Saharan Africa. It first appeared in Palestine: Crisis and Liberation *(Havana, Tricontinental, 1970).*

Israel's initial penetration in Africa came on a small scale in 1957 when her own national interest prompted her to seek political allies in the Third World. Israel was unhappy in 1956 because the Suez affair had identified her too closely with the interests of Great Britain, France, and the United States. It had reinforced Arab efforts to brand Israel as a "tool of imperialism" and provided too much hard evidence for political comfort. The growing strength of Muslim communities and the emerging Afro-Asian solidarity movement, born at the Bandung Conference in 1955, threatened to isolate Israel politically and economically. She sought to improve her international position by fashioning mechanisms which could undermine the emerging alliance between Asian, Arab, and African nationalisms. From their inception, these mechanisms have reflected the needs and interests of neocolonialism, even as they have pretended to subordinate themselves completely to African aspirations or have cloaked themselves in the rhetoric of idealistic mission.

The evidence shows that: (1) the U.S. government helped shape the style and substance of Israeli assistance programs to Africa; (2) the United States and its allies helped finance those programs through the use of the semicovert "third country" technique; (3) Israeli assistance programs have been concentrated in strategically important areas—particularly in specialized military training with direct "counterinsurgency" (i.e., counterrevolutionary) applications; (4) these Israeli programs serve the interests of a *relatively* small-scale Israeli imperialism and integrate nicely into a multinational U.S. imperialist strategy. We consider this exposition as part of the larger disclosure of those techniques with which Western interests seek to preserve their political hegemony and economic control over the peoples of Africa.

In fact, detailed information about Israeli programs is most readily available in little-known but revealing reports prepared by "experts" on the payroll of U.S. imperialism itself. Not surprisingly, the most complete survey and analysis of Israeli programs was prepared by a staff member of the U.S. Agency for International Development (USAID) responsible for administering the U.S. foreign aid program; *Israel and the Developing Nations: New Approaches to Cooperation* (1967) was written by Leopold Laufer, a State Department official and former policy adviser to the propaganda organ "Voice of America." A second—and unpublished—study is the work of a researcher for the Pentagon.

U.S. Strategists Decide to Use Israel

America's growing cadre of Africa strategists decided that an Israeli presence could be useful in Africa. The late Arnold Rivkin, an economist who headed the Africa Research Project at the Massachusetts Institute of Technology's CIA-organized Center for International Studies and later went on to a key role at the World Bank, was one of the first Americans to set out publicly the assumptions which underlay the U.S. decision to take advantage of the convergence of interests between the U.S. and Israel on the African front.

In the prestigious journal *Foreign Affairs*, Rivkin wrote in 1959 that Israel's moderate form of socialist development could serve as an important example to developing nations revolting against the West. "The Israeli model," he declared, "may well prove to be a sort of economic 'third force'—an alternative differing from the Western pattern, *but certainly far more compatible with free-world interests* than any communist model." (Our italics.) In this collection of proposals for sophisticated "free-world" policies to be coordinated by the United States, published as *Africa and the West,* he outlines the way the U.S. could support Israeli penetration:

> Israel's role as a third force might also be reinforced by imaginative use of the *third country technique.* A free world state wishing to enlarge its assistance flow to Africa might channel some part of it through Israel because of Israel's special qualifications and demonstrated acceptability to many African nations.[1]

Between 1951 and 1962, Israel received $15 million in aid and assistance from the United States. From 1950 to 1964, the UN and its specialized agencies—themselves often shaped and controlled by the U.S.—spent over $5 million on experts and fellowships for Israel.

The programs built a network through which U.S. expertise was "imported" into Israel only to be "exported" by Israeli nationals somewhat later. The United States was pleased with the "multiplier effect" that this aid had in broadening the impact of a U.S.-conceived strategy. Henry Chalfant, former U.S. Mission Director in Israel, quite frankly admitted this intention when he wrote:

> Israelis selected for training abroad were carefully chosen with a view to returning to Israel as disseminators of skill and knowledge to others. This "multiplier effect" is an essential element of any program, of technical assistance. ... The high quality of the trained Israelis is further attested to by the fact that Israel is now and has been in recent years transferring these acquired skills and knowledge to less fortunate people through a technical assistance program of her own.[2]

To preserve its credibility and enhance its effectiveness, Israel did not adopt American techniques wholesale, but modified them with a distinctive twist based on Israeli experience. Although Israel continues to require and receive foreign assistance, the size and scope of this technical training has decreased and changed in character over the years. Nevertheless, a development technology "Made in USA" has left its unmistakable mark on Israel's strategy and style.

The Scope of the Israeli Assistance Program

Israel's program of assistance to Africa assumes several basic forms: (1) highly trained Israeli "experts" are placed at the disposal of African states, often in strategically important positions; (2) various categories of African personnel, including students, civil servants, labor leaders, and military cadres are given specialized training in Israel itself; this training is

Table 1
Israeli Experts Serving Abroad and
Trainees Arriving in Israel, by Field
of Service or Training, 1958–66

Field of Service or Training	Total	Africa
	EXPERTS	
TOTAL	1,815	1,261
Agriculture	523	261
Youth organization	256	234
Engineering	64	42
Medicine and health	202	173
Education	106	102
Cooperation	24	21
Management	63	46
Construction and building	65	49
Social work	23	22
Miscellaneous	489	311

	TRAINEES	
TOTAL	9,074	4,482
Agriculture	2,264	805
Cooperation and trade unionism	1,048	664
Community development	712	493
Youth leadership	529	285
Medicine and health	265	211
Commerce, transport, finance, industry	156	37
Study tours and seminars	1,622	537
Individual academic studies	230	102
Miscellaneous	2,248	1,348

usually provided quickly and efficiently; and (3) Israeli businessmen and their government have set up joint economic enterprises with African states and private business.

In the first category, most of the important specialized assistance is military and paramilitary in nature and will be discussed in greater detail. Nonmilitary assistance programs utilize the "parallel training approach"—that is, while Israeli experts serve abroad, Africans are given specialized assistance in Israel. This assistance has been highly diversified, embracing everything from poultry training in Guinea to setting up national lotteries in Dahomey; from youth movement organizing in Gabon to pediatrics in the Upper Volta. The preceding table outlines the scope of these programs between 1958 and 1966.

Israel's agricultural programs are organized on military lines and carried out either directly by the military or agencies linked to it. Before he became defense minister, General Moshe Dayan took an active interest in shaping Israel's agricultural programs in Africa. This reflects the militarization of agriculture in Israel itself. Since the kibbutz system and most Israeli collective farms are closely tied into the national defense effort, this agricultural program has been organized on paramilitary lines. It is this highly political model of organization which Israel "exports" to Africa.

Israeli efforts seek to assist neocolonial states in mobilizing their populations for "development." In the area of youth mobilization, Israel developed the *Gadna* (Youth Battalions) and *Nahal* (Fighting Pioneer Youth), which have been used as models for similar programs in African states. In theory, these programs are nonpolitical; in practice, they create politically potent and militarily useful bodies. Laufer explains what they do:

Gadna (youth battalions for boys and girls aged fourteen to eighteen) offers sports, hiking, camping, crafts, group discussions, and cultural activities, as well as physical work and some paramilitary training. Nahal, which takes up where Gadna leaves off, is for young men and women of military age and includes paratrooper regular military training, followed by agricultural settlement in difficult or dangerous places.[3]

By 1966 Israeli experts had organized these "nation-building" programs in thirteen African countries: Cameroon, the Central African Republic, Chad, Dahomey, Ivory Coast, Liberia, Malawi, Niger, Senegal, Tanzania, Togo, Uganda, and Zambia. Other Israeli advisers carried on similar activities in Bolivia, Ecuador, Costa Rica, and Singapore.

Specialized training in Israel is provided on several levels. Government ministries offer courses, as do quasi-government agencies such as the Israeli labor complex, Histadruth. Histadruth, a nominally "socialist" but not anti-imperialist union, sponsors its own Afro-Asian Institute for Labor Studies and Cooperation in Tel Aviv, headed by Ellahu Elath, Israel's first ambassador to the United States. It turns out thirty to fifty "trained leaders" every three to four months. Significantly, this institute was launched with a $60,000 grant from the AFL-CIO in 1960; between 1960 and 1962 it received over $300,000 in scholarships and grants from the AFL-CIO and its affiliated national unions, such as the British Trade Union Congress (TUC). Disclosures by prominent journalists in the United States have since revealed that the international programs of the AFL-CIO are virtually integrated into and coexistent with the CIA's international labor strategy. African trade unions are highly political instruments and the training which takes place in Israel seeks to depoliticize them by pushing a "cooperative" orientation rather than a working-class, revolutionary, one.*

"The emphasis," admits Arnold Zack, a Harvard-trained ICFTU (International Confederation of Free Trade Unions) agent, "is on cooperation with other segments of society; comparatively little time is devoted to skills of building trade unions as a power force in the country."[4]

Most Israeli training programs are short-run and highly concentrated in nature. More than nine thousand "trainees" from the Third World have been exposed to Israeli seminars, conferences, and training courses. Only a few hundred students have spent more than a year in the country. Most courses are for middle-level personnel and concentrate, according to Laufer, on "transmitting new ideas and attitudes."

> The Israelis have learned [he reports] that trainees brought to Israel for short periods of highly intensive, controlled exposure usually carry away with them a more favorable image than those who stay for longer periods. . . . Since the exposure to Israel is selective, the trainees encounter the most attractive aspects of Israeli life and society.

These courses have enhanced Israel's political reputation on the continent while performing an important ideological and training function for imperialism.

---

* Another professionally run institute, the Center for Cooperative and Labor Studies in Tel Aviv, caters to the Latin American trade unionists and is supported by both the foreign ministry and Histadruth. "Occasionally," discloses Laufer, "the Center runs three-week seminars for South American trade unionists sponsored by the American Institute for Free Labor Development (AIFLD)." The AIFLD has been publicly exposed as a major CIA labor operation in Latin America which is openly funded by USAID.

Israel's interest in Africa is also prompted by economic considerations. As a geographically convenient source of raw materials and a market for Israeli goods, Africa has a natural attraction to businessmen. Trade between Israel and African nations is active and growing in volume. The volume of Israeli exports to Africa stood at $11.6 million in 1963; by 1965 it was $21.5 million. Notes Laufer: "It is probably more than a coincidence that the greatest increases have been in exports to those African countries (for example, Ethiopia, Ghana, Kenya, Nigeria, and Uganda) that also have an active technical cooperation program with Israel."[5] As a source of raw materials Africa is also crucial; the scale of Israeli imports from Africa is even more significant than exports and is growing. Samuel Decalo, another U.S. expert, has an interesting observation about the nature of this economic relationship:

> African imports of a number of Israeli commodities (e.g., furniture, cement, distilled soya oil) even if small in absolute figures amount to over 50 percent of total Israeli exports of these items. There are a number of other commodities (e.g., asbestos pipes, pharmaceuticals, carpets) of which Africa purchases over 25 percent of the Israeli exports with significant purchases of others below this figure . . . In like manner, Africa is Israel's prime supplier for a number of tropical products.[6]

Most observers think that Israel stands a good chance of *increasing* the extent and scope of these economic relationships.

The modes of Israeli economic investment tend to be deliberately designed to minimize suspicion on the part of Africans. By mid-1963, forty-two companies based on partnerships between Israeli and African public capital had been established. Explained *The Economist:*

Instead of demanding control, or concessions for long
periods, the Israelis almost invariably postulate as a condition of their participation that their shareholding *must*
be minority. Contracts are limited to five years, at the
end of which the local majority stockholders are given
the option of buying the Israeli interest out. . . . Companies jointly financed by Israeli and African public
bodies have been operating in Ghana, Liberia, Nigeria,
Sierra Leone, Ivory Coast, Dahomey, Niger, Upper
Volta, Senegal, Tanganyika, and two or three other
states.[7]

Israel's policy in this regard is motivated by shrewd economic reasoning. Explains Laufer:

. . . joint ventures have enabled Israeli companies to
enter new markets with relatively small capital investment and under the benevolent protection of the
governments of developing countries. Since in many of
these countries domestic markets are closely guarded by
long-established foreign or expatriate firms, the Israeli
firms might have found it difficult to establish themselves without the partnerships.[8]

The types of projects advanced with this method of Israeli
penetration have also tended to assist neocolonial governments with schemes which have a questionable benefit and
are hardly priorities for the majority of their impoverished
populations. For example, companies in which the Israeli
quasi-public firm, Solel Boneh, has been a partner have built:
an airport in Accra, luxury hotels in Eastern Nigeria, university buildings, eight hundred miles of road in Western Nigeria,
fancy Parliament buildings in Sierra Leone and Eastern Nigeria, and military installations in the Ivory Coast.

Israel's economic interest in Africa is a long-range one. Her limited economic involvement is in part a function of the tight control with which metropole powers and the United States seek to monopolize trade and retain preferences. But whatever its cause, this appearance of economic conservatism allows Israel room for considerable political maneuverability.

Israel and the International
Counterrevolution—Military Assistance

Israel comes into its own with sensitive and highly specialized military and police-intelligence training. A myriad of programs provide African states the type of military and police know-how required to build up effective internal security forces designed to protect those neocolonialist governments from being overthrown by their own populations.

Information about this dimension of Israeli penetration is veiled in secrecy. When a member of the Africa Research Group made a first attempt to seek out this information (by contacting a professor who has written about Israeli involvement in Africa), he was informed that "printed material on Afro-Israeli military information is pretty difficult to obtain. Whatever material exists is in Hebrew, much of it being classified." The professor, however, suggested that an inquiry be sent to Sanford Silverburg at American University in Washington, D.C.

Silverburg turned out to be more than just another academic. He is a professional researcher on the staff of the Center for Research in Social Systems (CRESS), a major research operation funded by the U.S. Army (to the tune of $1.9 million in 1967). CRESS was reorganized in 1966 following disclosures of its participation in the notorious Project Camelot, an intellectual espionage mission in Latin America.[9] It presently has two divisions: CINFAC, a Counterinsurgency

Information Analysis Center; and SSRI, a Social Science Research Institute which studies ways of improving the effectiveness of U.S. military personnel attached as advisers to the armed forces of other countries.

CRESS's interest in Israeli military programs in Africa is part of its larger responsibility for developing research which aids the Pentagon's commitment to preserve and defend the empire. The United States has been a long-term supplier of military assistance to Israel, as part of a broader policy in the Middle East. Between 1964 and 1967 military assistance to Israel amounted to $41.6 million, while total U.S. economic and military assistance was $1,127 million.[10]

Israeli military personnel are trained in the United States, as are soldiers from Arab countries. There are also a number of information-sharing arrangements between the Israeli and U.S. military establishments. In 1968 the Department of Defense financed close to $2 million worth of scientific research through thirty-two contracts at Israeli universities and research centers.[11]

Sanford Silverburg has spent five years on the CRESS staff, during which time he has also worked on graduate degrees at American University. While still attached to CRESS, he prepared a Masters thesis for the School of International Service (sic) entitled *Israeli Military and Paramilitary Assistance to Sub-Saharan Africa: A Harbinger for the Role of the Military in Developing States.* While concerned primarily with studying the Israeli military role in shaping the "nation-building" process—a notion very much in fashion among Pentagon officials and development planners—this document appears to be the most complete available nonclassified breakdown of the range and import of Israeli military programs.

At the outset of his study Silverburg acknowledges that data are hard to obtain, but nevertheless he manages (presumably through CRESS's resources) to pull together an impressive amount of evidence from a wide range of American, European, African and Israeli sources. In table 2, we outline the breakdown on a country-by-country basis.

The practical help Israeli military training provides the objectives of U.S. imperialism is best illustrated by the situation in the Congo, one of Africa's richest and most strategically located countries. The U.S. role in the Congo since independence is notorious: by the accounts of such men as Conor Cruise O'Brien, the United States played a determining role in structuring the government of the Congo after engineering a UN intervention which helped topple the Lumumba government and impose a servile one. The CIA was deeply involved in General Mobutu's original rise to power. At the prodding of U.S. corporate and financial interests, the United States maintained an active role in the Congo, particularly when organized rebellions and guerrilla movements began to threaten U.S. hegemony. In the course of developing effective counterinsurgency techniques, the U.S. Army ordered a study on "Witchcraft, Sorcery, Magic and Other Psychological Phenomena and Their Implications on Military and Paramilitary Operations in the Congo" (1964), which the academics at the Army-funded Counterinsurgency Analysis Center at American University provided. The report's conclusion is directly relevant to the role Israel came to assume. "Drawing upon the Belgian experience as well as that of Tshombe in Katanga," it noted, "it would appear that a more flexible approach to the military problem is to be found in the concept of elite troops: troops which are carefully trained and disciplined and which are well commanded." This military advice was accepted: only so as to diminish an already overextended and politically embarrassing *overt* U.S. role, it was the Israelis who took on the task of training the Congo's crack elite paracommando squadron.

Table 2

Israeli Military and Paramilitary Assistance Programs to Sub-Saharan Africa 1960–1966

Country	Year	Nature of Israeli Program
Cameroon	1966	Israeli Army officers set up Nahal-Gadna system in January.
Central African Republic	1960	50 study grants to individuals.
	1962	14 Army officers set up National Pioneer Youth with Israeli-trained staff (2-year contract).
Chad	1964	Student training by advisers sent to youth movement.
	1967	2 Israeli advisers killed in counterinsurgency operations with Chad Army against National Liberation Front of Chad.
Congo (K)	1963	243 Congolese paratroops sent to Israel for air training, including now President, General Joseph Mobutu.
	1964	Israeli advisers go to Congo to provide 100 more Congolese troops with parachute instruction, in October.
	1968	In March, Israelis train 35 more paratroopers in First Paracommando Battalion, considered "best unit."
Dahomey	1962	Israelis "advise" First Army Pioneer Company.
	1966	2 Israeli advisers administer Young Pioneers Youth Movement (USAID supported).
Ethiopia	1960–66	Israelis operate counterinsurgency program directed against Eritrean Liberation Front and Shiftas of Kenya.
		Israelis replace U.S. Special Forces "removed" after aborted coup by U.S.-trained Ethiopian officers.
		Substantial cooperation between Ethiopian and Israeli military operations includes: training for special forces, intelligence, counterinsurgency operations.
		Israel maintains major military mission graduating 500 men every 6 months.
		Israel cooperates with U.S. and Ethiopian military in establishing base at Jebel Hamid.
Ghana	[dates unknown]	Ghana Air Force and flying school organized, jeopardizing Britain's unilateral control.
		Israel provides assistance to Army, Navy units.
		British commercial interests force Israel out of Ghana.

Ivory Coast	1961	Nahal-Gadna-type program set up with help from USAID. *Service civique* revamped and revitalized, to consternation of French.
	1963	Army school for "civic action" established.
		On advice of Israel, Ivory Coast seeks to use Army in "national service."
		Israel equips Presidential Guard with Israeli-made Uzzi 7.66 mm submachine guns.
Kenya	1963	5 Air Force cadets and 30 Army personnel "unofficially" trained through 1963 (negligible program).
Malawi		Israel trains medical personnel.
		4 instructors help set up Malawi Young Pioneers Movement, paramilitary organization of 500 to 700 members.
Nigeria	1967	Army and police training provided.
		Israeli-made 11 mm mortars supplied.
		1967 charge that Israel also supplies weapons to Biafra denied by Israeli ambassador to Nigeria in January 1969.
Sierra Leone	1966	Israel helps set up Military Academy; 65 officers remain for 2 additional years.
Tanzania	1963	60 cadets trained in 193-day course.
		National Service Corps set up on Israeli model with Israeli assistance runs into trouble when 117 members are detained or discharged for disloyalty (no implication of Israeli involvement).
	1964	24 Naval Marine Unit cadets trained.
	1966	120 police receive paratroop training; unit assigned to maintain order, deter cattle rustling and, according to speculations, reserved for use against Zanzibar if necessary.
		Israel rumored to be involved with Tanzanian intelligence.
Togo	1961	7-man Israeli team organizes Agricultural Youth Corps using Gadna techniques.
		Experiments with *moshav* settlement schemes initiated.
Uganda	1963	15 Army officers, 5 pilots trained in Israel.
	1964	Air Force organized and trained.
	1966	Israel assumes all military training, supplies some planes, is alleged to be conduit for French assistance to Uganda.

What is significant about these Israeli programs is not their size but rather their strategic concentration in building up elite sections within increasingly important military institutions. That these institutions are also in countries which have most significant U.S. penetration (i.e., Ethiopia and Congo [Kinshasa]) is by no means coincidental. These programs give the Israelis, and through the Israelis, the United States, intimate access and influence in the internal development of the respective countries. "The granting of assistance—military or other—," admits Silverburg, "is also an open invitation to the donor to firmly establish its national interests in the recipient country, which may include inciting revolt and rebellion, though on a covert status."[12]

Since its involvement is motivated as much by the *international* interests of U.S. imperialism as by its own *national* interest, Israel takes great pains to work closely with the host government to avoid "misunderstandings." At the same time, Israeli programs are tied into a larger CIA and Western intelligence operation. Because of the very nature of intelligence-training Israeli agents provide Tanzanians, Ethiopians, and Congolese, Israel is deeply enmeshed in the sub rosa world of intrigue and covert political manipulation.

Hard facts about Israel's covert role are even more difficult to amass than information about military programs. There is evidence that Israel supported covertly a number of liberation movements which also enjoyed U.S. backing. The Israelis are reputed to be quietly assisting the Sudanese rebels and the discredited forces of Holden Roberto in Angola. On the diplomatic level, information obtained by the Israelis is often shared with local American embassies. In a recent interview, one observer said that such a practice is widespread and cited Uganda as one country in which the Israeli embassy serviced information needs of the other Western ambassadors and their staffs. In exchange, it is known that U.S. counter-insurgency and counter-guerrilla expertise has been shared with the Israeli military in its efforts to destroy the Palestine liberation organizations.*

Not all Israeli military and paramilitary programs or covert activities have been successful. They run up against the deeply-rooted problems and contradictions which plague all Western attempts to shape impoverished African states to suit their interests. Strategies to modernize armies as institutions for national integration and development have backfired when African army officers preferred a share of the power and privileges enjoyed now by the Western-backed neocolonial elites. Many of these soldiers are not motivated ideologically to seek political change and, when they do, prefer coup-style takeovers to the more "functional role" foreign experts prefer.

At the same time, foreign assistance, whether of the Israeli brand or another variety, cannot escape the central contradiction: countries which are oppressed by an imperialist system cannot develop with selective assistance by these oppressing powers. In fact, these programs only increase dependency and subordination. Mindful of their own long-run interests, the Israelis have limited their engagement in Africa to certain spheres, avoiding direct political identification with the imperialist powers. That "invisibility," however, is slowly being punctured—largely by Israel's own expansionist ambitions in the Middle East. Like their North American "Uncle," the Israelis have been forced into open counterrevolutionary warfare at home and abroad. The lessons of that identification are slowly filtering down among the African people.

---

* According to Silverburg, Israeli officers including General Dayan have visited Vietnam for on-the-spot investigation of counterrevolutionary warfare. Moreover, he "guessed" that "What We Learned" forms which U.S. soldiers fill out after encounters with the NLF "find their way to Israeli military officials." Silverburg thought the Israeli military was much more proficient in this regard than the U.S. has been in Vietnam.

Imperialism Finances Israel's Programs

Israel does not disclose the full extent of its aid program to Africa nor reveal who pays the bills. Funds are known to come directly from Israel's government, partner governments in Africa, international organizations, and to some extent private sources.

In 1966–67 Israel's Department of International Cooperation (Moshav) reported a budget of £10 million Israeli ($3.33 million). This figure, however, is very misleading. For one thing, Israeli costs are lower than the costs of comparable U.S. projects. In fact, the former director of the Department of International Cooperation of the Ministry of Foreign Affairs, according to Laufer, "told a group of U.S. visitors that Israel gets twice as much for its foreign aid dollar as does the United States."[13]

Nearly half of Israel's total program is financed by non-Israeli sources. The United States government, through the third-country technique, has been an important contributor to these programs. Exact figures on the U.S. contribution are hidden. Silverburg said it would be a waste of time trying to find out the exact figure. "These third-country arrangements," he disclosed in a conversation, "are usually handled with a tremendous amount of discretion. Even if you had some journalist's figures, he could be as much as a million dollars off." The Laufer report does mention some AID support for Israel's youth programs in the Central African Republic, Dahomey, and Costa Rica. It also mentions that "France has assisted youth projects in the Ivory Coast; and Great Britain and West Germany have reportedly given assistance to projects elsewhere in Africa."

Western support to Israel no doubt makes it possible for her to maintain an active program of penetration. Israel still earns more revenue from monies contributed from abroad than on monies obtained from exports. Without international

credits and contributions solicited abroad with the cooperation and complicity of Western powers, Israel could not survive economically. Its balance of payments problems have
always posed real difficulties for the economy. Without
financing from non-Israeli sources, her Africa programs
would be inconceivable. Acknowledges Laufer:

> Israel's achievement in having more than half its effort
> financed from non-Israeli sources is probably unique in
> the tangled history of postwar technical assistance
> operations. This shows how a small country, short of
> capital but with the will, and objective capacity, can
> generate a sizeable technical assistance program with
> little capital investment and negligible effect on its
> balance of payments position.[14]

Not all of the revenue for these programs comes directly
through the United States or imperialist powers. Some of the
expenses are met by recipient African nations. However,
these nations are often themselves dependent on Western aid;
hence the United States or some other ally funding an
African state enables it to afford the expenses of an Israeli
assistance program which itself is receiving disguised or covert
support through other channels. The United States could also
free local currency holdings in African states to help finance
Israeli training and assistance efforts.

U.S.-Israeli Coordination

There are many levels on which U.S. and Israeli "Africa
experts" exchange views and coordinate programs. Some of
these are governmental, but other, more important, exchanges
often take place on a private, nongovernmental basis through
meetings, seminars, and conferences. One such highly significant conference took place December 6–8, 1963, at Arden
House, formerly the plush Harriman estate, high above the

Hudson River near Bear Mountain, New York, now operated by Columbia University.

Sponsored by the National Committee for Labor Israel, a U.S.-based fund-raising outfit for Israel's Histadruth, the meeting brought together key U.S. and Israeli strategists to discuss programmatic approaches to foreign aid, the role of cooperatives and private enterprises and voluntary agencies, as well as some problems of Negro-Jewish relations. The list of the participants is impressive and instructive. The United States was represented by a number of experts with close links to the government, particularly the CIA. They include: Arnold Rivkin; Benjamin Rivlin, an Africanist who served with the OAS and State Department; Edmund Hutchison, a one-time RCA executive, then AID administrator; John A. Davis, the president of the CIA-funded American Society of African Culture (AMSAC); and the dean of the corporate-liberal Africanists, F. Taylor Ostrander, assistant to the chairman of the American Metal Climax Corporation, the major U.S. mining concern in central and southern Africa. Ostrander, who has served in a number of high government posts, is vice president of the Tools for Freedom Foundation, a CIA-supported program.

Israel was represented by top Histadruth officials. Others present include an official of the ICFTU, a representative of the World Bank, and an editor of *Fortune* magazine. Assistant Secretary of State Harlan Cleveland sent greetings to the meeting, and excerpts from the proceedings were published under the revealing title *The Free World and the New Nations* (A. S. Barnes and Co., 1964). Not only do the conception of the meeting and its content mesh nicely with the U.S. strategy outlined publicly by Arnold Rivkin, but, as Histadruth spokesmen made clear in more than one speech, the Israelis identified with the U.S.-sponsored "free world" mission in Africa and sought to assist it.

The Israeli Model: A Harbinger for the Future?

The Israeli experience has served as a model for similar ventures by U.S. client states and may be a harbinger of new perspectives and new modes of imperialist penetration in Africa, Asia, and Latin America.

The Israeli model interests U.S. policy-planners most as an example of an attempt at the mutual, multinational approach to aid. U.S. strategists want to get away from bilateral approaches because they tend to brand the United States politically as an interventionist. Global strategists would prefer to control the Third World through regional instruments (i.e., SEATO in Asia, OAS in Latin America, OAU in Africa). By directing broader regional groupings or multilateral assistance programs the United States can retain effective control with fewer political liabilities. They disguise the American role without limiting its power. What remains now is for the United States to work out the snags in such programs, develop new organs of cooperation, and more effective machinery for multigovernment planning. The experience with Israel is an important first step.

NOTES

1 Arnold Rivkin, *Africa and the West* (New York: F. A. Praeger, 1961), p. 89.

2 Leopold Laufer, *Israel and the Developing Countries: New Approaches to Cooperation* (New York: Twentieth Century Fund, 1968).

3 *Ibid.*, p. 110.

4 Arnold Zack, *Labor Training in Developing Countries* (New York: F. A. Praeger, 1967).

5 Laufer, *op. cit.*, p. 211.

6 Samuel Decalo, "Israel and Africa: A Selected Bibliography," *Journal of Modern African Studies*, March 5, 1967, p. 391.

7 *The Economist,* August 24, 1963.

8 Laufer, *op. cit.*, p. 148.

9 *See* I. L. Horowitz, *The Rise and Fall of Project Camelot*, 1968.

10 "U.S. Overseas Loans and Grants, Special Report," March 1968, p. 15.

11 Senator Fulbright inserted a complete list of all of the overseas defense research in the *Congressional Record*, May 1969.

12 Sanford Silverburg, *Israeli Military and Paramilitary Assistance to Sub-Saharan Africa: A Harbinger for the Role of the Military in Developing States* (Masters thesis, American University, 1968).

13 Laufer, *op. cit.*, p. 50.

14 *Ibid.*, p. 62.

The
Palestinian
Resistance

1. Origins of the Armed Resistance
Leila S. Kadi

The following introduction to the history of the Palestinian armed resistance appeared in the volume Basic Documents of the Armed Palestinian Resistance Movement, *published in Beirut in December 1969 by the Research Center of the Palestine Liberation Organization. It was prepared by the collection's editor, Leila S. Kadi, though the text reflects multiple authorship and draws freely on unacknowledged sources. Despite its "official" character as a PLO publication, its treatment of the splits and divisions within the resistance is accurate and generally free of polemic.*

Armed resistance, contrary to appearances, is not new to the Palestinian people. They have taken up arms against foreign rule since the British Mandate. The revolution of 1936 represented the peak of the Palestinian struggle against both the British Mandate and Zionism. It followed a long period of political struggle by the Palestinian people exemplified in memoranda of protest, demonstrations, strikes and attempts at dissuading Britain from supporting the Zionist movement.

The distinguishing feature of the 1936 popular revolution is that the traditional Palestinian feudal, religious and bourgeois leadership had nothing to do with its outbreak. The man who played a leading role in preparing for the revolution was Izz al-Din al-Qassam, a simple man who had contacted the leader, Haj Amin al-Husseini, requesting an appointment as a roving preacher to prepare for the revolution. Al-Husseini refused this request, saying: "We are working for a political solution to the problem."

Undiscouraged, Qassam went ahead and organized secret cells among the poor workers and peasants. On November 14, 1935, Qassam fought his first battle against the British forces in the Jenin area where he was killed. Although the Qassam movement was unable to achieve any of its major aims, it still challenged the traditional leaders before the people.

The second phase of the revolution started on April 15, 1936. Qassam's secret organizations renewed their operations from the rural areas and the revolution spread from the north of Palestine to the south. On April 19 the city of Jaffa witnessed a massive popular uprising. The British forces reacted by blowing up whole quarters of the city. In response, the "national committees" of the people declared a general strike.

On April 25, the national committees forced the Islamic Council and various other groups to disband their political organizations and form the Arab Higher Committee to lead the people's struggle through a general strike and armed revolution. The leaders acceded to the proposed radical measures under obvious massive popular pressure, generated by Qassam's armed resistance movement.

When the British failed to crush the revolution or prevent it from spreading, they turned to the pro-British Arab rulers to use their influence to convince the Palestinian people to end the revolution and negotiate peacefully with Britain. The Arab rulers' response, headed by Nuri al-Sa'id, was positive.

Sa'id visited Jerusalem on August 26, 1936, and asked the Arab Higher Committee to take all possible measures to end the strike and disturbances, promising that the Iraqi government would negotiate with the British government to satisfy the legitimate demands of the Arab people of Palestine.

The Palestinian people rejected the principle of Arab mediation and carried on their armed struggle until the rulers of Trans-Jordan, Saudi Arabia, Iraq and the Yemen intervened and sent cables to the Palestinian people telling them to "keep quiet."

In spite of the popular rejection of Arab mediation, the Arab Higher Committee issued a statement announcing its approval of the principle of Arab mediation, and urging the Palestinian people to end the strike and the disturbances as of October 12, 1936. With this statement the second phase of the Palestinian revolution came to an end. It clearly revealed the Palestinian people's readiness to adopt the method of armed struggle and reject the logic of negotiations with Britain by foiling the efforts of the Arab rulers to mediate between them (Palestinians) and the British government. Moreover, the second phase gave clear indications of the hesitation and continuous efforts of the traditional Palestinian bourgeois and feudal leadership to agree to any mediation to end the revolution and start political negotiations with Britain. The important element during this phase was the interference of the Arab rulers, who belonged to the same class structure as the Palestinian leaders and imposed their position on the Palestinian people.

The third phase of the Palestinians' armed revolution is marked by the assassination on September 27, 1937, at the hands of the revolutionaries, of L. Andrews, Acting District Commissioner in Nazareth. The Arab Higher Committee issued a communiqué condemning this act. In this phase the antagonism between the rural masses and the bourgeois feudal leadership came into the open. The British authorities reacted by escalating their acts of repression and terror. Members of the Arab Higher Committee were imprisoned and others fled the country.

The people's revolution spread and was concentrated in the provinces of Nablus, Galilee and the northern district. At the beginning of 1938 the revolutionaries were in full control of the villages of these areas where they had wide influence.

The weak point of the revolution was the absence of a unified, politically aware leadership which could be responsible for coordinating military action between the different areas. As for the traditional feudal leadership, some of its members were in exile while others were cooperating with the British authorities to destroy the revolution. The revolution suffered under some severe handicaps. First of all there was the constant personal bickering for leadership by the bourgeois and feudal Palestinian parties and their attack on the revolution itself, both in terms of condemning it before the Palestinian people and then by conducting negotiations with Britain. There was also the lack of any proper military coordination on the different fronts. Thus the revolution gradually became weaker and less effective. With the outbreak of World War II the revolution came to an end. The reactionary traditional leadership continued its efforts to solve the problem through negotiations with the British government. The latter sent commissions of inquiry and then issued the White Paper of 1939 which limited Jewish immigration and promised Palestinian independence in the hope of securing a calm situation in Palestine throughout the war years.

The occupying power imposed rigorous laws on the Palestinian people. It meant death for a Palestinian Arab to be found carrying a gun. This penalty, however, was not imposed on the Jews. Thus during the course of the war, it was the Jews who were being armed (often with British assistance), while the Palestinians were kept under surveillance.

The war period witnessed in Palestine an alliance between the traditional Palestinian leadership and the other Arab rulers who wanted the Palestinian people to terminate all violence against British rule. By the end of the war the Zionists were ready to fight the now-unarmed Palestinians. The Palestinians were in no way ready to face the Zionist onslaught that was unleashed against them, and the Arab armies that eventually came to their aid were too inefficient and ill-equipped. In addition the Arab feudal and bourgeois regimes were primarily concerned with maintaining close relations with Britain and the United States. The Palestinian leadership, in turning over the fate of the Palestinian people and their struggle to the reactionary Arab rulers, went back to the same tragic course of 1936.

The year 1948 saw the establishment of the state of Israel and the Arab Palestinian people's loss of their homeland and dispersal to refugee camps.

The first reaction of the Palestinian people after this disaster was to resist any kind of rapprochement that would lead to a final settlement with the state of Israel. Examples of this opposition are to be found in the following:

1. The publication in 1952 of a secret weekly bulletin, *Nashrat al-Thar,* by the Committee for Resisting Peace with Israel. This committee was mainly composed of students at the American University of Beirut. These same students were among the group that formed the nucleus of the Arab Nationalist Movement (ANM) founded by a Palestinian, Dr. George Habash. He obtained his degree in medicine from the American University of Beirut in the early fifties. After his graduation Habash practiced in Amman for a few years. Then he devoted himself to the ANM and became one of its key figures. *Nashrat al-Thar* was very effective and had a widespread distribution among the Palestinians in refugee camps up to 1954. It played a role in uncovering various secret attempts to eliminate the Palestine problem through a final

settlement with the state of Israel. Such a settlement could only mean that the Palestinians would remain forever after in a state of diaspora. The bulletin's effect was mainly among Palestinians in Lebanon, Syria and Jordan, while its influence on those in the Gaza Strip was negligible.

2. During the years 1953–54 the United Nations Relief and Works Agency (UNRWA) put forward many projects aiming at the rehabilitation of the Palestinian refugees by constructing permanent residence units. Rehabilitation meant the end of their existence as refugees and their acceptance of the state of Israel as a *fait accompli*—which meant the loss of Palestine. In order to counteract the rehabilitation projects, the Palestinians lauched mass demonstrations, organized general strikes, and destroyed many of the housing units set up by UNRWA. The rehabilitation projects were put forward again by Dag Hammarskjöld in 1959 in the form of a plan for the integration of the Palestinians in the economic life of the Middle East. The Palestinians opposed this plan by holding the Arab Palestinian Conference in Beirut in 1959. The rejection of the plan by Palestinians compelled the Arab governments to oppose it, thus forcing the UN to withdraw the plan.

3. Alongside the political struggle of the masses of the Palestinians, small Palestinian groups residing in the Gaza Strip, Syria and the West Bank took the initiative by undertaking commando action inside Israel. These commando raids, which penetrated deep into populated areas of Israel, prompted the latter to carry out a large-scale raid on Gaza on February 28, 1955, and assassinate two commando leaders, Salah Mustafa and Mustafa Hafez. These guerrilla groups were not based on, connected to, or part of any political organization, but were trained and led by Egyptian army officers. These groups were disbanded after the 1956 tripartite aggression on Suez.

Politically active Palestinian groups considered that the

Arab governments were mainly responsible for the 1948 defeat and thus they became affiliated to, and actively participated in, national Arab parties such as the Baath and the Arab Nationalist Movement. These parties called for Arab unity, which Palestinians believed was the road to a strong unified Arab state capable of confronting Israel and liberating Palestine.

With the establishment of the United Arab Republic, on February 22, 1958,* the Palestinians were convinced that they were on the brink of liberating Palestine. Historical developments proved them wrong. During the three years of unity the UAR government attempted to build up popular Palestinian organizations such as the Palestinian National Union in Syria and Gaza. These organizations were unpopular and ineffective since they were imposed from above.

At the same time, in 1959, a secret monthly magazine of limited circulation, *Our Palestine*, began publication in Beirut. *Our Palestine* called for the Palestinization of the Palestine problem. This meant that the Arab governments should give the Palestinians a free hand to work for the liberation of their country. Later on, it became known that the sponsors of *Our Palestine* were the Fateh group. This group came into existence out of the discussions of Palestinian students in the Gaza Strip who had suffered under the Israeli occupation of 1956 and were concerned with the problem how best to win back Palestine, admitting the Arab governments' inability to do it for them. Little by little, they became convinced that the Palestinians must take their cause into their own hands. Yasser Arafat became their leader.

Arafat (his code name is Abu Ammar) was born in Jerusalem in 1929. His career, in a way, mirrors the history and thrust of the Palestinian commandos. He spent his early childhood in a house within a stone's throw of the Wailing

---

* The union of Egypt and Syria under Nasser's leadership.—ED.

Wall. When the Arab-Israeli fighting of 1948 ended, Arafat found himself with his parents a refugee in Gaza. He managed to go to Cairo to study engineering at Fuad I (now Cairo) University, where he majored in civil engineering. As chairman of the Palestinian Student Federation he helped, in his own words, to "lay the basic foundation for our movement." While studying he also acted as a leader and trainer of Palestinian and Egyptian commandos who fought the British in the Suez area, served the Egyptian army as a demolitions expert and fought against the British and French at Port Said and Abu Kabir in 1956. After a brief period as an engineer in Egypt he obtained an engineering job in Kuwait in 1957, where he stayed until 1965. Meanwhile he traveled among the scattered Palestinians to recruit members for the organization. Soon cells were formed in Kuwait and among students in West Germany. The initial development was slow and went against the trends of the period.

The Myth of Arab Unity: 1957–1967

Between 1957 and 1967, talk about Arab unity reached its climax but, at the same time, rivalry between the various Arab governments became even more acute. Aspirations for Arab unity were so deeply held by the people that they constituted a reality which had to be considered. Equally significant was the interaction and confusion of the various political movements: Nasserist, Baathist, Arab Nationalist, etc., regardless of their country of origin. In this context, the Palestinian national question was not a simple one, even more so because, through the idea of unity, the existence of Israel made it possible for many Arab governments to redirect popular aspirations towards external objectives and an outside enemy. Certain Arab states (for example, the UAR and Tunisia) accused the Fateh militants of being agents of

CENTO.* President Nasser realized that the war in the Yemen had dragged on for a much longer period than was expected and was thus costing the UAR treasury more than it could afford. This led to pressing internal economic problems which threatened the effectiveness and development plans of his regime. President Nasser was of the opinion that the industry and economy of the UAR should be more developed before embarking on a war against Israel. The UAR was of the opinion that Fateh was trying to involve it in war with Israel at a time when Arab unity had not yet been achieved and the UAR's economy was not yet well developed. Thus in his opening speech to the Second Palestinian National Congress which was held in Cairo on May 31, 1965, President Nasser declared: "We do not have a plan for the liberation of Palestine." Moreover, 1965 produced the first Arab leader who publicly declared that the Arabs should solve the Palestine problem by signing a peace treaty with Israel. Thus the strictly clandestine character of various Palestinian resistance movements until 1967 was due less to the Israeli enemy than to the attitude of Arab states, where Palestinian militants were often put under house arrest, thrown in jail or even worse. Fateh will never forget that one of its first partisans was killed in 1965 by the Jordanian army.

With the failure of the Syrian-Egyptian union in 1961, the concept of unity as the road to the liberation of Palestine collapsed. Palestinians realized that the attainment of unity was an almost impossible task; and that they could not afford to wait until all of the Arab world was united. They started to talk of an independent Palestinian entity and action. As a result, more than thirty Palestinian organizations, most of which had only a small membership, were set up. This large

* This treaty organization replaced the Baghdad Pact and is composed of the non-Arab Muslim states (Iran, Pakistan, and Turkey) which have connections with the United States.—ED.

number of organizations was ample proof of the Palestinians' desire to work seriously and independently for the liberation of their homeland. At the same time it indicated that a strong, effective organization was lacking.

The triumph of the Algerian revolution in 1962 gave more weight to the principle of independent Palestinian activity. The Algerians were able to recruit material and moral support from various Arab regimes and, through armed struggle, to attain their independence. Some Palestinians thus believed that they could adopt the same kind of policy if they took the initiative and maintained their freedom of action.

During this period Fateh, which is the reverse initials of *Harakat al-Tahrir al-Watani al-Filistini* (Palestine National Liberation Movement), strove to create the nucleus of a political organization recruited from among the Palestinian intelligentsia. Since 1962 Fateh has concentrated all its efforts on starting military action but was faced with the problem of the shortage of means to embark on such an activity. In 1964 Fateh held a conference to discuss this question and the majority of the members voted for starting military action on January 1, 1965, in spite of the shortage of means. Those who opposed this decision proposed that military operations should be started under another name rather than Fateh so that, in the event of failure, Fateh might continue its preparations and its secret activities. The proposal was accepted and it was agreed to use the name of al-Asifah for the first military operations. Fateh announced that *it* was al-Asifah after the tenth military communiqué, but the leadership decided to continue using the name of al-Asifah because it had become a historic name.

On Nasser's initiative, the first Arab summit conference, held in Cairo between January 13 and 16, 1964, was convened to discuss Israel's plan for the diversion of the waters of the Jordan River. The UAR was of the opinion that Syria, Jordan and Saudi Arabia were trying to involve it in war with

Israel in order to stab it in the back. The UAR held that it would not let itself be pushed into a battle with Israel before the attainment of unity between all Arab countries. Thus President Nasser was suspected of having no intention of getting into war with Israel when the latter would start pumping water from the Sea of Galilee down to the Negev. The conference issued a communiqué in which it decided to organize the Palestinian people to enable them to play their part in liberating Palestine and in determining its future.

The immediate background of this decision can be found in the session of the Arab League Council held on September 15, 1963. At that session, the council studied the problem of Palestine in a more constructive manner than usual by affirming the "Palestine entity" at the international level; by establishing the bases for action through the organization of the people of Palestine; and by making them assume responsibility for their national cause and for the liberation of Palestine.

The first decision taken by the Council of the League was the appointment of Ahmed Shukeiri as the representative of Palestine at the Arab League. Shukeiri is a Palestinian lawyer who had been assistant secretary general of the Arab League, later a member of the Syrian delegation to the United Nations, and then the U.N. delegate of Saudi Arabia. The council also asked him to carry out consultations with representatives of the people of Palestine for the formation of a new general government in exile. Furthermore, he was asked to visit various Arab capitals to discuss the means which the Arab governments would place at his disposal for the fulfillment of this task.

Shukeiri began his tour of the Arab states on February 19, 1964, to discuss with Palestinians and the Arab governments the drafting of the Palestine National Charter and the draft constitution of a liberation organization, on which the "Palestine entity" would be based.

Shukeiri visited Jordan, Syria, Bahrain, Qatar, Iraq, Kuwait, Lebanon and the Sudan. He met the then president of the Yemen Republic, Abdullah Sallal, in Cairo. His tour ended on April 5, 1964. Upon his arrival in Cairo, Shukeiri made a statement in which he announced that he had held about thirty conferences with the Palestinian people, during which he had met thousands of them. At these conferences he had explained the Palestine National Charter, and the basic system of the liberation organization.

On May 28, 1964, the Palestine National Congress, in which members of Fateh participated, opened in Jerusalem. It unanimously elected Shukeiri as chairman of the Congress. It was held under the supervision of the Arab League, and under the auspices of King Hussein, and attended by two hundred forty-two Palestinian representatives from Jordan, one hundred forty-six from Syria, Lebanon, Gaza, Qatar, Kuwait and Iraq. The most important resolutions adopted by the Congress were the following:

1. Establishment of a Palestine Liberation Organization (PLO) to be set up by the people of Palestine in accordance with its statutes.

2. Appeal to all Palestinians to form professional and labor unions.

3. Immediate opening of camps for military training of all Palestinians, in order to prepare them for the liberation battle which they affirmed could be won only by force of arms. The Arab governments were urged to admit Palestinians to their military academies.

4. Establishment of a Palestine National Fund to finance the PLO. The sources of revenue would include annual subscriptions, to be paid by every Palestinian over eighteen years of age, loans and grants to be offered by Arab and friendly states, contributions to be collected on national occasions, and the revenue from issuing Palestine Liberation Bonds by the Arab League.

5. Election of Ahmed Shukeiri as chairman of the executive committee of the PLO.

The second Arab summit conference, which was held in Alexandria from September 5–11, 1964, welcomed the establishment of the Palestine Liberation Organization. (It also fixed the obligations of each Arab state towards the PLO.) The conference endorsed the decision taken by the PLO Executive Committee to establish a Palestine Liberation Army to be stationed along the Gaza Strip and the Sinai Peninsula.

The creation of the PLO raised the hopes of the Palestinian people. It absorbed a number of the small organizations that had been set up earlier in the sixties. Fateh, which was at that time operating only on the political level, clandestinely, and the Palestinian branch of the Arab Nationalist Movement (ANM) and a few other small organizations maintained their separate identity, in spite of the fact that they participated in the PLO national congress.

Up to this time Fateh was the sole organization which called for the adoption of the principle of armed struggle as the only means for the liberation of Palestine. Furthermore, Fateh believed that the Palestinians should start armed struggle irrespective of the reaction or plans of the Arab regimes. The Palestinian branch of the Arab Nationalist Movement called for coordination between the Palestinian armed struggle and the plans of the progressive regimes, mainly the UAR. The logic behind this thinking was to avoid a premature confrontation between Israel and the Arab states. They feared that Fateh's action would force the involvement of the Arab states, and the UAR in particular, in a war with Israel. Yet despite this Fateh embarked upon reconnaissance operations inside the occupied territories in 1963. On July 14 of that year Fateh suffered its first two casualties.

In 1964, the Palestinian branch of the ANM formed a military group to undertake reconnaissance operations inside the occupied territories and to establish a network and arms caches. This decision was adopted at a conference held in September 1964 that included representatives of all the Palestinian members of the ANM. The basic principles that were adopted at this conference were the following:

1. Armed struggle is the only way to liberate Palestine.

2. All secondary conflicts should be subordinated to the conflict with imperialism and Zionism.

3. The different revolutionary groups should be unified.

On November 2, 1964, the first casualty claimed by ANM was killed by the Israeli army in an unplanned clash. At that time the ANM refused to disclose the name of the man or to give any details about the circumstances that led to his death. This was done to avoid any hindrance of its preparations and to maintain secrecy.

On January 1, 1965, Fateh's first communiqué was published in the Lebanese press announcing the start of its military activities in the occupied territories. At this early stage these activities were not clearly described for the reason that the Arab regimes and their mass media were tacitly opposed to the principle of Palestinian guerrilla warfare. The Palestinian people remained passive, awaiting the Arab states, especially the UAR, to bring a favorable end to their problem. Fateh was an isolated movement trying to prove that Palestinians could fight, could confront their own problem and could escape the control of the various Arab states, especially Jordan, which was hostile to any possibility of a change in the status quo.

Jordanian police checks on the refugee population made any political activity extremely difficult. In Cuban terminology, the Palestinian resistance began as a "foco," as a nucleus employing armed violence without any political preparation of the population it was trying to involve. But while the strategy of the "foco" as applied within the framework of class struggle has shown itself to be ineffective in

Latin America, the armed nucleus of the Palestinian resistance, due to the military collapse of the Arab states, was successful within the framework of a national movement. Naturally this strategy was imposed by the circumstances and by the nature of the national movement of which Fateh is the nucleus.

The Arab regimes continued to oppose independent guerrilla warfare until June 5, 1967, except for Syria, which found in Fateh the embodiment of its slogan repeated since 1965 calling for a popular war of liberation.

The military grouping of the Palestinian branch of the ANM came to be known as Abtal al-Audah (Heroes of the Return). It started its military operations in November 1966, under internal pressure from the members of the ANM who urged that the reconnaissance activities should be transformed into actual military operations. A few months after its emergence Abtal al-Audah became associated with the Palestine Liberation Army (PLA) for financial reasons. Shukeiri welcomed this step because he wanted to bring the commando organizations under the control of the PLO in order to compete with Fateh. The Palestinian branch of the ANM then formed another military group, which carried out its first operation in the occupied territories a few days before the June war.

The Palestine Liberation Army (PLA) did not play an active role prior to June 5, 1967. Yet in the six-day war the PLA troops stationed in the Gaza Strip fought bravely against the Israeli forces.

Growth of the Armed Struggle

The overwhelming defeat, in June 1967, of the Arab regimes took the Arab people by surprise. This defeat proved that dependence on the Arab governments and armies for the liberation of Palestine would lead nowhere. It proved that the idea of Arab unity, which was considered to be the road to Palestine, was far-fetched under existing conditions. The Arab masses were isolated and could not play their proper role in the war because the existing regimes feared their people—in case they armed and trained them—more than the enemy. Thus the role of the people was limited to observing the defeat of their armies, the occupation of the whole of Palestine, Sinai and the Golan Heights. The Palestinians took it upon themselves to act, continue the war against the enemy, rally the Arab people to their side and make them play their proper role in retrieving Palestine, Sinai and the Golan Heights from Israeli occupation. Thus directly after the June war a number of conferences were held (in Damascus) in which representatives of the various commando groups participated. The PLO was in touch with what was going on. The purpose of these conferences was to formulate a Palestinian response to the defeat. The only formula that was approved was that of armed struggle. Nearly half of the Palestinian Arab people were now under the yoke of direct Israeli occupation. However, these meetings did not lead to any practical results; Fateh renewed its military operations unilaterally in August 1967.

Abtal al-Audah merged with two other groups to become the Popular Front for the Liberation of Palestine (PFLP). PFLP started its military operations on October 6, 1967, and the first military communiqué was published on December 21, 1967.

The re-emergence of several Palestinian politico-military organizations underlined the need to coordinate and unify their activities. This prompted Fateh to call, on January 4, 1968, for a meeting of all Palestinian organizations, including the PLO and PFLP. The conference was held in Cairo between January 17 and 19, 1968. The PLO and PFLP refused to attend this conference on the grounds that some of the organizations invited did not have a significant military or political weight. Nevertheless, Fateh held the meeting, at the end of which the Permanent Bureau for the Palestinian Armed Struggle was set up. This Bureau included, in addition to Fateh, eight lesser organizations. It ceased to exist on the political level shortly after the convening of the fourth Palestinian National Congress, held in Cairo in July 1968. However, on the military level, the military wings of these organizations merged with al-Asifah.

On July 10, 1968, the fourth Palestinian National Congress was held in Cairo and was attended by representatives of the different commando organizations, including al-Sa'iqah. Al-Sa'iqah is a Palestinian group which has very close associations with the Baath party ruling Syria. The fourth National Congress was held in the absence of Ahmed Shukeiri, who had been forced to resign from the presidency of the PLO after a long struggle between him and the majority of the Executive Committee backed by the rank and file of the PLA in Syria. Some other Palestinian organizations had played a role in the pressures which caused his resignation. They accused him of having single-handed leadership harmful to the Palestinian struggle. They also believed that he subordinated the struggle to political maneuvering.

The Congress elected Yehya Hammouda as acting president of the PLO Executive Committee. Formerly he had been president of the Jordanian Lawyers' Association; however, since 1957 he had been barred from Jordan because he was accused of being a communist. Hammouda was given the job of contacting the Palestinian commando organizations and holding the fifth Palestinian National Congress within a period of six months.

With the collapse of Arab military strength, the Palestinian guerrilla movement gained momentum and strength very quickly. This was most obvious in Jordan, where there was no fast military build-up of the conventional armed forces as was the case in the UAR. The commando organizations armed themselves with great rapidity and in only eighteen months. Fateh, for example, was able to train thousands of combatants, while it had taken the same organization seven years (1958–65) to complete the structure of its first politico-military nucleus. Soon the commando organizations came to control the mass of the Palestinian population, especially in the refugee camps in Jordan. With the battle of Karameh, March 21, 1968, the commando groups (and particularly Fateh) emerged as undisputed leaders of the Palestinian population. Political education was intensified among the refugees with the aim of rediscovering their Palestinian identity. It was also about this time that the resistance was able to consolidate its military bases, the state of Jordan included, and to turn them into relatively secure bases, first of all in the Ghor mountains, where a great number of fighters have been trained. The resistance movement, in short, asserted itself in the Arab world, obliged Israel to take account of its existence, began to mobilize the Palestinian population, and set up the beginnings of an administrative infrastructure.

The armed struggle, intended to win popular support, began to bear fruit. Soon, the impression made by the resistance on Arab public opinion overtook the influence of Baathism and Nasserism and imposed itself upon the mass of Palestinians. All this led even King Hussein to declare in one of his press conferences after the Karameh battle, "We are all *fedayeen*."

Under these quickly changing circumstances a potential conflict was developing between the resistance movement and the Jordanian regime. One manifestation of this conflict was the official acceptance by the Jordanian regime of the peaceful settlement of the Arab-Israeli conflict on the basis of the UN Security Council resolution of November 22, 1967. In contrast to this we have the firm and unambiguous rejection by the entire Palestinian resistance movement of this sort of settlement. Another manifestation of the conflict was the confrontation which occurred in October 1968 between the commando organizations and the Jordanian authorities. The commandos were anxious about rumors of contacts between Jordanian and Israeli officials for a peaceful settlement. This led Fateh and PFLP to issue separate statements proclaiming their determination to carry on the struggle at all costs.

Fateh issued a statement on October 20 asserting that it was not opposed to peace and stability in the area; what it did oppose was surrender and acceptance of the *fait accompli.* It rejected any attempt by the United Nations to find a peaceful solution on the basis of the UN Security Council resolution of November 22, 1967. Further, it declared that it was determined to continue fighting at all costs. The statement of the PFLP issued on October 22, 1968, accused the "reactionary Palestinian right" of selling out the true interests of the Palestinian people to "counter-revolutionary forces." It compared the proposed peaceful solution to the disaster of 1948.

The PFLP also asserted that these were critical moments for the Palestinians; and it was up to the liberation movement to resist with all the means at its disposal the Security Council's resolution, and to condemn outright any Arab country that adopted a hesitant attitude to the Palestinian problem. Any attempt by the "reactionary Palestinian right" to depict this attitude as an "interference in the internal affairs of the Arab countries" was part and parcel of the "reactionary Zionist imperialist" conspiracy to liquidate the Palestine problem.

The first open and serious clash between the commando groups and the Jordanian government occurred on November 4, 1968. Tahir Dablan, a close associate of the Jordanian intelligence services, who had set up an armed group, *Kataib al-Nasr* (Battalions of Victory), provoked an incident with

Jordanian security forces to provide them with a pretext for opening fire on the Palestinian organizations. Immediately the Jordanian Royal Guard took up positions in the streets of Amman and around three camps—al-Wahdat, Hussein and Schneller. They shot at the people there and several deaths resulted. In addition, they bombarded the arms and food depots belonging to Fateh. A curfew was imposed in Amman by the Jordanian authorities. King Hussein urged Yasser Arafat to negotiate a compromise. Shortly afterwards a Palestinian emergency council was set up which, in principle, was composed of all the Palestinian unions, parties, organizations and armed groups.

This council included a bureau of military coordination which was dependent upon it. The Palestinian organizations were driven to tighten up their ranks by the political context as well as by the necessity of uniting to form a national force in the face of Israel. The palace made the various Palestinian movements sign an agreement of fourteen points which, among other things, stipulated that there should be coordination between the military forces of the Palestinians and the Jordanians and which called for the formation of a unified staff and prohibited commando operations south of the Dead Sea. The agreement served the purpose of restoring peace between the commandos and the regime and was never implemented.

The guerrilla groups issued a statement announcing that agreement had been reached between the two sides, but without giving any details. On Wednesday evening Fateh, in a broadcast from Cairo, had this to say in the wake of Jordanian events: "Fateh does not agree to commit suicide with Arab bullets. The Palestinian organizations are alone competent to punish those Palestinians who deviate from the revolutionary line and we reject controls which, under slogans of 'coordination' and 'cooperation,' are designed to liquidate us." Fateh went on to say that "Arab frontiers must remain open for our operations and we demand the immediate liberation of Palestinian revolutionaries detained in Arab prisons. The insecurity of Palestinian fighters inside Arab frontiers cannot continue and we cannot guarantee to remain quiet in the future. We shall not pay the price of a peaceful settlement and we call on all Arabs to disown the Jarring mission.*

One of the most interesting aspects of the crisis was the attitude taken by Egypt. According to *al-Ahram* of November 7, the guerrilla organizations dispatched an open letter to President Nasser asking for his personal intervention to settle the crisis. Nasser, however, took the position that, despite his anxiety at what was going on, he did not wish to interfere for fear that his move would be misconstrued; also Jordanian sovereignty had to be taken into account. Finally, on November 10 a decree was issued by the Jordanian Minister of the Interior to the effect that arms could only be carried by those given a special permit by the government. This decree was in blatant contradiction to the agreement concluded between the Jordanian authorities and the principal guerrilla organizations.

In accordance with the resolution adopted by the fourth Palestinian National Congress the PLO Executive Committee held several meetings with the different commando organizations. From these meetings a formula of representation for the National Assembly of the PLO was drawn up. This formula gave thirty-three seats to Fateh, twelve to the PFLP, twelve to al-Sa'iqah, eleven to the executive committee of the PLO, five to the PLA, one seat to the National Fund of the PLO, three seats to students', workers' and women's organizations, and twenty-eight seats to independents.

PFLP rejected the formula and refused to participate. It proposed to establish instead a front for all organizations to

* Gunnar Jarring had been appointed by U Thant to organize negotiations between Israel and the Arabs. He resigned in failure in 1971.—ED.

be formed on an egalitarian basis, i.e., one organization, one vote. Fateh, on the other hand, agreed to the formula and issued an important political statement a few days prior to the convening of the Congress. In this statement Fateh announced its belief in the PLO as a general and proper framework for Palestinian national unity and said that it would participate in the conference and the PLO Executive Committee.

The fifth Palestinian National Congress was held between February 1 and 4, 1969, in Cairo. At the end of the Congress a new executive committee was formed headed by Yasser Arafat—official spokesman of Fateh. The new executive committee was composed of four representatives of Fateh, two of al-Sa'iqah, three independents and one from the old PLO executive committee.

At the end of this Congress a statement was issued. It declared that the Palestinian cause was facing the danger of liquidation in the interests of Zionism and imperialism through the UN Security Council resolution of November 22, 1967. It further warned against everything that went under the name of peaceful settlements, including the Soviet project to lay down a timetable to implement the Security Council resolution. It also rejected any Arab policies or international interventions which contradicted the Palestinians' right to their country. It objected to any form of tutelage over Palestinian affairs and particularly over the development of the rising Palestinian resistance movement.

The statement warned against the "defeatist deviationists" who wanted to liquidate the Palestinian cause in favor of a spurious Palestinian entity subservient to Zionism and imperialism. Furthermore, the Congress drew up a plan to augment the effectiveness of the Palestinian resistance. This included, above all, a call for the unification of guerrilla action and financial resources, and the strengthening of the Palestinian Liberation Army.

Since this plan required additional finances the Palestinians were called upon to give more money and the Arab states to meet all their financial commitments to the Palestinian Liberation Organization. It urged Arab states to facilitate the residence, work and movement of Palestinians found on their soil.

After the fifth Congress Fateh announced that it would retain its organizational independence.

A Split in the PFLP

Towards the end of January 1969 an open conflict arose within the ranks of the PFLP. As previously mentioned the Front had originally consisted of three separate groups which had agreed to operate together, including the Arab Nationalist Movement. The ANM as a whole was undergoing a sharp shift to the left. This did not happen with the same speed and decisiveness everywhere in the Arab world, but it became clear that with the internal splits taking place most ANM members were in the leftist camp, whose organ of expression is the Beirut weekly *al-Hurriyah*. It was only to be expected that this conflict should make itself felt in the Popular Front for the Liberation of Palestine. The conflict persisted until Dr. Habash returned to Amman, following brief imprisonment in Damascus. However, the Front refused to participate in the Palestine National Congress under the pressure of the left-wing group.

On February 10, 1969, the Beirut weekly *al-Hurriyah* carried a statement by the left-wing faction of the PFLP (under the leadership of Naef Hawatmeh, a Jordanian graduate of the Arab University in Beirut who joined the ANM in the fifties, and early in the sixties became one of its leading members). It pointed out that at a decisive PFLP conference held in Amman in August 1968 the progressive wing gained the day in its call for a revolutionary policy linked with the toiling masses. According to *al-Hurriyah*, the moderates ostensibly approved the conference proposals, but acted in a manner which is contrary to these proposals. For example, on January 28, 1969, they arrested three members of the progressive wing in the cultural club of one of the refugee camps in Amman. Then five more were arrested in al-Bakaah camp, and six others in various places.

The progressives called for an immediate meeting of the coordinating bureau of the moderate wing of the PFLP, declared that while the Front had been exposing the "reactionaries" and "petty bourgeois" and their lukewarm attitude towards the Palestine cause, and while it had been challenging the Zionist enemy in the occupied territory and outside it, "opportunist pockets" had appeared within the Front's own ranks who sought to impede its revolutionary progress. These were a group of "adolescent café intellectuals" who subscribed to scientific socialism in name only.

On February 24 the Beirut weekly *al-Hurriyah* officially announced that the progressive wing of the PFLP had broken away and formed an organization to be known as the Democratic Popular Front for the Liberation of Palestine (DPFLP).

The causes behind this split can be summarized as follows:

The Marxist group, led by Naef Hawatmeh, who was behind the split, called for breaking off all relations of subservience with the Arab regimes whether they were progressive or reactionary. Furthermore, this group strongly criticized the other Palestinian organizations, especially the PLO and Fateh, on the grounds that, like the progressive Arab regimes, they were led by the "petty bourgeoisie" and its ideology, which had proved its failure in the 1967 defeat. The new Marxist group called for a long-term war of popular liberation against imperialism and Zionism. They also called for the establishment of a Marxist-Leninist party completely committed to the ideology favorable to the dispossessed peasants and workers (the Asian proletariat).

On the other hand the majority of the PFLP, led by George Habash, while agreeing to the basic analysis of the Hawatmeh group, believed in maintaining certain relations with the progressive Arab governments. These relations they see as necessary to secure financial and military support vital for the survival of PFLP and the resistance movement in general.

As for the Palestinian people, Habash maintained that the war with Israel is a national liberation war which requires the recruitment of the widest sections of the Palestinian people, a great number of whom are "petty bourgeois." Thus, to alienate and antagonize the "petty bourgeois" class would bring a heavy loss to the national cause. At the same time, Habash stressed that the leading cadres of PFLP should be in the hands of those who are committed to the ideology of the proletariat.

2. Inside Fateh

Gerard Chaliand

*Veteran French journalist and author Gerard Chaliand
(best known for his reporting from North Vietnam and
guerrilla-controlled areas of Portuguese Africa) visited
the Middle East in early 1969. His full report on the
Palestinian resistance, from which this excerpt is taken,
appeared in* Le Monde Diplomatique *in March 1969.*

Between Israel and the Arab States

The scene is a Fateh training camp in Syria, about forty
miles from Damascus. In a stony plain, in the open country,
are two large buildings. A short distance away are bare hills.
It is here that a hundred and twenty men, dressed in camou-
flage and rubber boots, are being trained: they run in close
formation, led at a fast pace by an easy-striding instructor.
Every morning they have two hours of physical training:
long-distance running, combat course, jiu-jitsu, and karate.
The standard of work is good and, in spite of severe weather
conditions, some of the *fedayeen* are stripped to the waist.
The course, which lasts for two or three months, is quite
difficult, with strict discipline and a very full timetable. It is
strictly forbidden to take alcoholic drinks and meals are
eaten standing up. The meals are sometimes interrupted by

one of the leaders, at whose order the trainees immediately
come to attention. This winter is bitterly cold with strong
winds blowing but, whatever the weather, the training is
interspersed with long night marches. All the individual arms
which, like the famous "Klashnikov," are usually of Soviet
model and Chinese manufacture, are carefully greased. The
leaders in charge of military training have to break the habits
inherited from a backward society and to inculcate into their
men a sense of discipline in which precision, efficacy and
punctuality have their place. In this sense the training of the
commandos introduces a modern element into a traditional
society. Weapons are plentiful and the course aims at forming
combatants capable of using the rifle, the mortar, the machine gun, the bazooka and the rocket. There are also specialized classes dealing with the techniques of dynamiting.

All the leaders are Palestinians, most of them under thirty.
The greater part of them come from comfortable back-
grounds and have studied in Arab countries. Apart from the
military instructors—of whom there are five—and the physical
training instructor, there is a leader who is responsible for
general discipline in the camp, and a political commissar. The
recruits are young—from seventeen to twenty-five years old—
and, apart from two Turks and a Yugoslav, they are all Palestinians. The Turks are left-wing and are close to the Turkish
Workers party. For them the Palestinians' struggle is a just
one and they take part in it out of a sense of internationalism, not out of Islamic solidarity. The Yugoslav, a Serb, preferred not to be questioned. In principle the simple trainee
has the right to criticize his leaders but I did not have occasion to witness a concrete example of this. Political formation is of a much lower standard than military training. Certainly there are political books: Castro, Guevara, Mao
Tse-tung, Giap, Rodinson,* General De Gaulle's memoirs, and

* Maxime Rodinson teaches Islamic history at the Sorbonne; he is the author of
various Marxist histories and analyses of the Arab world.

also *Mein Kampf.* In view of my surprise at the inclusion of the latter work, the political commissar explained that it was necessary to read everything and that, as the Israelis behave like Nazis, it is useful to know something about the Nazis.

The general intellectual level is underdeveloped, and if we do not consider the presence of revolutionary books as the expression of an integrated political culture, it can be seen during discussion on precise points (not in general declarations and stock phrases) that the theoretical tools are embryonic and the ideology confused. From Fanon they take the description of the psychology of the colonized and the need to resort to violence; from Guevara, the texts advocating the need for armed conflict; from Mao, the concept of the prolonged war; from Debray, whose works are extensively translated into Arabic, the idea that the party is useless, for "the guerrilla nucleus is the party in gestation." The only elements which are in some way integrated are those that can be integrated by a national movement, which is what Fateh really is. On the other hand, there is a very strong feeling of national identity among both staff instructors and Palestinian militants and, although the Palestinians claim to be an integral part of the Arab world, they consider that most—if not all—Arab regimes have dodged the Palestinian problem while pretending to solve it.

It is easy to cross the frontier between Syria and Jordan if you are in the company of Fateh militants; there is little or no control, either by the police (wearing a uniform which is clearly of British origin, and a spiked helmet), or by the Bedouins of the royal guard in their traditional dress with a straight dagger in their belts. Fateh also has offices at the frontier. The countryside belonging to what is left of Jordan is very beautiful: mountain roads winding between narrow gorges, hills eaten away by erosion, narrow valleys with sparse vegetation, leafless poplars, white and fragile like birch trees. Sometimes we skirt a camp of refugees who are spending this winter of wind and heavy rains under canvas. The country is dotted with sad little towns as far as Amman, which itself is nothing but a large, desolate market-town, flanked by low houses. The main street brings to mind those seen in "westerns." At some distance from the town center, in a building guarded night and day by armed *fedayeen*, Fateh has its public relations offices, modestly furnished, with maps on the walls. Here Fateh leaders, speaking English and French, welcome visitors, answer questions, and arrange programs according to individual demands. For myself, I was refused only one thing, which was to take part in a commando operation; all my other requests were granted.

The east bank of the Jordan river—the present State of Jordan—is riddled with Palestinian resistance bases. Most of them are bases of Fateh which is, without doubt, the backbone of the resistance. For greater security some visits take place at night, by Landrover. Often, where the nature of the land permits, a base will prepare one or more caves which are used for meetings. Ammunition, which is always plentiful, is also stored there. There is, among the *fedayeen*, a considerable number of Palestinian students who have recently returned from the countries in which they were studying. Many of them have studied law, commerce, or the arts. Those who have been educated in Western Europe seemed to me to be the least inclined to consider the Egyptian experience under Nasser as an example of socialism, while most of the others regarded the structure of the United Arab Republic as revolutionary.

There are no political commissars attached to these bases where the young *fedayeen* have been for some months—since the end of their military training—but sometimes there are discussions and explanations with a visiting leader. Daily life in the bases is less arduous than the intensive training received by the recruits. But discipline is still very severe. During discussions with the *fedayeen*, the shock caused by the defeat of June 1967, and by the exodus from the West Bank which many of them experienced, is clear. The difficult living conditions of the Palestinians prior to June 1967, which were then endured with a kind of bitter resignation, are now deeply felt and are regarded as absolutely intolerable. On many occasions, I noticed that the *fedayeen* in no way consider themselves as an elite, nor do they disdain the refugee population. They do not have a commando mentality, but a very clear awareness and feeling that they are fighting *for* the refugees, of whom they themselves form an organic part. This feeling is a guarantee for the continuation of a close relationship with the mass of refugees.

Near the River Jordan

The bases which are closest to the territory occupied by Israeli troops are less than three miles from the river Jordan. It is possible to drive through the region during the daytime, and the frequent checks made by the Jordanian police do not apply to Fateh vehicles. On the way we passed Iraqi units whose tents were well hidden but who drew attention to their presence by spreading out their multi-colored washing in the open only a few yards away. Many petrol pumps have no petrol and this is only one of the numerous signs of the economic upheaval that Jordan has suffered since the last war. Not far from El-Shuna—a large village almost completely destroyed by Israeli planes—lower down on the other side of the Jordan river, Jericho can be seen through field-glasses. Cars arrive, coming from the West Bank after having crossed the Allenby Bridge, which the Israelis have left open to allow the West Bank Palestinians to come and go freely.

Away from the road, everything is mined in this no-man's-land which extends on this side of the river Jordan. Not far away, carefully hidden beneath thickly branched trees, a

Fateh commando section has dug solidly constructed shelters deep enough for a man to stand up in. This camp was set up less than fifteen days beforehand and will soon be abandoned to prevent its position becoming known. Around the camp, mounted on jeeps, are heavy Czech and Chinese machine guns as protection against air attack. Like all the bases I visited, this base also has rockets. About twenty *fedayeen* live here and these take part in physical training every morning and in operations at night. The latter were much reduced during the month of January as torrential rain had swelled the waters of the Jordan, making it very difficult to cross the river. Before each operation, a reconnaissance patrol is sent out so that, if there is an Israeli ambush waiting for them, losses will be kept to a minimum. Political explanations made to visitors—regardless of who they may be—always insist that the combat in which the Palestinian resistance is engaged is not directed against the Jews as such, but against the Zionist state, which has deprived the Palestinian people (who for centuries lived in the territories now occupied by the Israelis) of its just rights.

The Ashbal

In addition to the bases and the training camps, Fateh has set up two camps for the *ashbal* (young tigers), boys of ten to fourteen years, to give them political and military training. We were able to visit one of these camps not far from the al-Bakaah refugee camp. This camp trains three hundred young boys, with the consent of their parents, and in most cases there is already a member of the family in the *fedayeen*. The boys are split into two groups, one of which comes in the morning and the other in the afternoon. The other camp, which was opened seven months previously, has a hundred and fifty boys. It is led by two instructors. According to the instructors, many parents still feel some reticence with regard to these camps, and in fact there could be more trainees, as there is no lack of instructors. The *ashbal* are young boys who do not go to school: those who follow the UNRWA classes (the UN organism responsible for the refugees) are not accepted—they must carry on with their studies. Reading and writing are taught in the camp. In this way as well as the triple program—sports, political and military—the boys spend most of their day at the camp before returning to sleep with their families in the refugee tents. The very first members of the *ashbal*, who started on the course seven months ago, continue their training and should, in principle, join the *fedayeen* when they reach the age of fifteen. Meanwhile they are an active ferment of militant nationalism in the refugee camps and especially in the midst of the other young people, whether at school or not.

The group that we visited trains for three hours every afternoon. Monday: shooting practice with the Chinese submachine gun, the "Shmaisur"; judo; history of Palestine. Tuesday: close combat; lessons about the refugees and the action of Fateh; football. Wednesday: target practice with the "Klashnikov"; history of Palestine; obstacle race. Thursday: target practice with the Belgian F.M.; free sport. Friday: fifteen-mile march. Saturday: close combat; combat course; rifle practice (Egyptian Model); political formation. Sunday: close combat; machine-gun practice; political formation; football.

After June 1967

Undoubtedly the future will uncover tangible proof that President Nasser only committed himself to the blockade of the Tiran Straits, and the verbal escalation which ensued, for tactical reasons, without any intention of starting hostilities. The fact remains that the Arab armies were defeated, some of them—like the Syrian army—without having really fought at all. Apart from strictly military considerations, there were, as some observers noticed, social and political reasons for the defeat: in Syria, a precarious regime which preferred not to risk the military apparatus which was the guarantee of its survival; in the UAR, a caste of officers belonging to the largely privileged administrative middle class who had little desire for any change in the status quo. Taking into account the social structure of the Arab countries, it is not possible for any of the regimes to undertake a popular struggle similar to that taking place in Vietnam.

On June 30, 1967, Fateh held a clandestine conference and decided to resist. Al-Asifah trained an ever-increasing number of volunteers. Operations were re-opened in September and the armed struggle soon aroused a feeling of belonging to a national collectivity among the Palestinian people. Fateh operations were at first directed against towns in west Jordan: Nablus, Ramallah, Jerusalem. Within the occupied territories themselves there was very little popular support; everything had collapsed under the shock of the defeat. The commandos could only get into contact with relatives, friends, or former neighbors. Very soon Israeli repression disrupted the embryo of a resistance network. Palestinians who helped the resistance had their houses blown up. Fateh had to modify its strategy, but the struggle had given it prestige, and the repression—though at first discouraging—heightened the tension with the occupying power which the Israeli authorities, by the introduction of liberal measures, had tried not to provoke.

To limit its losses, which were numerous because of the Israeli use of helicopters and lack of cover, Fateh decided, in a second stage, to send in its commandos from the outside—namely from Jordan—for rapid harassing operations that would keep the enemy always on the lookout, oblige him to mobilize all his human resources, and threaten his economic life. At the beginning of 1968, after Ahmed

Shukeiri had left the direction of the PLO in December, Fateh invited the resistance movement to unite, not at the top but at the level of active combat. But in spite of the fact that a bureau of coordination was set up, no progress was made towards this unity until February 1969.

On March 21, 1968, the battle of Karameh took place. A sizeable Israeli column, preceded by tanks with air cover, crossed the Jordan. The Palestinian commandos, who could have avoided a confrontation, received the order to stand fast and held out for twelve hours. Israeli losses were not inconsiderable and some tanks were left behind on the field of battle. According to the Israelis this battle was of small importance; but for the Palestinian resistance, Karameh represented an important turning point. For the Arab states (King Hussein had his photograph taken mounted on a ruined tank), as well as for the mass of the Palestinian people, Karameh was an act of *armed propaganda.* The Palestinian resistance organizations, who had knowingly broken the rules of guerrilla warfare, wanted to prove that even without tanks or planes it was possible to fight against the victors of the six-day war. The Israelis, who only drew up a military balance-sheet of this battle, ignored the psychological importance of this *fedayeen* victory, however modest, for the defeated Palestinian masses.

A Meeting with Yasser Arafat

Yasser Arafat enumerated Fateh's principles to me, indicating the general line of the movement, during a much-interrupted conversation in a cave some score of miles from Amman and not far from a large town. At night we climbed a steep path guarded by lookouts hidden behind the rocks. The large cave was furnished with tables and chairs and was equipped with a telephone which rang at least half a dozen times in less than an hour. Yasser Arafat was taking leave of quite a big delegation. On the table there was a "Klash-nikov." Arafat is of small build, with a quick eye and an economy of gesture. His thinking is precise and flexible and he is not verbose. During our conversation he recalled the difficulties that the Palestinian resistance had experienced before emerging as an autonomous force. He considers as a very positive development the fact that not only Arab public opinion but also world public opinion has begun to be aware of Palestinian national reality. This is a reality that the state of Israel has tried to conceal, because if the threat which hangs over Israel, according to Zionist propaganda, is aimed at sensitizing an opinion which quite rightly remembers Nazism, the Palestinian people have *in fact* been wronged by the establishment of Zionist colonization. The Israeli author-ities, Arafat said, call the commandos "terrorists," but all national resistances have been called this—in France, for example, during the Nazi occupation. The aims are military and economic; reprisals against civilians have only been made in answer to Israeli attacks: it was after the bombing of Irbid and Kafr-Kasr that a bomb was left in Jerusalem, and after the bombing of Salt that the attack on Tel Aviv took place. As regards the extension of commando operations, Arafat thinks that these will very shortly be multiplied, as soon as the mobility of the commandos enables them to strike more deeply into the occupied areas. The *fedayeen* are gaining in-creased experience as they improve their level of combat. Operations such as those against the phosphates factory at Sodom, the plastics factory at Beersheba, the petrol refinery at Elath, and the Dodge assembly plant at Nazareth will become more numerous. According to Arafat, what gives Israel its strength is the fact that for it the war is decisive. But, he added, we offer the population the choice of remain-ing in Palestine. Israel's weak spot is the fact that it is en-gaged in an unjust war—our struggle is beginning to prove this to the world. When I asked him if the Palestinian resistance would accept a compromise imposed by the great powers, with the agreement of the Arab countries, Arafat pointed to the machine gun and replied, "We will carry on the struggle."

At the beginning of the year, while the Israeli air force continued its policy of trying to turn the Arab states against the resistance movement, by bombarding Naga Hamadi (UAR), south Jordan, and Beirut airport, the movement was establishing itself and becoming a force to be reckoned with. Private and state aid given to it has become increasingly important. Well-informed circles in Lebanon estimate that the annual collection receipts of Fateh are worth at least £2 million sterling.

With the organized mobilization of the Palestinian population—which has still to be developed—one of Fateh's problems is to raise the political quality of its middle-level cadres, which is at present a weak spot. At the moment they are hurrying to organize the refugees, because the time factor is all-important in this year, 1969, when the great powers must try to intervene. At the same time, the movement is trying to create an atmosphere of permanent military mobilization within the population. And the recent steps toward unifying the Palestinian organizations are aimed at creating a national popular army. In effect, at the moment, the resistance only asserts itself on the level of commando operations and it will require an organized—and thus political—action to reach a stage of greater effectiveness. Certainly the conflict is a national one, and it is natural for Fateh to be a broad national movement whose first interest is national identity. In any case the political context of the region would not long tolerate any other kind of movement. But it seems that the distrust of political bargaining and of verbalism has been turned, in the case of many leaders, into a refusal of all politicization, leaving the movement's ideology—conscious and unconscious—impregnated by the region's conservatism. Officially the nature of the future state is defined in a simple formula: "The land will belong to those who liberate it."

In spite of the accusations by rival groups denouncing its right-wing tendencies, there are also Marxists in Fateh, but in an individual capacity, not as part of a current or group. As far as I know, none of these has a key post—except possibly one of the "independents" who was elected to the PLO Executive Committee last February. With regard to the Arab states, Fateh's position is clear: no intervention in the internal affairs of the Arab states as long as the states do not intervene in the affairs of Fateh. So it seems unlikely that the movement will, at the moment, take the initiative of calling into question the status quo in Jordan, especially as such an action would be sure to worry the other Arab states which harbor refugees, and where a considerable number of commandos are stationed. Also such an action might eventually incite Israel to occupy the east bank of the Jordan.

Fateh and the Refugees:
Hospitals, Schools . . . and Men

Since 1968, Fateh has begun to set up a network of public health installations. There are seven clinics under the direction of doctors and surgeons, seven social centers directed by nurses, and a convalescent home where there is also a clinic for performing serious operations. The hospital we visited not far from Amman is called "Palestine" and it was opened last November. The doctor in charge is a Palestinian who was in practice in Saudi Arabia up to 1967, when he returned to put himself at the service of the resistance. He does not receive any salary for his services. The hospital has a surgical block and a blood bank. There is another one at Salt. According to the figures I was given, these hospitals each receive about five thousand patients each week. Treatment, medicines and operations are all free. The UNRWA hospitals and dispensaries, although they provide important services, are inadequate to meet the medical needs of the Palestinian population and Fateh is trying to make good this lack. Among the numerous diseases requiring treatment are: malnutrition, dermatosis, anemia, and tuberculosis. Infant mortality is thirty-two per thousand. According to Fateh's doctors, the food that the refugees receive from UNWRA is far below the fifteen hundred calories officially announced by the United Nations. There is a serious lack of proteins. The medicines most used in the movement's clinics are multivitamins, antibiotics and dermatological products.

Each clinic has a social center consisting of four nurses who make regular visits to the camps to explain the principles of hygiene to the women. The medical staff, including the doctors, try to pin down the refugee population in order to eliminate diseases, but there are many problems. The refugees move their tents quite often, either because of climatic conditions or because of the instability inherent in being refugees. Sixty nurses have just been trained by Fateh doctors, who give training consisting of a month's theory and a month's practical work, with four hours' study each day.

Apart from the health problems of the refugee population, Fateh naturally has to provide for the medical needs arising from commando warfare. Before he is finally accepted, each future combatant undergoes a series of physical and psychological examinations, the aim of the latter being to determine the candidate's degree of combativeness and will power. Thirty to forty kilometers of mountain have to be covered alone, without food, carrying arms and a pack. After this test, the men are examined and accepted or rejected.

Along the whole length of the river Jordan, close to the frontier, Fateh has tried to create small underground medical posts, with a doctor-surgeon to each post. These are for the treatment of the wounded who are brought back on stretchers by their comrades. These posts, of which there are still only a few, are equipped with plasma and are able to give blood transfusions; each *fedayee* carries a disc with his blood group upon it. The surgeon of the post can perform quite difficult operations but the most serious cases are transferred to hospitals in the interior.

A concrete two-story building on the outskirts of Amman is the school "Jerusalem" set up by Fateh for the orphans of the combatants who have died in action, the *Shouhada* (martyrs). The refectory, kitchen, dormitories and classrooms are all kept very clean. There are six teachers who each earn fourteen dinars per month (about forty dollars). Fifty-five girls aged six to twelve are boarded at the school. They are all very neatly dressed. They have been chosen because they have no families and had been living in the refugee camps. According to age, they have four to six hours of lessons each day and the rest of the time is taken up with organized leisure activities. They are taught Arabic, arithmetic, the history of Palestine from the Ottoman occupation to the present day, and the geography of Palestine and the Arab world. During the year another school will be opened to accommodate a hundred girls and also a school for boys. The teachers are young and speak quite good English.

The "Jerusalem" orphanage is the first school set up by Fateh. As yet there are no classes given by the nationalist leaders in the refugee camps themselves. The movement hopes to establish some in the future but there are difficulties, mainly lack of personnel. Moreover, the creation of a double power in so many areas by Palestinian organizations in Jordan raises problems. Unlike the UNRWA schools, the orphanage diffuses a nationalist ideology: girls follow special courses to become nurses, older ones are taught how to handle arms. On Fridays (the weekly holiday), the children visit the movement's bases round Amman.

At the Schneller Camp

The Schneller camp, which is about eight miles from Amman, houses about fifteen thousand refugees. It is one of the biggest camps and its tents stretch out from the road right up to the bare hills. There are few flat surfaces in Jordan; few tents have the good fortune to be on really flat land. Multi-colored washing is drying in the winter wind. There is only one water pump for the whole camp and corrugated-iron toilet cabins have been put up some distance away. Usually refugees coming from the same village put their tents together so that they will continue to feel some sort of group security. The tents are meant to house five to six persons but sometimes there are eight sleeping in them. Some of the children go to school regularly, the rest go only sporadically depending upon the season, their family, and the UNRWA schools. Very few of the adults have any work; the majority of them live on the spot and have no other activity but that of existing. There is a clandestine organization in the camp, linked to Fateh: a reliable nucleus of leaders who can, when necessary, mobilize the whole camp, as happened when there was a confrontation with Jordanian troops on November 4, 1968. However, there is not at the moment a systematic organization of the camp into sections with active participation by the population.

In the middle of the camp, Fateh has—with the help of the population—built a medical center of corrugated iron which, according to the figures I was given, receives five thousand patients a week. The small clinic is full of people and outside several hundred more are waiting. The clinic is run by a young Palestinian doctor and three nurses. Surgery hours are from 9 A.M. to 1 P.M. each day. By 10:45 the number of patients received is close to a hundred. The doctor, who got his degree in Cairo, is not paid any salary. He joined the movement at the beginning of 1968. Most of the cases exam-

ined are due to malnutrition. There are many cases of dermatosis, rheumatism and infantile diseases. The clinic has a good
supply of medicines which are carefully set in order. Thanks
to this clinic, Fateh also asserts its political presence.

Haniya, refugee, aged seventeen:

I come here to be treated because it is our own hospital.
The doctor says I have rheumatism in my hands and
that is why I am in pain. It hurts me to close my fists
and this is because it is damp in the tents. We don't pay
anything here: everything is given by the *fedayeen.* May
God give them long life!
    I came here in 1967. Before that I lived in Jericho.
Then my father died and we left with my brother. Before, we had a house and I went to school. Now I don't
go to school any more and we are beggars. We left everything behind us and came from Jericho to Amman on
foot. My brother was without work for eleven months.
Now he earns thirty piastres a month and we are able to
survive. What I want more than anything is to go back
home.

Khitam Abdellatif, refugee, aged forty:

At that time (in 1948) we lived near Ramallah. We were
a peasant family: the land was ours and we cultivated it
ourselves. We also had some cattle. Then we were
attacked and had to flee. I remember that we spent the
night in a cave in the mountains. After a time, when we
had walked a long way, we were put in an UNRWA
camp at Ramallah. Quite a long time afterwards, we
found some very poorly paid work but we were able to
eat and we survived, thanks be to God. Then, when we
had begun to earn a little more and the family was in

good health, suddenly the same thing happened again. They came back and took everything and we left with just our shoes, the veils for our heads and very little else. We walked for three days.

We arrived in Amman like street beggars and we knocked on the doors. My eight children were hungry. Soon the smaller ones fell sick with parasites in their intestines and they had to sleep on the floor with a shawl for their only blanket. Then we were sent to the camp of Jarash and we were given bread. If you could manage to get the bread it was all right but if you couldn't it was just too bad. A few days later they gave us flour and we made our own bread. This flour was our only food and I made a paste from it and gave it to the children with water. Two months afterwards, winter arrived and suddenly there was torrential rain and even snow, and the tent let everything in. My youngest child died of cold in the snow and mud.

The leader of the camp met the authorities, who got in contact with the king but all we got was to be taken by lorry near to a river close to the Kasr-El-Damia bridge, where the Israelis fired on us. So we fled and hid in the Salt mountains. We waited and then we came back to Amman on foot, walking for a whole day. Then we were brought in by lorry to this place. At first they didn't give us anything, either for eating or sleeping. Then somebody, a German called Schneller, said, "What's that! Are you leaving them here without anything?" The UNRWA sent us tents and food. Life isn't easy here. My oldest child, who is fourteen, goes to the UNRWA school. My husband is sick but he would like to work, even if he is badly paid. We eat the hard broad beans and the kidney beans given to us by UNRWA with a little oil and some bread. For my youngest child, I also receive a little milk each day. We depend on God and the *fedayeen*. It is enough for us that they bear arms because they are going to give us back our country. After what we have already suffered we can willingly put up with more in order to be able to live with our heads held high.

Let us take a look at the refugee situation as it was prior to June 1967.

UNRWA (United Nations Relief & Works Agency, for the welfare of Palestinian refugees in the Near East), set up in 1950, notes: "No solution has appeared as regards the Agency's fundamental problem: the growing gap between its resources and the needs it has to meet." The number of refugees continues to increase. At the end of May 1967 it had reached a total of 1,344,576. The Agency reports, "The distribution of foodstuffs has remained limited by the ceiling imposed for rations, and the number of children registered who do not benefit from the distribution of rations has reached 284,304."

Not all the registered refugees live in the Agency's camps. Those outside the camps live in the towns and villages of the host country but they have roughly the same food and health services. The Agency points out: "From an economic point of view their situation is no different from that of the refugees living in the camps."

The New Exodus

It was against this background that the war of June 1967 provoked a new exodus involving at least 350,000 refugees. This is in addition to the 350,000 persons who were displaced from the occupied regions of southern Syria, the west bank of the Jordan and the Gaza strip. The Agency reports that the elementary needs of most refugees have only just been met in the "villages" under canvas. "The inhabitants of

the camps set up in the Jordan valley were also exposed to
the physical danger of military operations and they fled once
more to the high plateaux, far from the valley. For many of
them it was the fourth displacement within a year." After the
exodus towards east Jordan, the office estimated that there
were still about 245,000 registered refugees on the west bank
of the Jordan. In addition to the 494,000 registered refugees
in east Jordan, the Jordanian authorities have counted
246,000 displaced persons. This means that the total number
of refugees and displaced persons in east Jordan is 740,000.
In 1968, 590,000 refugees were receiving UNRWA rations,
which meant that 150,000 refugees were left without any
help. Six tent "villages" have been set up on the high plateaux of east Jordan, accommodating 78,400.

The Agency's report says that in Gaza "the sequel to the
war has been painful and prolonged and the Agency's services
have suffered the consequences of repeated incidents and
security measures such as curfews, interrogations, and deten-
tions, sometimes followed by the demolition of houses. In
addition, economic activity, always precariously balanced in
Gaza, is stagnant and the Agency's services, especially food
rations, are in ever greater demand. It is thought that between forty and fifty thousand refugees have left Gaza since
the hostilities (this was the figure given on June 30, 1968).
The Agency estimates that there are still about 265,000 refugees living in Gaza. At present it distributes 206,638 rations
to those enrolled on its registers, and another 2,435 to hard
cases." During the second half of 1968, there was a steep
increase in the occurrence of acute poliomyelitis in compar-
ison with the level for the previous two years. Other diseases,
including measles and tuberculosis, have also shown a marked
rate of increase in 1968 among refugees in east Jordan and in
Gaza. Finally, the report points out that "in the villages
under canvas, where schools have been set up in tents, winter
storms, flooding and a series of military actions (resulting in a

new exodus of refugees in February and March 1968) have interrupted the education programs."

The Resistance and the Arab Masses

Certain Middle East regimes are threatened by the combined actions of Israel and the Palestinians. If we consider the nature of the national movement, it is very unlikely that the Palestinian resistance can, on its own, radically modify the situation of the region. But the Palestinian struggle extends beyond its promoters to the extent that it mobilizes the Arab masses. In addition, certain Arab nationalists have transferred to the Palestinian resistance the hopes which they formerly placed in Nasserism and in Baathism. For the moment, the Palestinian resistance can only have an *indirect* influence on the Arab countries: it is a ferment, but it is limited by the fact that it is a national movement. Is it possible, at this stage, for it to be more than a national movement? The Jordanian regime has everything to lose by the extension of the Palestinian resistance. The least external shock could disturb the delicate equilibrium of the Syrian ruling group, surrounded by rival clans. The Nasserian regime, representing the most important Arab country (in which national cohesion is strongest), has begun since the defeat to swing to the right. The legend surrounding the head of state is crumbling and he is trying not to be outflanked by his right wing. He has no other alternative. This situation is the direct result of a deliberate policy, continued for many years, which has only strengthened the importance of the middle and lower middle classes. The Baathist regime in Iraq is the only one not to suffer the defeat of 1967, since it came to power a year later. Considering its relative geographical distance and the regime's need to win popularity, it is highly likely that, simultaneously with a series of nationalizations, it will make a high bid for the nationalist lead. This will make it even more likely that it will supplant its Baathist rival (Syria), which has lost the Golan Heights.

All these factors will weigh upon the Palestinian organizations and resistance (quite apart from the financial pressures that can be exerted by states that provide subsidies), in the context of the efforts towards conciliation to be made by the great powers, on the basis of the UN resolution of November 22, 1967. The possibility of a large-scale reprisal operation by Israeli forces cannot be excluded. Nevertheless, world peace does not seem to be in any real danger in the Middle East. Neither of the great powers is directly involved in the conflict and they have the same interest in maintaining the status quo in this part of the world. It is hard to see why the Soviet Union is more likely to intervene in this conflict than in Vietnam.

Moreover it must be pointed out that, at the present time, the balance of military strength is greatly in Israel's favor. Formerly it was the Arab states which refused the mediation of the great powers; now it is Israel. The Arab governments, especially the UAR, are in favor of a negotiated settlement, because they need peace in order to recover, by diplomatic means if possible, the territory lost during the war. So that, apart from Israel, the only element which is strongly opposed to the intervention of the great powers is the Palestinian resistance.

Israel's preoccupation with obtaining secure frontiers, and if possible recognized ones, gives it at the present time an expansionist posture which it will soon have to confirm or deny. It is well known that there is a strong tendency towards an expansionist direction within the ruling strata, feeding on the Israeli population's need for security. The population is kept in a state of mobilization by every possible means; the gap between "hawks" and "doves" is very narrow.

The development of the Palestinian resistance has put an end to any possibility of creating a Palestinian state on the

West Bank against the will of the fighters, as some Israeli leaders wanted. The Palestinian resistance, regarded by the Israelis from a purely military angle, has been under-estimated. At the beginning of the year, the Israeli authorities did not think that they would have to face Palestinian pop-ular demonstrations in the occupied territories. After eighteen months of relative calm, widespread strikes and street demonstrations against the occupation have exploded. These are the *political* consequence of the occupation and of the armed action of the commandos. This is the normal cycle in any occupation. In spite of their efforts to create a certain economic well-being, the Israeli authorities have not escaped it. All experience has proved that nationalism is a more powerful lever than prosperity. *The essential effect of the armed struggle has been to re-structure an uprooted and atomized society which had lost the desire to struggle.* In this sense, the resistance has re-created a sense of identity, and awakened the Palestinian national consciousness.

In the short term there seems to be very little possibility of a negotiated solution to the Palestinian conflict. Given the relative strength of the forces concerned, the ultimate aims of the Palestinian resistance seem unattainable. But a Palestinian state will come into existence, the result of a compromise, certainly, but not of a yielding. Apart from the Palestinians themselves, the strength of the Palestinian resistance lies in the fact that it enjoys the undivided support of the people of the Arab states. This means that any pressure which might be exerted on the Palestinian resistance by the governments of the region, to bring about a compromise which would be detrimental to the Palestinian people, has very little chance of succeeding.

3. Strategy for Revolution

Popular Front for the Liberation of Palestine

*After Fateh, the best known of the Palestinian resistance
groups is the Popular Front for the Liberation of
Palestine (PFLP), which gained prominence globally
through its hijackings in 1969 and 1970. Unlike Fateh,
the PFLP is explicitly Marxist in its analysis and also
Leninist in its insistence on the leadership role of a
vanguard party. Although critical of the Soviet Union
and unequivocal in ranking Mao with Marx, Engels and
Lenin in the revolutionary pantheon, the PFLP refrains
from taking sides in the Sino-Soviet dispute. Its position
on the split follows the third-world–oriented stance of
Cuba, North Korea, and North Vietnam. The report
excerpted here follows the model of Mao's 1926
"Analysis of the Classes of Chinese Society." It was
formulated at a PFLP conference in February 1969 and
published in the PLO's* Basic Political Documents of
the Armed Palestinian Resistance Movement.

It is necessary to define the forces of revolution on the
Palestinian level from the point of view of class. To say that
the Palestinian people, in all their classes, are in the same
revolutionary situation *vis-à-vis* Israel, and that all classes of
the Palestinian people have the same revolutionary capacity
in the light of their being landless and outside their country,

is an unrealistic and unscientific statement. This statement could be valid if the totality of the Palestinian people lived under the same material conditions. Since the totality of the Palestinian people are not living under the same conditions, scientifically it is impossible to ignore this fact, and these different conditions and resultant differences in the adopted attitudes must be discussed.

It is true that a great majority of the Palestinian people were driven from their country in 1948 and found themselves in almost similar vagrant conditions. It is also true that those who remained in Palestine were constantly threatened with the same fate. Yet during the last twenty years the conditions of the Palestinians have been settled and have taken definite class dimensions. Thus to claim that the whole of the Palestinian people are landless and revolutionary is erroneous. During the last twenty years definite class interests have become the determining factors in the attitudes adopted by the Palestinians. The Palestinian bourgeois class has its own land and interests. These interests have made it important for that class to look for stability and security.

In determining the revolutionary forces on the Palestinian level it is necessary to start from a class point of view. Arab and Palestinian rightist thought tries to nullify or dilute the class concept and invalidate all attempts to explain the present circumstances with reference to this concept. For example, it claims that the class concept cannot be applied to the Palestinians and the underdeveloped countries because it is not as well defined as in the developed capitalist countries. It is wrong, they say, to treat the class concept in the underdeveloped countries as one treats it in the developed ones.

Other rightist elements claim that in the phase of national liberation the struggle is between the totality of the people and the forces of imperialism. The phase of national liberation is not a phase of class struggle. Class struggle is justified during social revolution; at the time of national liberation, the conflict between classes should be made subordinate to that between the totality of the people and the foreign imperialist. Furthermore, rightist thought declares that Israel represents a special kind of imperialism which threatens the Palestinian people in all its classes. Thus, the problem is not a class problem but that of a struggle between the Zionist existence and the Arab Palestinian existence.

To allow this kind of thought to go unchallenged would mean total loss and the inability to identify the true revolutionary forces which form the core of the revolution. It would also mean that the revolution would be led by a certain class which cannot carry the revolution to its conclusion and draw up radical revolutionary programs which can ensure victory in the battle.

The class structure in an underdeveloped society differs from that of industrial societies, where there is a strong class of capitalists and a very large class of workers, and the struggle between them is violent. This situation does not obtain in underdeveloped societies. However, the latter are also class societies, in which there are exploiting classes represented by imperialism, feudalism and the bourgeoisie, and exploited classes represented by the workers and peasants. Thus each class has its own attitude with regard to the movement of history and the revolution. The upper classes are conservative and are for the status quo and resist historical changes. The lower classes are revolutionary, want to change and contribute to the movement of history. In other words, discussing the characteristics of underdeveloped societies is scientific as long as it objectively analyzes the differences between the characteristics of the class structure of the underdeveloped societies and those of the developed ones. If the discussion abrogates the question of classes or if it lessens the differences of attitude to be adopted by these classes with reference to the question of revolution, the discussion becomes biased and unscientific.

For example, the Arabs live in an underdeveloped and an unindustrialized society, yet the people live under very different circumstances. In Amman the rich live in Mount al-Luwaybidah, workers and peddlers in Mount al-Nazif, and still others in camps. The attitude of these different groups of people with regard to the revolution could not be the same. The Arabs should face forcefully all theories which attempt to conceal the objective facts of the classes. Are the sons of all classes represented on the battlefield? Or are the great majority of the fighters the sons of workers and peasants? If this is the case, then why does not the political thought of the revolution conform to the actual objective facts?

Workers and Peasants: the Core of the Revolution,
Its Basic Material Class and Its Leadership

The classes of the revolution on the Palestinian battlefield are *the workers and the peasants.* These classes daily suffer from the oppressive exploitation practiced by world imperialism and its allies in the Arab homeland.

Workers and peasants are the ones who fill the camps of misery in which the great majority of the Palestinians live. When one talks about the camps, this means, in fact, talking about a class structure which represents the workers, peasants and destitute petty bourgeois Palestinians. The Palestinian bourgeois class does not live in the camps.

When one appeals to the workers and peasants—inhabitants of camps, villages and city slums—and makes them politically aware, provides them with the organization and means of fighting, then one will find the material and the solid base for an historical revolution of liberation. The setting up of this solid backbone to the revolution will make it possible for a class alliance to be made which will serve the revolution's purpose without exposing it to vacillation, deviation or abortion.

The Palestinian Petty Bourgeoisie

Who is this class? What is its size? What is its stand with regard to the revolution? What are the relations that exist between the petty bourgeoisie and the workers and peasants —the very stuff of revolution?

The petty bourgeoisie includes craftsmen and manual industrial workers, petty intellectuals such as students, elementary and high-school teachers, petty officials, shop-owners, lawyers, engineers and physicians.

The petty bourgeoisie in the underdeveloped countries is numerous and can form a high percentage of the people. Thus it is necessary to realize that any discussion of this class will center around a great number of the people. Therefore, it is necessary to define the position of this class on a clear scientific basis. Otherwise a great error which will affect the progress of the revolution will be committed through giving more credit to the role of this class in carrying out the revolution than it deserves.

In any discussion of the petty bourgeoisie, it is difficult to define its class features. One part of this class lives comfortably with all its basic requirements taken care of, and it attempts to rise to the level of the bourgeois class. Another part cannot attain subsistence level; thus they are nearer to the revolution and more inclined to change. It is necessary to study in detail the class structure of the petty bourgeoisie and the stand of each of its sections at each stage of the revolution.

Generally speaking, it can be said that the petty bourgeoisie could be an ally of the revolution and its basic class, the workers and peasants, during the stage of democratic national liberation. But such an alliance should be on an enlightened basis to avoid its infiltrating into positions of leadership and subjecting the revolution to vacillation, deviation and stagnation. This class is an ally of the revolution, but not the basic material of the revolution. The revolution could not be led by members of the petty bourgeoisie, its programs or its strategy.

The application of these rules is very delicate and difficult. The petty bourgeoisie, in addition to its numerical size, has two important qualifications: awareness and education. If the workers and peasants are not aware, organized and capable of leading the revolution, the petty bourgeoisie will use this alliance to infiltrate into the leadership of the revolution.

To defeat the petty bourgeoisie in its attempt to lead the revolution without undermining the basic conflict with the enemy, the other classes—namely, the peasants and workers —should know when to ally themselves with it and when to struggle against it. Otherwise the struggle will lead to the following problems:

(1) Either the struggle between the petty bourgeoisie and the workers and peasants will be at the expense of the struggle against the enemy.

(2) Or the petty bourgeoisie will succeed and take over the leadership of the revolution.

The struggle against the petty bourgeoisie should be limited to a definite stand or a problem which the people sense. As a result of its class structure, the petty bourgeoisie will adopt attitudes which are sometimes vague, compromising and vacillatory. The meaning of this analysis is that occasions will arise when the organizations of the petty bourgeoisie will adopt such attitudes. Here the people can justify the struggle against the petty bourgeoisie, call for it and be on our side. As an example we can cite the incident which occurred on November 4, 1969, when the reactionary Jordanian government attempted, intelligently, to attack guerrilla action by striking against one of the guerrilla organizations. The PFLP took a definite stand, led the battle and uncovered the vacillatory stand of compromising organizations. The masses sided with the PFLP and, in spite of shortcomings, it succeeded in foiling the reactionary plan.

Settling the question of class leadership among the Palestinians is not an easy task. It will not be accomplished in a short period, and it should not take the form of a permanent struggle. It is wrong to think of this matter in unrealistic terms. Settling the problem of class leadership among Palestinians in favor of the workers, peasants and the poor class will take a long time, and ought to be accomplished without undermining our basic struggle and at a time when the people can justify and understand the considerations and reasons for the struggle.

At this time the presence of the petty bourgeoisie at the head of the national Palestinian movement should be objectively understood. Without such an understanding it will become difficult for the working class to head this leadership successfully. The reason for the presence of the petty bourgeoisie at the head of the Palestinian national movement is, first, that this class, during the stages of national liberation, is one of the classes of the revolution. Second, the petty-bourgeois class is numerically large. Third, because of its structure, this class is educated and competent. Thus, in the light of the ambiguity of the working-class structure—concerning political awareness and organization—it is natural that the petty bourgeoisie should head the alliance of classes which are against Israel, imperialism and Arab reaction. To this should be added the special characteristics of the Palestinian petty bourgeoisie and the difference between it and the Arab petty bourgeoisie which heads the Arab national regimes. The Palestinian petty bourgeoisie has raised the slogan of armed struggle and is leading it now. In addition, the fact that it is not in power makes it more revolutionary than the Arab petty bourgeoisie, which aims at preserving its interests and remaining in power by avoiding a decisive and long-term struggle against the camp of the enemy.

The Palestinian Bourgeoisie

The Palestinian bourgeoisie is in reality a commercial and banking bourgeoisie whose interests are interlinked and connected with the commercial and banking interests of imperialism. The wealth and riches of this class are the result of finding markets for foreign goods, insurance agencies and banks. Thus in the long run it is against the revolution, which aims at destroying the existence of imperialism and its interests in our homeland. The destruction of imperialism implies the destruction of the wealth of the bourgeoisie. Since our battle against Israel is at the same time against imperialism, this class will stand by its interests, in other words, with imperialism and against the revolution.

The Palestinian bourgeoisie which is living in Palestine under the Zionist occupation—even if it has not overtly joined Israel—is not a force of the revolution. It will objectively remain the class through which the enemy will try to abort the revolution and stop it in the middle of its course.

As for the Palestinian bourgeoisie which is living now outside Palestine, its interests—at the moment—are not contradictory to guerrilla action as long as the latter, at this stage, is performed within a limited theoretical, political and fighting field of vision. Thus, occasionally, it supports guerrilla action with part of its surplus wealth. But the revolutionary development of the Palestinian national movement, which will make it openly struggle against imperialism, will make this bourgeoisie adopt the attitude which will objectively conform with its class interests.

Actually we confess that certain sectors of this bourgeoisie will be an exception to the rule, and, because of the special nature of the Palestinian problem, they will remain on the side of the revolution and will not work against it. But these exceptions should not override the general rule which governs the stand of this class with regard to revolution.

The bourgeoisie, numerically, only forms a small percentage of society. Bourgeois society is merely half of one
percent of the whole society. Furthermore, this class is not
the one which carries arms or is ready to fight and die in
defense of the freedom of the homeland and the people. In
other words, any attempt to visualize this class analysis of the
forces of revolution in terms which would squander and
disrupt the forces of the nation and bring about an internal
struggle within them is unscientific and false. The revolution—in the light of this analysis—does not lose an active
fighting force. On the contrary, it gains clarity of vision and a
correct definition of the positions of the forces of revolution;
it puts the poor classes in a position where they can assume
responsibility for leading the revolution and mobilizing their
forces to the greatest extent. In the light of this analysis the
vision of the war of liberation will be a nationalist one in
which the great majority of the people will stand against
Israel, imperialism and Arab reaction under the leadership of
the poor, whose misery and poverty are caused by imperialism and reaction.

The Method of Organizing the Mobilization of Palestinian Revolutionary Forces

The political organization armed with the ideology of
scientific socialism is the highest form for the organization
and mobilization of the forces of the working class. This
truth has been clearly proved by all the revolutionary experi-
ences witnessed in this century. The Chinese, Vietnamese and
Cuban experiments, in addition to the October Revolution,
assert this truth.

But ... what of the petty bourgeoisie? The petty bourgeoisie, according to our analysis, is one of the forces of the
revolution. Can we mobilize it within this framework? If the
answer is negative, then what is the organizational framework

within which all the forces of revolution can be assembled and mobilized?

The majority of the Palestinian petty bourgeoisie will not be organized within the framework which is based on a political party organization armed with the ideology of scientific socialism. Revolutionary socialist thought is not the thought of this class. The petty bourgeoisie feels uncomfortable in front of a solid, committed and disciplined party organization. It prefers to commit itself to a general liberal thought which does not go beyond the general liberation slogans, and to vague political organizations which do not require of it more than it is capable of giving. In other words, the petty bourgeoisie will not be organized within this framework. It will join the other Palestinian organizations which do not clearly adopt the ideology of scientific socialism and the revolutionary political party organization. In the light of what has been said, the organizational form capable of comprehending all the forces of revolution is that of the political party committed to the ideology of scientific socialism. This ideology can mobilize the workers and peasants on a grand scale, and calls, at the same time, for the setting up of a national front through which an alliance can be established between the workers and peasants—the basis of the revolutionary classes—and the petty bourgeoisie, as one of the forces of the revolution.

The proposed wide, national front, is, in our opinion, the realization of national revolutionary Palestinian unity. If the implication behind Palestinian national unity is the gathering together of all the forces of revolution in the phase of democratic national liberation to resist the basic enemy as represented by Israel, imperialism and Arab reaction, then this form will attain such an aim. The meeting of the three classes within the framework of the front—even from the numerical point of view—represents the great majority of the Palestinian people. As for national unity, which is called for by certain elements, the aim of this is to ensure infiltration, by the traditional bourgeois and reactionary leadership, into the ranks of the revolution to destroy the idea of organizing a revolutionary political party, and to dilute the clarity of political revolutionary thought. Clearly this does not serve the revolution.

From what has been said the lines of our position with regard to the relations among the Palestinian forces and the problems at this level become clear:

(1) We consider Palestinian national unity as essential in the mobilization of all the forces of the revolution to resist the enemy camp. On this basis we should adopt a definite stand in this direction.

(2) The form of national unity is the creation of a front in which all the classes of the revolution—workers, peasants and petty bourgeoisie—should be represented.

(3) We should attend actively to the mobilization of workers and peasants in one revolutionary political organization armed with the ideology of scientific socialism. On this basis we should actively attempt to unify all the left-wing Palestinian organizations which, through dialogue between them and through their experience, can commit themselves to such an analysis.

(4) The petty bourgeoisie will not join an organization committed to scientific socialism and strong political organization. Thus it will join those Palestinian organizations which raise general liberal slogans, avoid clarity in thinking and analyzing class structure, and exist in an organizational form that does not require of the petty bourgeoisie more than its capacity. In other words, the petty bourgeoisie will fill, in the first place, the ranks of Fateh and the Palestine Liberation Organization (PLO).

(5) On this basis, and on the basis of our understanding of the basic conflict, the nature of the present phase and the necessity of national unity to assemble all the forces of the

revolution to resist Israel, we should work for the establishment of a national front with Fateh and the PLO which can
offer the war of liberation the necessary class alliance, on the
one hand, and protect the right of each class to view the war
and plan for it in accordance with its class vision, on the
other.

This is our vision of the forces of the Palestinian revolution
and the form of its mobilization.

The Forces of Revolution on the Arab Level

The strategy of the Palestinian war of liberation requires,
generally speaking, the mobilization of all the forces of
revolution in the Arab states, and, more specifically, of those
surrounding Israel. The PFLP stresses the link between the
Palestinian question and the Arab one, and the need for
uniting the Palestinian liberation movement and the Arab
liberation movement. The PFLP further stresses the strategic
necessity for an Arab "Hanoi" as a revolutionary base which
can bring about such unity.

Although we do not say that the mobilization of the
revolutionary forces on the Arab level is the direct responsibility of the Palestinian revolution, yet we can say that the
destiny of the Palestinian revolution and armed resistance—
guerrilla action—depends on the degree of its unity with the
revolutionary strategy which aims at mobilizing the forces of
revolution in Jordan, Lebanon, Syria, Egypt, Iraq and the
remaining Arab states. The dilemma of the Palestinian resistance movement is not only due to the fact that it has not
fulfilled the subjective conditions—ideological, strategic and
organizational—which have been fulfilled by the successful
national liberation movements in this age, but it is also due to
the fact that the resistance is living under hindering conditions caused by the Arab states. These states threaten to
liquidate the resistance movement by applying the Security

Council resolution instead of being a revolutionary support giving the movement strength, widening its area of operation and doubling its force.

The road which will lead to victory is: armed struggle against Israel and the imperialist interests in our homeland; extending the front of armed struggle which resists Arab reaction, the interests and military bases of imperialism in the Arab homeland; laying siege to Israel through a strategy of popular liberation warfare on all fronts—Syria, Egypt, Lebanon, Jordan and inside the territories occupied before and after June 5. The important thing is not that the Palestinian people should register a heroic stand through guerrilla action, but that it should achieve liberation (victory). The road to liberation, in the light of our definition of the enemy camp, is that of a revolutionary Palestinian Arab front bringing guerrilla action to fruition, protecting this action and extending it until it encompasses Israel from all sides and confronts all the enemy forces which give Israel aid and protection.

The strategy of revolutionary Arab action conforms in its broad outlines to the strategy of Palestinian revolutionary action. The basis of this conformity is the similarity of the conditions which have existed in the Arab states throughout the present period. In the light of Israel's occupation of Sinai and the Golan Heights, its existence and presence as a stepping-stone for imperialism to strike at any Arab nation— in spite of the class and economic transformations which have taken place in Egypt, Syria, Algeria, Iraq in the direction of socialism—the Arab states are living in the stage of national liberation, namely, the stage of national democratic revolution.

But Arab capitalists and feudalists are, even today, the ruling classes in certain Arab states. The rule of these classes is exemplified in the reactionary regimes of Jordan, Lebanon and other Arab states. These regimes are linked, as far as their interests are concerned, with world imperialism under the leadership of the U.S. In spite of the partial and outward conflicts between these regimes and Israel, it is nonetheless true that such partial conflicts are based on an objective meeting of interests with world imperialism. Thus these regimes realize that their basic conflict is with the movement of the people. From this one can conclude the relation of the armed struggle—Palestinian at the moment and Arab in the future—is one of conflict with these regimes in spite of any temporary tactical positions that may be forced on both.

As for the critical situation which confronts the Palestinian armed struggle and the Palestinian liberation movement, this is a result of its relations with the Arab nationalist regimes, and especially those nationalist regimes bordering Israel, namely, Egypt, Syria and Iraq.

Any daring revolutionary evaluation of these regimes should be based on the June defeat, its result and significance, in addition to what has followed this defeat in the form of strategy, programs and attitudes. Any attempt at mitigating the significance of this defeat, its meaning and lessons cannot but be an attempt at serving certain interests or an emotional unrealistic view of matters which is far from being scientific, objective and frank.

The June defeat has resulted in the total occupation of Palestine, in addition to the Golan Heights and Sinai. It has also resulted in the dispersal of hundreds of thousands of Palestinians and the degradation of a nation. A revolutionary position is the one which will not give false accounts of events, negotiate, or dilute a clear view of the matters, and by which we can understand and analyze the defeat, and be able to see the political and military strategy necessary to secure resistance and victory in the war.

The Palestinian and Arab people, and the Arab nationalist political parties and organizations, used to consider the Arab nationalist regimes as revolutionary and progressive, and capable of liberating Palestine and fulfilling the aims of the people. When the June war was declared the people and these forces did not expect a defeat similar to the June one. The June defeat has proved the great error in the way matters were viewed. There was error in our knowledge of the enemy and our determination of it and our evaluation of its plans and strength. In addition, there was an error in determining the phase, and a greater error in evaluating the totality of the revolutionary presence which was stifled by these national regimes and by the Arab nationalist organizations and institutions.

The Aim of the Palestinian War of Liberation

That Israel is an aggressive state hostile to our people is indisputable. The creation of Israel has meant for our people their expulsion from their homeland, the seizure of what was built by their own efforts and toil, their dispersion in different parts of the Arab homeland and the world, and the gathering of the majority of the Palestinians, with no hope and future, in the camps of misery and wretchedness, scattered in Jordan, Syria and Lebanon.

The fact that Israel is an expansionist imperialist state at the expense of the Arab land and its people is indisputable. As far as we are concerned, it is an experience which dissipates all false claims. The "national home" for the Jews in Palestine became the "State of Israel," within the borders stipulated by the 1947 UN Partition Resolution, then it expanded to include Israel with the pre-June boundaries, larger than those drawn by the 1947 UN resolutions, and then it expanded to include the whole of Palestine, Sinai and the Golan Heights.

The fact that Israel is a base for imperialism and colonialism on our land, which they use to destroy the revolutionary movement and keep us subservient to them in order to plunder and exploit our wealth and efforts, is obvious and indisputable. As far as we are concerned this is not a theoretical conclusion. It is a reality which we have lived during the 1956 tripartite aggression, the 1967 June war, and which we will continue to live as long as Israel remains in our land.

The truth about our war of liberation has been distorted— and will continue to be distorted—as a result of the following: the creation of the Zionist movement has been linked to the persecution of the Jews by the Europeans; the establishment of the state of Israel has been linked to the Nazi persecution of the Jews during World War II; the domination of the imperialist and Zionist influence on great parts of world public opinion; the existence of certain political forces which claim that they are progressive and socialist, in addition to the Soviet Union and other socialist countries which supported the establishment of the state of Israel; the mistakes committed by certain Palestinian and Arab leaders in the manner of their conduct of the war waged against Israel.

The Palestinian liberation movement is not racist or hostile to the Jews. It does not aim at the Jewish people. Its aim is to break Israel as a military, political and economic entity based on aggression, expansion and organic unity with the interests of imperialism in our homeland. It is against Zionism as a racist aggressive movement in alliance with imperialism which has capitalized on the suffering of the Jewish people to serve its interests and those of imperialism in this rich part of the world, which is the gateway to the countries of Africa and Asia. The aim of the Palestinian liberation movement is the establishment of a national democratic state in Palestine in which the Arabs and Jews can live as equal citizens with regard to rights and duties, forming an integral part of the democratic progressive Arab national existence which will live peacefully with all the progressive forces in the world.

Israel has carefully portrayed our war against it as a racist war aiming at the destruction of every Jewish national and throwing him into the sea. The aim behind this is the gathering together of all Jewish nationals and their mobilization for a war of life or death. A basic strategy in our war against Israel should aim at exposing such a falsification, and addressing the exploited misled Jewish masses and pointing out the contradiction between their interest in living peacefully, and the Zionist movement and the ruling forces in the state of Israel. Such a strategy will ensure the isolation of the fascist group in Israel from the remaining progressive forces in the world. It will also ensure for us, alongside the growth of the progressive armed resistance and the classification of its identity, the widening contradiction which objectively exists between Israel and the Zionist movement, on the one hand, and the millions of exploited and misled Jews, on the other.

The Palestinian liberation movement is a progressive national movement against the forces of aggression and imperialism. The link between the interests of imperialism and the continued existence of Israel will make our war against the latter basically a war against imperialism. On the other hand the link between the Palestinian liberation movement and the Arab progressive movement will make our war against Israel that of a hundred million Arabs in their progressive, national and unitary struggle. The battle of Palestine today, and all the objective circumstances surrounding it, will make the war a starting point for the attainment of the interconnected aims of the Arab revolution.

Lastly the Palestinian war will be, as far as the Palestinian and Arab people are concerned, an introduction of the Arabs into the civilization of the age and a transition from the state of underdevelopment to the requirements of modern life. Through our war of liberation we shall acquire political awareness of the facts of this age, and we shall throw aside delusions and learn the value of facts. The habits of under-development, exemplified in surrender, dependence, individuality, tribalism, laziness, anarchy and extemporization, will change, through the war of liberation, into the realization of the value of time, organization, accuracy, objective thinking, the importance of collective action, planning, total mobilization, interest in education and acquisition of all its weapons, knowing the value of the human being, freeing woman—half of society—from the bondage of decadent habits and customs, the basis of nationalism in confronting dangers, and the supremacy of this connection over tribalism and regionalism. Our long-term national war of liberation implies our fusion in a new way of life and our starting point on the road of progress and civilization.

4. The August Program

Democratic Popular Front for the
Liberation of Palestine

By 1968 a definite split had developed in the Popular
Front for the Liberation of Palestine. A left faction, led
by Naef Hawatmeh, articulated its position in the form
of a self-criticism which was accepted by the PFLP as
its "Basic Political Report" at an August 1968 meeting.
The Hawatmeh faction argued in the coming months that
the criticism was accepted only nominally; in February
1969 they left the PFLP to form a rival claimant to the
mantle of Marxism-Leninism. The new party took the
name Democratic Popular Front for the Liberation of
Palestine and the August 1968 program stood as their
fundamental position paper. It was published in English
in pamphlet form by the Palestine Solidarity Committee
at the State University of New York at Buffalo.

Lessons from the 1967 defeat

Since the 1948 disaster the national Palestinian and Arab
revolutionary movement has entered a new phase with regard
to class, ideology and politics. In the light of the bankruptcy
of the feudal-bourgeois regimes and leadership, which wholly

allied themselves with the counter-revolutionary forces after the disaster, the national resistance movement began to adopt new class, ideological and political definitions. The basic features of such definitions could be traced back to World War II. The emerging petty bourgeois class, which perceived the bankruptcy of the feudal-bourgeois class with regard to the solution of national liberation dilemmas, adopted an active nationalist policy hostile to colonialism, imperialism and Zionism.

The new leadership proposed the establishment of an alliance between workers, peasants, the poor and the military. Thus, the petty bourgeoisie began to play the role of the leading class as their ideology became dominant.

This national struggle, which is basically a class national struggle, was expressed in the changing class, economic and political programs—officially represented in the United Arab Republic, Syria, Algeria and to an extent in Iraq—which aimed at disrupting the alliance between feudalism, capitalism and imperialism. This leadership also attempted to solve the dilemmas of national liberation and the democratic national revolution. It broke up the feudal economy, which was bourgeois and *comprador* in nature, and established an economy which depends in the first place on light industrialization. It attempted to solve the problems of the agricultural sector of the economy in favor of the wage-earning peasants and the poor. All this was done to establish an economic base, independent of world capitalism; and a national political and social base, hostile to colonialism, imperialism and Zionism; and to build modern, organized, national armies with which to protect the homeland and liberate Palestine. In face of the fierce national-class struggle, the forces of counter-revolution did not wait long. They began to plan the 1956 Anglo-French-Zionist aggression to liquidate the regime which was hostile to imperialism, reaction and Zionism, and which threatened the interests and basis of the counter-revolutionary forces in Palestine and the Arab world. After the 1956 aggression, neo-colonialism—headed by the United States of America—attempted to patronize the Arab national liberation movement. But the national regimes resisted this encirclement and continued to fight their national battle against traditional colonialism and neo-imperialism. This continued in accordance with their hesitant petty bourgeois class nature. Eventually the Americans were convinced of the failure of their policy of peaceful encirclement to break the Arab national liberation movement, to liquidate the Palestine problem in the interest of Israel, and to re-arrange the class and political map of the Arab world for the benefit of the bourgeois-feudal regimes, which act as the material and political base for imperialism in the area and guarantee the security of the state of Israel.

Thus it was not the Arab reactionary regimes, but the nationalist regimes and the whole Palestinian and Arab national liberation movements who were responsible for the June war. Why did they fail? And with what work program did they face the June defeat?

Theoreticians of the Palestinian and Arab petty bourgeoisie, feudal reactionaries and the bourgeoisie proper gave explanations and analyses of the defeat which were limited to the educational, technical and cultural superiority of Israel and American imperialism, which is far superior technically to any underdeveloped country in Asia, Africa, or Latin America. This group of analysts concluded that to be able to defeat Israel we should become superior to it in education and technology.

Another group of petty bourgeois and feudal intellectuals attempted to explain the defeat in terms of technical military faults committed by this army or that, such as their unpreparedness in the face of the devastating surprise attack on the Arab air forces.

The Palestinian and Arab petty bourgeois and reactionary

theoreticians and analysts deliberately neglect the facts of modern history in their analysis of the Arab defeat in June. They ignore the basic reasons for the acceptance of the six-day defeat, in spite of the heated slogans prior to June 5, such as "inch by inch," "popular liberation war," "the policy of the scorched earth." These slogans formed the material objective antecedents to the following result: the June defeat. If the educational and technical superiority of Israel and imperialism is the main cause of the defeat, what is the explanation for the ability of the North Vietnamese people to confront half a million American soldiers in addition to half a million soldiers of the Saigon government? If we did not have the ability as a weak and underdeveloped country to resist and fight the United States, how can the ability of the Vietnamese and Cubans to fight against American imperialism be explained? And if the defeat was a result of a vast number of technical military faults, how can one explain the acceptance of this defeat and the disappearance of the above-mentioned slogans, particularly at a time when Vietnam is conducting its popular revolutionary war "inch by inch," both in word and deed, and its war is not devoid of setbacks and defeats?

There are in Vietnam and Cuba national regimes composed of the proletariat and poor peasants which use the material, cultural and moral potentialities of their countries to solve the dilemmas of national liberation and the democratic national revolution. This is achieved by liquidating all the material and moral class concessions (feudal and bourgeois) and by the establishment of the solid material base for economic and political independence through heavy industrialization and agrarian reform. In society, the revolutionary classes head the alliance of classes and political forces which oppose feudalism, capitalism and imperialism. Such a national economic and political program can mobilize and arm all the revolutionary classes to solve the dilemmas of national liberation and foster the struggle against imperialism and neocolonialism. Under such circumstances the slogan of popular liberation acquires its practical connotations where the working and poor masses are organized into a popular militia force, partisan phalanges, and the regular national army in order to defeat imperialism and the local forces in alliance with it.

In the Arab world the problem is different: the circumstances and composition of the Palestinian Arab national liberation movement were responsible for the June war, and it is that movement which must be responsible for the reversal of the June defeat. The petty bourgeois class occupies the leading role in the Palestinian and Arab national liberation movements and this class has led the entire range of the class, political, economic and military changes within the ideological, class and political structure of the petty bourgeoisie. In June 1967, this program was the one which was defeated. The economy that was set up by the petty bourgeoisie could not resist the Zionist-imperialist attack because it was a consumer economy based on light industrialization and agrarian reforms (the redistribution of land to raise self-sufficient production). Such an economy—following the closure of the Suez Canal—was forced to retreat and ask for assistance from the reactionary oil-producing countries, to be able to sustain itself.

The petty bourgeois regimes had to choose between two alternatives. The first alternative was to follow the Vietnamese and Cuban experience by drastically changing the national work program of their countries. This could be accomplished by mobilizing the material, human and moral capabilities of society and the national Palestinian and Arab liberation movements, and by arming the masses and waging a revolutionary popular liberation war. This war should be directed against all the interests and bases of colonialism, Zionism and reaction in alliance with colonialism; and should apply the slogan "fighting Israel and those supporting Israel" by resisting all the counter-revolutionary forces which support Israel or which interact with those who support Israel. By doing so the balance of power would start to shift to the side of the national Palestinian and Arab liberation movements, and the possibility of antagonizing the United States would become practical. Moreover, Arab human superiority —waves of fighting people—would overcome the Israeli-American technical superiority, as happens daily in Vietnam and Cuba.

The second alternative was to stick to the positions and programs which prevailed before June 1967 and which resulted in the June defeat. This would mean that the national Palestinian and Arab liberation movements would be forced to retreat continuously in the interest of Israel, imperialism, and Arab reactionary forces in alliance with both neo- and traditional colonialism. This is what actually took place.

The Policy of "Non-Interference"

Reactionary Palestinians who, following the June defeat, put forward the slogan "non-interference in the internal affairs of the Arab countries" arbitrarily separated Arab affairs from developments in the Palestine problem. When it attempts to imitate the Algerian experience, the slogan forgets, or pretends to have forgotten, that the subjective and objective characteristics that connect the Palestine problem with developments in the Arab world and the policies of imperialism in the Middle East, radically differ from those of Algeria. Moreover, these reactionaries have previously determined to neglect the particularities of Israel and its difference from all other kinds of neo- and traditional imperialism.

Israel represents a dynamic society which has expansionist aims in the area in addition to Palestine. As a society it is superior to the underdeveloped Arab countries in the educational and technical fields. This makes its expansionist policy easier. The relationship between Israel and American imperialism necessitates the amalgamation of the national Palestinian and Arab liberation movements. In addition, Palestine is a part of the Arab world and its future is related to that of the Arab countries.

In spite of all this, reactionary Palestinians neglect the facts of history and put forward the slogan "non-interference in the internal affairs of the Arab countries." This has quietly overlooked defeatist Arab stands with regard to the problem of Palestine. All groups of the resistance movement, including the Popular Front for the Liberation of Palestine, went along with this reactionary demagogic slogan which was interpreted as "non-interference in the Arab stand *vis-à-vis* the Palestine problem." Not one of the resistance groups has passed a critical judgment on the June defeat or on Arab responsibility for this defeat after twenty years of preparation for the liberation of Palestine. Because of the principle of "non-interference in the internal affairs of the Arab countries," not one group has openly condemned the stands taken *vis-à-vis* the Palestine problem and the Security Council resolution. It is ridiculous to find Haj Amin al-Husseini, who sold out the 1936 revolution, openly criticize certain Arab leaders' statements regarding the Security Council's resolution in *Le Monde,* in May 1968, while all the groups in the resistance movement, including the Popular Front, kept quiet about these developments in the Palestine problem.

The Popular Front openly condemns this slogan in the context in which it has been practiced for the last fifteen months. The resistance movement is not expected to substitute for the national liberation movements in the Arab countries, but it is expected openly to criticize the stands adopted by the Arab governments towards the Palestine problem and put the blame on those responsible for the defeat. If the resistance movement keeps quiet about the Arab governments with regard to decisions pertaining to the Palestine problem, then it will be plotting against Palestine.

The Question of Palestinian National Unity

The resistance movement has neglected the modern history of Palestine in its understanding and application of the problems of "national unity." The policies adopted towards the question of national unity were reactionary and wrong. This has led to placing the reactionary classes at the head of the resistance movement. This leadership is the same one which has led the national Palestinian liberation movement and the national revolution to its failure throughout the modern history of Palestine. At a time when the sons of the revolutionary classes of poor workers and peasants and revolutionary intellectuals fight for the liberation of the homeland and rejection of the Zionist occupation, the military leadership of the resistance movement has placed political leadership in the hands of rich feudal capitalist groups which have had nothing to do with the armed struggle throughout the modern history of Palestine. The resistance movement has understood the slogan of "national unity" in an inverted manner. Thus the concept of national unity was formulated under the leadership of feudal elements, bankers, big merchants and reactionary Palestinians. The starting point was participation in the "Jordanian national front," which was composed of Palestinian and Jordanian reactionary elements, under whose hands the people have suffered many hardships. The final point was the creation of the National Palestinian Congress, which is composed of reactionary Palestinian elements headed by bankers and big contractors whose condition for joining the Congress was that they should be given its leadership, while the Popular Front and Fateh should form its left and right arms.

Palestinian national unity is a political necessity. But what sort of national unity? The sort of national unity which accomplishes liberation. It leads the resistance movement on the road to victory by mobilizing and arming the Arab masses. It awakens their basic and collective capabilities in the long struggle of resistance. This resistance will depend upon violence in the face of an enemy whose strategy is to deliver rapid blows and accomplish swift victories.

This unity is the unity of all classes and political forces under the leadership of the revolutionary patriotic classes which have carried arms throughout the modern history of Palestine. It is the sons of these classes who have answered the call to arms since June 1967. The modern history of the people of Palestine, and that of popular liberation wars in all underdeveloped countries, proves that the workers and peasant classes are the ones who are prepared to carry arms and fight a long-term war against the enemies of national liberation, namely, imperialism and its agents.

Thus the Popular Front openly declares its condemnation of the slogan "national unity" in its present context and application. Furthermore, it condemns and openly criticizes its previous practices, starting with its participation in the Jordanian national front and finally in the National Palestinian Congress.

The Dilemma of Existing Resistance Movements

The Palestinian national liberation movement is of the same ideological, class and political structure as that of the Arab national liberation movement led by the petty bourgeois class. At the same time it represents one of the weakest groups in the national liberation movements in the area. This is the case because of a number of subjective and objective characteristics, headed by the contradictions of the Palestine problem and the large number of nonproductive human beings among the dispersed Palestinian people.

From here we can touch on a basic characteristic of the Palestinian liberation movement. The petty bourgeois class, the leader of the Arab Liberation movement, was able to eliminate the forces of feudalism and the bourgeois class from a leading position within the national movement, and was able to expose the alliance of these forces with colonialism and imperialism. Yet the Palestinian petty bourgeois class failed to remove this incapacitated bourgeois class from playing a national role. Thus the petty bourgeois class was able continuously to infiltrate the leadership of the national liberation movement and make it serve its ideological, political and class interests. Consequently—and following June 1967—the Palestinian right, supported by the Arab right, was able to dominate the resistance movement through demagogic slogans and lead it within the scope of its theoretical and political beliefs. These beliefs serve the interests of the bourgeoisie and those of Arab reaction and destroy the means by which the Palestinian and Arab national movements can save themselves from imperialist-Israeli occupation. In the final analysis, these policies do not serve the resistance movement. They tend to transform it into a tactical means of bringing pressure to bear. This pressure aims, first, at containing the national revolutionary uprising of the Arab masses. Secondly, it aims at minimizing the concessions to be made by Arabs in order to ensure the implementation of the Security Council resolution, which threatens the Palestine question, in its entirety, with liquidation. The leadership of the petty bourgeois class has failed to salvage itself and the leaders of the resistance movement. The reasons for this failure are: its adoption of hesitant ideological and political policies; its failure to comprehend the basis of a nationalist policy; and the domination of the ideology of the reactionary right over important sectors of the resistance.

In spite of the belief that a popular war of liberation is the course of action to be adopted in order to achieve the liberation of Palestine and in spite of the high morale among the Palestinian people, the leadership of the resistance movement, namely, the bourgeoisie and petty bourgeoisie, has put the resistance movement in a critical historical situation which has transformed it into a means of pressure.

The Course of National Salvation

The road to national salvation requires strong wills from the members of the resistance movement. National salvation rejects whatever is existing and pushes forward on a new course—the course of transforming the resistance movement into an organized mass movement. It is armed with political, material and radical national ideologies under the leadership of vanguard fighting forces equipped with political consciousness and the ideology of the proletariat, hostile to Israel and imperialism and its allies throughout the Arab land.

The vanguard of the proletariat will bring about the national unity of all classes and political forces which are hostile to counter-revolution. These must be committed to a program of arming the people for a long-term war under the leadership of the revolutionary fighting forces in a wide national liberation front.

The spirit of resistance will spread among the Palestinian people; it needs the vanguard which will lead it on the road of national salvation. Such a vanguard, through analysis and criticism of the Palestinian liberation movement, has not yet been born.

The young elements among the members of the resistance movement and the Palestinian people who are armed with a consciousness of scientific ideology should lead the dialectical movement to bring forth such a vanguard, which will lead the people with all its classes and national political forces on the road of victory, the road of a long-term war.

5. Jews and Arabs: One Future
Naef Hawatmeh

*The Marxism of the DPFLP, like that of the PFLP,
is eclectic. Sympathetic to China, Cuba, and North
Vietnam, the party nonetheless does not repudiate the
socialist states of Eastern Europe. In this article, the
DPFLP's leading theorist offers Yugoslavia and
Czechoslovakia as possible models for a federally
constituted Palestine embracing Jews and Moslems.
Hawatmeh also explores the possibility of concrete
solidarity between Palestinian and Israeli socialists. The
article originally appeared in* al-Hurriyah *on January 12,
1970. It appears in the* Merit *pamphlet* Documents of
the Palestinian Resistance Movement *(New York:
Pathfinder Press, 1971).*

The Palestinian resistance movement sees the Security
Council resolution as a reactionary and imperialist solution of
both the Palestinian and the Israeli questions. This view is
incompatible with that of most of the Arab regimes, which
either accept the resolution, or reject it in theory but in
practice work along with it; Saudi Arabia is a case in point.
What then is the solution?

The resistance proposes a democratic solution of the problem that calls for long-term political, ideological, and armed

struggle. For only if the struggle is carried on in all three fields can it assume its truly practical and objective significance. The democratic solution proposed rejects all the chauvinistic solutions, whether Arab or Israeli, which were in existence until June 5, 1967: Israeli expansion, or massacring the Jews and throwing them into the sea, etc. It also rejects the reactionary solution offered by the Security Council resolution. What it is striving for is the right of the Palestinian people to decide their own future in their own territory, which was seized from them by a nationalist, Zionist, and imperialist act of usurpation in 1948, and the construction of a democratic popular state in the whole of the territory of Palestine in which Arabs and Jews will enjoy equal rights and obligations, everyone being entitled to develop his national culture in a democratic, progressive spirit. The constitutional form assumed by this state is not important—it may be a unitary state, or a federal one on the model of Yugoslavia or Czechoslovakia, or anything else.

With this end in view DPFLP submitted to the Sixth National Palestinian Congress that met in Cairo in early September 1969 and, at the same time, to the Palestinian and Arab masses, a "proposed democratic solution of the Palestinian and Israeli problems." Obviously, this solution can only be achieved through long-term ideological, progressive, popular armed struggle; and it must be supported by the common struggle of all progressive and democratic forces in the area, especially in the ranks of the Palestinian resistance movement, Israeli society and progressive Jews. This proposed democratic solution, in fact, calls on all progressive Israelis and Jews to organize themselves into an armed popular Palestinian front to ensure the day-by-day objective implementation of this solution. For as progressive and democratic trends grow stronger in the ranks of all the Palestinian resistance organizations, this solution will impose itself all the more forcefully on the citizens of Israel. Israeli reaction cannot always be watching Israeli society, and reactionary Zionist culture must inevitably disappear as progressive trends grow stronger in the Palestinian and Arab national liberation movement.

With this progressive aim in view, DPFLP has called for a dialogue to be initiated with Israeli organizations which follow an anti-Zionist and anti-imperialist line, although they have not yet arrived at a decisively progressive attitude in their understanding of the Palestine problem and the nature of the composition of the state of Israel. Such Israeli organizations are Rakah and Matzpen. DPFLP has published in *al-Hurriyah* several analyses of Matzpen, and in its pamphlets has clearly drawn the distinction between the attitude of this organization and that of the Zionist left (Mapam) and the Iraeli reactionary forces.

The radical democratic solution of the Palestine problem is a long and complicated question in an area thick with reactionary regimes that are allied with colonialism and imperialism and steeped in a rightist reactionary culture. To use a Marxist expression—the prevailing culture is the culture of the predominant classes. It is an area, too, in which an essentially Zionist state has been established—a state with a double character, with chauvinistic and expansionist ambitions. It has organic links with colonialism and imperialism and, with its reactionary Zionist culture, plays a double role in the area, in addition to the fact that it is a state established on the conquest and the national usurpation of the people of Palestine. "A people that persecutes another people cannot be a free people," Marx said, and his saying has been borne out by the course of ancient, medieval, and contemporary history.

In the Arab world, as is the case with the peoples of all backward countries, the only way to rout the counterrevolutionary forces and to defeat them by imposing solutions which will ensure that the people can choose their own future by themselves and in their own territory, is by adopting the Vietnamese method—the method of a popular war of liberation to overcome the technical superiority of imperialism, Zionism and reaction. This is the course being followed by the Palestinian resistance movement, in preference to traditional wars in which victory must go to the triple counteralliance. In spite of the crisis which is now besetting the Palestinian resistance movement as a result of the composition of a number of its petty bourgeois leadership cadres, the left wing of the resistance, in bearing arms against imperialism, Zionism, and reaction, is also fighting ideologically and politically for the development of the resistance movement along progressive and democratic lines. The daily growing victory of Vietnam is the result of a popular war led by a united liberation front in which the revolutionary Communist party plays the central role in leading the operation of national liberation and the democratic revolution.

However complicated the Palestinian and Israeli questions, it is only through the insistence of the resistance movement, and its left wing in particular, on breaking the reactionary regimes and rejecting reactionary solutions, that a new trail can be blazed towards the liberation of the peoples of the Middle East. Even if, for local and international reasons which cannot be discussed in the present context, the ruling and dominating regimes in the area succeed in imposing reactionary solutions and repressing the Palestinian resistance movement which rejects such solutions, the resistance movement will have achieved an important revolutionary advance if it sows the seeds of a violent democratic revolution in the Middle East in the near future. For the course of history is forward; adverse forces may sometimes compel it to take a step backwards, but this is only a preparation for two steps forward.

6. Towards a Democratic State in Palestine
Fateh

The following document represents Fateh's most mature and comprehensive statement concerning the liberated Palestine for which the movement is fighting. Ironically, it was presented on the eve of the civil war in Jordan, in September 1970, at the Second World Congress on Palestine, held in Amman under the auspices of the General Union of Palestinian Students. The full text was carried in the United States by Liberation News Service in their bulletin of October 15, 1970.

The Palestine Revolution and the Jews

It is almost a year since the Palestine liberation movement, Fateh, declared officially and for the first time, a political program spelling out the ultimate objective of the liberation struggle. The declaration stated: "We are fighting today to create the new Palestine of tomorrow; a progressive, democratic and non-sectarian Palestine in which Christian, Moslem and Jew will worship, work, live peacefully and enjoy equal rights." The statement added, "Our Palestinian revolution still stretches its welcoming hand to all human beings who want to fight for, and live in, a democratic, tolerant Palestine, irrespective of race, color or religion."

The statement was repeated, explained and amplified by Fateh representatives in every international gathering attended by a Fateh delegation. The official spokesman of Fateh, Abu Ammar [Yasser Arafat], was quoted by several journalists as saying that "once we defeat the enemy and liberate Palestine we will create a home for all of us."

Abu Eyad, one of the leaders of Fateh, stated in a long interview with the editor of *al-Taleea* (June 1969) that the Palestinian revolution condemns persecution of human beings and discrimination in any shape or form and that Fateh would help Jews anywhere if they faced persecution at the hands of racists. Abu Eyad said that he would be willing to give these Jews arms and fight with them.

This was not just a fantastic propaganda claim; it was put into effect a few weeks later when Fateh students protected a Jewish professor, Eli Lobel, in Frankfurt, Germany, from assault and attempted murder at the hands of Zionist German thugs last July. Fateh protected Jewish members of Matzpen [the Israeli Socialist Organization] in Germany after their lives were threatened in the same incident.

Profile of a Democratic Palestine

Difficulties and Limitations. It is quite difficult and risky at this early stage of the revolution to make a clear and definitive statement about the new liberated Palestine. Realism, rather than romantic daydreaming, should be the basic revolutionary approach. We do not believe that victory is around the corner. The revolution does not underestimate the enemy or its imperialist allies. What will happen during the years of hard struggle for liberation cannot be easily predicted.

Will the attitude of Palestinian Jews harden, or become more receptive and flexible? A further drift to the right, the stepping up of anti-Arab terrorism—in the Algerian O.A.S.

tradition—followed by a voluntary mass exodus on the eve of liberation would pose a completely different problem and would be quite regrettable.

On the other hand, joining the revolution and working with it will lay firmer ground for the new Palestine. The revolution is striving hard to achieve the second alternative.

Guerrilla operations are basically directed at the military and economic foundations of the Zionist settler-state. Whenever a civilian target is chosen, every effort is made to avoid the loss of civilian life—though one would find it hard to distinguish civilians and non-civilians in this modern spartan society where every adult is mobilized for the war. Hitting quasi-civilian areas aims at the psychological effect of shocking the Israelis into realizing that the racist-militaristic state cannot provide them with security when it is conducting genocide against the exiled and oppressed Palestinian masses.

In the Dizengoff Street bomb (Tel Aviv), Fateh guerrillas delayed the operation three times to choose a place (in front of a building under construction) and time (12:30 A.M.) to maximize noise but to minimize casualties. The result: few were injured, but thousands were shocked and made to engage in serious rethinking.

In conclusion, despite all uncertainties, there is the hope, the vision and the behavior of the Palestinian revolutionaries, designed to achieve a better future for their oppressed country. Answers must be thought out and found for myriad questions relating to this future. Even if the answers are tentative, they will start a dialogue which provides the road towards maturity and fulfillment.

1. *The Country*. Pre-1948 Palestine—as defined during the British mandate—is the territory where the democratic, progressive state is to be created. The liberated Palestine will be part of the Arab homeland and will not be another alien state within it. The eventual unity of Palestine with other Arab

states will make boundary problems less relevant and will end the artificiality of the present state of Israel, and possibly that of Jordan as well.

The new country will be anti-imperialist and will join the ranks of progressive revolutionary countries. Therefore, it will have to cut the present life-links with, and the total dependence on, the United States. Therefore, integration within the area will be the foremost prerequisite.

It should be quite obvious at this stage that the new Palestine discussed here is not the occupied West Bank or the Gaza strip or both. These are areas occupied by the Israelis since June 1967. The homeland of the Palestinians usurped and colonized in 1948 is no less dear or important than the part occupied in 1967.

Besides, the very existence of the racist oppressor state of Israel, based on the expulsion and forced exile of part of its citizens, is unacceptable to the revolution in even one tiny Palestinian village. Any arrangement accommodating the aggressive settler-state is unacceptable and temporary. Only the people of Palestine—its Jews, Christians and Moslems—in a country that combines them all is permanent.

2. *The Constituents.* All the Jews, Moslems and Christians living in Palestine or forcibly exiled from it will have the right of Palestinian citizenship. This guarantees the right of all exiled Palestinians to return to their land whether they have been born in Palestine or in exile and regardless of their present nationality.

Equally, this means that all Jewish Palestinians—at the present, Israelis—have the same right, provided, of course, that they reject Zionist racist chauvinism and fully agree to live in the new Palestine as Palestinians. The revolution therefore rejects the supposition that only Jews who lived in Palestine prior to 1948 or prior to 1914 and their descendants are acceptable. After all, Moshe Dayan [minister of defense] and Yigal Allon [deputy minister] were born in Palestine before

1948 and they—with many of their colleagues—are diehard racist Zionists who obviously do not qualify for a Palestinian status; whereas newcomers may be anti-Zionists and work ardently for the creation of a new Palestine.

In the interview referred to earlier, Abu Eyad, one of the officials of Fateh, reasserted that not only progressive Jews but even present Zionists willing to abandon their racist ideology will be welcome as Palestinian citizens. It is the belief of the revolution that the majority of the present Israeli Jews will change their attitudes and will subscribe to the new Palestine, especially after the oligarchic state machinery, economy and military establishment are destroyed.

3. *The Ideology.* The Palestinians, in the process of and at the time of liberation, will decide on the system of government and on the political-economic-social organization of their liberated country. (It should be repeated at this juncture that the term Palestinians includes those in exile and under occupation and Jewish settlers.)   A democratic and progressive Palestine, however, rejects by elimination a theocratic, a feudalist, an aristocratic, an authoritarian, or a racist-chauvinist, form of government. It will be a country that does not allow oppression or exploitation of any group of people by any other group or individual; a state that provides equal opportunities for its people in work, worship, education, political decision-making, and cultural and artistic expression.

This is no utopian dream, for the very process of achieving the new Palestine inherently produces the requisite climate for its future system of government—i.e., a people's war of liberation brings out new values and attitudes that serve as guarantees for democracy after liberation.

Witness changing attitudes toward collective work in refugee camps in Jordan and Lebanon. Palestinians and other sisters and brothers joining them in volunteer work and livelihoods. They are not exploited or enslaved labor. The values of human life change. Unlike Israeli napalm raids and indiscriminate killing, Palestinian guerrillas kill sparingly and selectively.

New forms of human relations emerge. No master-slave relation can be attained among fighters for freedom. Increasing awareness of the international dimensions of their problems and discovery of who backs the oppressor and who supports the oppressed create new responsibilities to the international community, especially to the supporters of liberation and democracy.

Therefore, Palestinians after liberation will not accept subjugation from anybody and will not reintroduce oppression against any group, for this would be a negation of their *raison d'être* and an abdication of their revolutionary existence.

This is quite obvious in Palestinian refugee camps in Jordan and Lebanon. After twenty-two years of oppression, humiliation and manipulation by secret police and local exploiters, the camps have awakened to the revolution. In the process, the exiles have broken their bonds, have thrown out the secret police and its spies and allied exploiters and have instituted democratic self-management.

Medical, educational and social services are being provided locally through the revolutionary organizations in a self-help fashion that has brought back dignity and self-respect. Crime rates in these camps have drastically gone down to 10 percent of their prerevolutionary magnitude. Self-discipline has replaced the police. The new militia is providing the link between the revolutionary avant-garde and the mass base. Democratic checks are built in. These Palestinians will not accept oppression and subjugation from anybody and will not enforce it on anybody else.

Newsmen and other foreign visitors have discovered that nowhere in the Arab world can they find people as mature and tolerant vis-à-vis the Jews as in the camps of Jordan and Lebanon, and especially among the *ashbal:* the "young tigers."

These young Palestinians (eight to sixteen years old) are almost totally free of any anti-Jewish biases. They have a clearer vision of the new democratic Palestine than that held by bourgeois city dwellers. These young people are the liberators of tomorrow. They will complete the destruction of Israeli oppression and the rebuilding of the new Palestine.

If the democratic and progressive new Palestine is utopia, then the Palestinian guerrillas and camp dwellers are starting to practice it.

The Transition and After

It is quite logical to expect specific transitional collective accommodations immediately after liberation, and even a few remaining in the normalized permanent state, i.e., some collective or group privileges besides the purely individual privileges. Jews—or non-Jews, for that matter—would have the right to practice their religion and develop culturally and linguistically as a group, besides their individual political and cultural participation. It seems quite logical, for example, to have both Arabic and Hebrew as official languages taught in government schools to all Palestinians, Jews or non-Jews.

The right of free movement within the country and outside it would be guaranteed. Palestinians desirous of voluntarily leaving the country would be allowed to do so. Immigration would be restricted in a transitional period to the return of all exiled Palestinians desirous of return. In a normal permanent state, however—subject to agreed-upon regulations and the absorptive capacity of the country—immigration would be open without discrimination. Freedom of access, visits, extended pilgrimages and tourism would be guaranteed—subject of course to the normal regulation—to all

Jews, Moslems and Christians of the world who consider Palestine a holy place worthy of pilgrimage and meditation.

Is the New Palestine Viable?

Several well-intentioned critics maintain that even if the creation of the democratic Palestine is possible, it will not survive for long. Their basic contention is that the population and cultural balance will heavily favor the Jews in the new Palestine. This—in their argument—will lead either to an explosive situation or to the domination of the new Palestine by the Jews and a possible reversion to a neo-Zionist state in disguise.

The argument is serious and looks quite plausible given the present set-up and the European dichotomy of the "Arabs" as a backward group and the "Jews" as a modern one.

As for population, the Jews in Palestine today number 2.5 million compared to 2.6 million Palestinian Arabs (Christian and Moslem) in the occupied territories before 1967 and in exile.

Birth rates and net natural growth rates are higher among Arab Palestinians than among the Jews in Palestine.

Immigration, however, has been the major cause of growth in the Jewish ranks. Nevertheless one must consider the fact that 250,000 Jews have permanently left Palestine (emigrated) since 1949 in a period when relative security prevailed. Most of the emigrants were European Jews, whereas most of the new immigrants were Arab Jews who found it very difficult to stay in their countries after the creation and survival of the aggressor settler-state of Israel.

The process of the revolution will inevitably increase the tempo of emigration, especially of those beneficiaries of a racist state who will find it very difficult to adapt to an open pluralistic society. Parallel to that development will be the increasing modernization of the Arab countries and toler-

PFLP
POPULAR FRONT FOR THE LIBERATION OF PALESTINE

BEKÆMP
IMPERIALISMEN

POPULAR FRONT
FOR THE
LIBERATION OF PALESTINE

EL AL

EMBASSY
UNITED STATES OF AMERICA

ation of all minorities including the Jewish citizens. Fateh is already engaged in serious negotiations with several Arab countries to allow Jewish emigrants to return, to give them back their property, and to guarantee them full and equal rights.

These factors are expected, on the whole, to maintain relative population balance in Palestine.

The pace of social and educational development is increasing rapidly among the Arab Palestinians as well. It is estimated that the number of university graduates among the Palestinians in exile exceeds fifty thousand.

Palestinians have successfully played the role of educators, professionals and technicians in several Arab countries, especially those in the Arabian Peninsula and North Africa. Arab Palestinians faced this cultural challenge in pre-1948 Palestine and managed in the relatively short period of thirty years to compete effectively with the Jews in agriculture, industry, education and even in the field of finance and banking. Armed with this spirit of a victorious revolution, hopefully in comradeship with a significant number of Jews, the Arabs of Palestine will become effective and equal partners in the building of the new country.

Integration of Palestine within the Arab region will add to its economic and political viability. The present Arab boycott will obviously be replaced by economic aid and trade, a goal which the settler-state of Israel completely failed to achieve, remaining thus an American ward and protégé during its entire existence.

Conclusion

The democratic, non-sectarian Palestine still lacks full clarity and elaboration, but this is the best that can be done at this stage of the arduous liberation struggle. Through armed struggle the Palestinians have outgrown their bitterness and prejudice in a relatively short time. A few years ago, discussing this proposal would have been considered as a complete sell-out or high treason. Even today, some Arabs find it difficult to accept the proposed goal and secretly—or publicly—hope that it is nothing more than a tactical propaganda move.

Well, it is definitely not so. The Palestinian revolution is determined to fight for the creation of the new democratic and nonsectarian Palestine as the long-term, ultimate goal of liberation. Annihilation of the Jews or of the Palestinian exiles and the creation of an exclusive racist or theocratic state in Palestine, be it Jewish, Christian or Moslem, is totally unacceptable, unworkable, and cannot last. The oppressed Palestinian masses will fight and make all needed sacrifices to demolish the oppressive, exclusive state.

The Israeli racists are greatly irritated by the idea of a democratic Palestine. It reveals the contradictions of Zionism and bares the moral schizophrenia that besets world Jewry since the creation of Israel. The Israeli Jewish professor Eli Lobel and the French Jewish writer Ania Francos were threatened and molested by Zionists for their sponsorship of a democratic Palestine as the ultimate goal of liberation. The Zionists are stepping up their campaign to discredit the idea, especially among the Jews.

Their effort has been in vain. The forces of logic and the effect of years of persecution in exclusive societies at the hands of racists are opening the eyes of Jews and others in the world to the only permanent solution that will bring a lasting peace and justice to our Palestine: building a progressive, open, tolerant country for us all.

Black September

1. Skyjack
Interview with Leila Khaled

In June 1970 U.S. Secretary of State William Rogers announced his "peace plan" for the Middle East, and it was quickly accepted by both Jordan and Egypt. The Marxist parties (PFLP and DPFLP) concluded that the two Arab states would take prompt action to crush the resistance movement. The Popular Front responded with multiple hijackings, beginning Sunday September 6. A $24 million Pan American jet was hijacked, flown to Cairo, and blown up to protest both the U.S. role in the Middle East and UAR acceptance of the Rogers plan. Two more jets were successfully hijacked that same day and flown to an impromptu "Revolution Airport" in the desert northeast of Amman; three days later a BOAC jet was forced to land in the same area, where PFLP commandos had dug trenches to defend themselves against Jordanian government intervention. More than four hundred airline passengers were held for varying durations, as the PFLP demanded release of imprisoned comrades held in various parts of Western Europe. Among those imprisoned was Leila Khaled, who was captured in an unsuccessful attempt to hijack an El Al jet on September 6. The following interview, released by Liberation News Service at that time, describes her previous successful hijacking and gives a vivid personal account of the motivations and politics of the hijackers.

Isn't it something awful that I could see my home town again only when I hijacked a plane? But there it was—Haifa—away on the left just past the pilot's head as I sat behind him looking out of the cockpit windows. As we came down to twelve thousand feet for the approach to Lydda airport the whole lovely coast of my country, occupied Palestine, which some people call "Israel," came into sight.

It was a fine, clear day, but I had little time to enjoy the view because we were approaching the most exciting and dangerous point of our adventure. Although the pilot had so far done everything I told him, would he, somehow, land the plane at Lydda? Or would the Israelis be able to force us to land?

It had all begun two days earlier in Rome. This was my first visit to Europe and Rome is a wonderful city. I was very tired when I arrived, and I slept for ten hours solid.

Then the evening before the flight I walked through the city from the Borghese Gardens to the Fountain of Trevi. Of course, I threw the traditional coins in the fountain, which means, I hope, that I'll see Rome again: but will the Italians let me in next time?

There was a woman singer in a cafe near the fountain and I just sat and listened for two hours. The only other things I did were to buy myself a bottle of French perfume and to confirm my booking for the flight next day to Athens at the TWA office.

I couldn't eat dinner that night and it was three in the morning before I could get to sleep and when I awoke I had no appetite for breakfast either. I was hungry, but I'm accustomed to hunger because of my commando training and also because, when I was young, there were times when there wasn't very much food at home.

In the morning—this was August 29—I had to do some shopping at a very chic shop on the Via Veneto. I bought some very big sunglasses, a leather shoulder bag and a large-brimmed hat which alone cost fifteen thousand lire. Wickedly expensive, I know, but this was all part of the uniform—I had to look like someone who usually traveled first class.

Back at the hotel I got dressed. I'm not very interested in clothes but it seemed a waste of money to have things burnt when we blew up the plane after landing so I put as little as possible into my suitcase. I put two dresses in my handbag and wore two trouser suits, one on top of the other. The lower one, with psychedelic flowers, was borrowed and I wanted to return it; the top one was in very smart white cotton, sleeveless, and I wore sandals.

Because flight 840 was late we had to wait an extra half hour in the lounge. I spotted the young man who was the other member of the "Che Guevara" commando unit. I didn't know him and had only seen his picture. Apart from a secret sign of recognition we took no notice of each other.

This extra wait was an anxious time and two other things upset me before we got on the plane. I noticed an American lady with four young children who seemed very happy and excited about their trip. I then realized, with a shock, that something dreadful could happen to them if anything went wrong. I love children and I wanted to tell the lady not to travel on this flight. But when I thought of some of our Palestinian children, who had nothing in life, I felt a bit stronger and braver.

The second incident was in the bus going out to the plane. A man sat next to me and asked me where I was from, and I let him believe I was from Bolivia. Then he told me that he was a Greek returning to Athens after spending fifteen years in Chicago and that his widowed mother would be waiting at the airport.

This was another shock. I felt it particularly because we Palestinians know what it is to be away from one's country and I too had a widowed mother waiting for me at home. He went on talking but I didn't hear the rest of what he said.

My friend and I were in first class because that section is nearer the cockpit. But there were only five first-class passengers in all, so that the three cabin crew fussed over us a great deal, which was exactly what we did not want. Not long after take-off, the two of us seated ourselves in the front row nearest the cabin door. We both refused drinks before lunch—I don't drink anyway—and then we both refused lunch, because we didn't want to have trays on our laps hemming us in. But when the stewardess exclaimed at this, and so as not to be conspicuous, I ordered coffee and my friend a beer. He also asked for a pill, to suggest that he was feeling ill.

We didn't get rid of the cabin crew that easily. Instead of lunch they brought us a huge trolley laden with fruits and cakes and, to our dismay, parked it in front of us to help ourselves, completely blocking the way to the cabin door. We had been ordered to take over the plane thirty minutes to an hour after take-off since the Rome-Athens flight takes only ninety minutes, and we were approaching the deadline. We didn't want to ask the hostess to remove the trolley because that could have appeared suspicious. Finally, after what seemed an age, she took it away and another passenger, who had been using the lounge seat right next to the cabin door, also moved away.

The way was clear and we could get into the cabin without having to frighten anyone—that's the one thing we wanted to avoid: frightened people can do foolish things.

I asked for a blanket and the hostess tucked it in around me. My friend gave me a strange look, wondering whether I was becoming afraid. To reassure him I took out my toilet case and combed my hair. Then I looked at my watch and showed him five fingers, signaling that in five minutes we would go into action—I was in charge of the operation. Underneath the blanket—this was why I wanted it—I took a pistol out of my shoulder bag and tucked it into the top of my pants. And then a grenade. I took out the safety pin.

Just as everything was ready, one of the hostesses carrying a tray came out of the cabin door; it opened outwards and she held it open with her elbow. We took this chance. My friend, holding his pistol and grenade, brushed across the front of the hostess and through the door. When the hostess saw the weapons she screamed, "Oh no," and threw her tray down—that was the only violence we had in the plane during the whole journey.

As we went towards the cockpit my friend called out, "Don't move. Now you have to listen to the orders of the new captain." While he was speaking he heard the captain saying into his radio: "Two armed men have come into the cabin. This is a hijacking."

My part in the actual takeover was to stand facing down the plane to control the passengers with my pistol and grenade. But when I stood up with the grenade in my hand and reached for my pistol, I felt the pistol slipping down my leg inside my trousers. I hadn't eaten for a day and the waistband was loose.

It was such an anti-climax that I laughed. Instead of brandishing a pistol, there I was, bending over with my back to the passengers and fumbling for my weapon up the leg of my trousers, of two trousers actually. The captain swiveled round in his seat to see the new captain but all he could see of "him" was the top of a large, white, lady's hat.

Having retrieved the wretched pistol I put it into my pocket, never to take it out again—too scaring and too much like Hollywood.

You can't imagine the look of total astonishment on the face of the captain when I went into the cockpit and announced, "I'm the new captain." Poor man, what did he see?—me, in my sleeveless suit, floppy hat and sandals. "I'm the new captain," I said; "take this as a souvenir—it is the safety pin from this grenade," and held it under his nose.

"It's a free hand grenade now. If you don't listen to my orders, I'll use it, and the plane and everyone in it will be blown up."

"What do you want?" the pilot asked.

"Proceed directly to Lydda airport."

"Lydda?" the co-pilot asked. "Aren't we going to Athens?"

"You understand English," I replied.

We sat down in the two seats just behind the pilot. The grenade was in my left hand and it stayed there until we landed. My friend put his away but he kept his pistol out.

I asked the captain to give me his wireless headset and he was so flustered that he tried to put it on over my hat. "Excuse my hat," I said, and pushed it back. I had had a ribbon specially sewn on so that I could hang it round my neck: I very much wanted to save that hat.

I tried to raise Rome airport but there was no answer. I then turned to the flight engineer and asked, "How many fuel hours of flight do you have?" I knew the answer because I had read this off the fuel gauge. I was sure he would tell me a lie and he did: "Two hours," he said.

"Liar. I know you have three and a half hours. It's there on the fuel gauge. Why did you lie to me? The next time I ask you anything and you lie to me, I'll break your neck."

"Why are you so angry?" the captain asked.

"Because I don't like liars," I replied. I wasn't really angry. I wanted to scare them a little so they would take orders. The engineer didn't say a word for the rest of the flight.

The time was now about 15:20 hours.

The dials and switches and lights in a plane's cockpit may seem bewildering but we had been thoroughly trained and I knew what the dials meant. I had a thorough knowledge of the Boeing 707.

Having put the crew in its place the next thing was to speak to the passengers on the intercom. Our message was:

Ladies and Gentlemen:
Your attention, please. Kindly fasten your seat belts.

This is your new captain speaking.

The Che Guevara Commando Unit of the Popular Front for the Liberation of Palestine, which has taken over command of this TWA flight, demands that all passengers on board adhere to the following instructions:

1. Remain seated and keep calm.

2. For your own safety, place your hands behind your head.

3. Make no move which would endanger the lives of other passengers on the plane.

4. We will consider all your demands, within the safe limits of our plan.

Ladies and Gentlemen, among you is a passenger responsible for the death and misery of a number of Palestinian men, women and children, on behalf of whom we are carrying out this operation to bring this assassin before a revolutionary Palestinian court.

The rest of you will be honorable guests of the heroic Palestinian Arab people in a hospitable, friendly country. Every one of you regardless of religion or nationality is guaranteed the freedom to go wherever he pleases as soon as the plane is safely landed.

Ladies and Gentlemen, our destination is a friendly country, and friendly people will receive you.

Thank you for your cooperation. We wish you a happy journey.

The person we were after was General Rabin (the former Israeli chief of staff), who we knew had been booked on that flight. But he seemed to have changed plans at the last minute. I suppose prominent Israelis find it safer to travel on airlines other than El Al nowadays. Then I broadcast our message to the world:

The Popular Front for the Liberation of Palestine informs you that its Che Guevara Commando Unit is now in complete control of the Boeing plane belonging to Trans World Airlines, flight 840, on its way from Rome to Lydda airport in the Occupied Palestinian Arab territory.

Captain Shadia Abu-Ghazali, who has taken over command of this plane, and her colleagues request all those concerned to use the following call sign in their communication with the aircraft: POPULAR FRONT—FREE ARAB PALESTINE. And let it be clear that unless the above-mentioned call sign is used in communicating with the plane, we will not care to respond.

Thank you.

Shadia Abu-Ghazali was my code name. The original Shadia was a resistance fighter in PFLP. She was killed in October 1968 at the age of twenty-one.

After this I handed over our new route map to the captain. We did not follow the usual air traffic lane over Athens and Nicosia. Instead we went straight down the Greek coast, then southeast over Heraklion in Crete and eastward to Lydda. Not a very interesting flight because it was almost all over the sea at thirty-three thousand feet.

When the captain went on to the new course I noticed that he kept turning to port so as to go southwestward. He may have been trying to take it up to the American Wheelus airbase near Tripoli in Libya. But I was watching the compass and ordered him back on course. After that I told him exactly when to turn and on to what bearing number on the compass.

After fifteen minutes my friend reminded me that the passengers still had their hands above their heads. I looked into the cabin and so they did. I apologized for inconveniencing them and asked the hostess to serve them with whatever they wanted to eat and drink, champagne if they wanted it. Otherwise, throughout the flight we had no contact with the passengers or cabin crew.

We tried hard to get on to friendly terms with the three crew members but had no luck. We asked them if they wanted anything to eat or drink but they refused. We offered them our cigarettes but they refused those too. They didn't ask a single question about us. From time to time the captain would turn round, look at me and shake his head unbelievingly. The only human contact was when the co-pilot, like a child in school, asked if he could go to the toilet.

The pilot kept glancing at the grenade in my left hand, so finally, to reassure him, I put my arm across his back and tapped him on the left shoulder with the grenade: "Listen— I'm accustomed to this thing. Don't be afraid." A little later I scratched my head with the grenade to show him just how familiar with it I was, but I doubt whether he was reassured.

15:55 hours. Compass bearing 140 degrees.

There were long, uneventful periods during this eventful flight that were punctuated only by the messages I broadcast to the countries we flew past or over—Italy, Greece, the UAR, Lebanon and Syria. These messages explained what we had done and appealed for support "for the just struggle of the Palestinian people," and ended with the words, "Down with U.S. imperialism and Zionism. We will win." The co-pilot looked at me angrily every time I mentioned America.

I also spoke, spontaneously, to the passengers over the intercom to explain our struggle. "We have hijacked this plane because we want to cut the roots that feed Israel. Don't go to Israel because there is resistance on land and en route: tell this to your friends. We want to go back to our country and we can live with the Jews because we lived with them before." We tried to explain things to the crew but they were an unreceptive audience.

16:10 hours. Compass bearing 112 degrees.

The exchange of messages I had with Cairo Airport, in Arabic, was amusing. They were flabbergasted when a woman's voice told them what had happened and where we were going. I first had to tell them that I wouldn't respond till they used our own call sign. Then, the breathless response came from Cairo something like this: "You Popular you Front you Free you Arab you Palestine! Why-are-you-going-to-Israel?" And I replied, "Yes, we are going to Israel—to liberate it!"

Soon after this, things became serious as we began our descent to Lydda. Of course, we had no intention of landing there—that possibility was the one thing that worried us. But we wanted to fly over our enemy's city just to show him we could do it.

"Descend to one-two-zero," I told the pilot, and the co-pilot chipped in, "You mean twelve thousand feet?" "You know what I mean."

So we began the long descent and out of the haze the coast of Palestine gradually grew clearer.

"What shall we do when we get to twelve thousand?" the pilot asked. "Let's have a round twice," I replied, and made a swinging gesture with my left hand—the pilot's eyes, as always, following the grenade; "we want to have a picnic over our land."

Needless to say, my exchanges with Lydda airport were not friendly. The controller was very excited and shouted at me angrily the whole time. Having switched to the Lydda wavelength, I first read a message in Arabic for our people in Occupied Palestine. I tried to speak to the airport tower in Arabic but they wouldn't reply. "TWA 840?" they kept calling, so I responded, "Shut up! This is Popular Front Free Arab Palestine. We will not respond unless you use this call sign. We are coming down. We are landing. Give us space."

I said this just to frighten them, because I don't think the Israelis wanted us to land any more than we wanted to land there. My words seemed to have had the desired effect because Lydda tower shouted back, "Don't come down, don't come down, or else we'll send Mirages to shoot you down."

And I told them: "Here is Free Arab Palestine. What can you do about it? I don't care for my life. This is our land. We want to die over our land. But you will be responsible for the lives of the crew and passengers." (While all this was going on at about twenty thousand feet, my friend held the intercom microphone near my mouth so that the passengers could hear the exchange, which couldn't have been very comforting for them.)

There were more threats of Mirages from the ground and when I glanced ahead there they were, two of them, just in front of us. We were still descending, but the captain said to me, "We can't descend any more. It's too dangerous with these Mirages in front." This, evidently, was how the Israelis were trying to prevent us from landing. The co-pilot then asked to speak to Lydda. He explained to them:

"We have to follow her orders and descend or else the aircraft will be blown up. Clear the air. And, don't keep calling TWA 840. This is Popular Front." Perhaps because of his words, the Mirages moved out a little, though they still stayed with us and we descended to twelve thousand. We then did three big turns over Lydda and Tel Aviv. We were seven minutes in all over Tel Aviv: enough to make our point. My final message to Lydda, just to keep them worrying, was, "Bye-bye for now, but we are coming back!"

17:12 hours. Compass bearing 350 degrees.

I gave the pilot a compass reading for a course due north and he suggested that we climb because we were using up too much fuel at twelve thousand feet. I told him to go up to twenty five thousand.

In a very few minutes Haifa was before us—the hump of Mount Carmel, the harbor below it and over to the right the oil tanks and the cement factory with its long plume of white smoke. "This is my city," I told the crew. "Take a good look at it. This is where I was born."

From maps I had a rough idea of the area in which our house stood and I think I identified this area but the city slipped away beneath us much too quickly. I felt like asking the pilot to make a turn over my home town so that I could have a better look at it but we were really running low on fuel and every minute counted now.

Just that fleeting glimpse, and a few dim childhood memories are all that link me directly, personally, with my home in Palestine. I was born in April 1944, so I was just under four when my mother, with us eight children, left Haifa some time in March 1948.

That was how my family became "refugees." But no Palestinian is really a "refugee." We are displaced persons or evictees. For if we were refugees and had found refuge, we would not want to go back to what we had left. Because we didn't leave of our own free will, but were pushed out according to a deliberate Zionist plan, we want to go back, but haven't been allowed to. This determination to return makes us Palestinians unique among all the "refugees" of the world.

As the plane crossed the frontier between Israel and Lebanon, the co-pilot, looking rather worried, asked, "Are we going to Beirut?" "That is none of your business," I told him. "We don't have much fuel left, you know," he replied. "I know that, and I also know how to swim, should anything happen."

I, too, was worried about our fuel situation but I also was tremendously excited as we flew over the beautiful blue bay that lies beyond Ras Nakura. On the point opposite the Ras is Tyre, which is where we have lived since leaving Palestine. Our apartment is almost on the beach and I thought I could just about pick it out. Little did my mother know that one of her daughters was flying high above her head. I visited her on my last evening in Lebanon and even told her I would be home for dinner. I knew she would be anxious but I had to keep things secret. I had also left the usual farewell letter in case something happened.

I could see the waves breaking on the beach where I had learned to swim. That is how we passed our time. Tyre had no cinemas then and we had no money to go to them even if there had been any. Away to the right, at the head of this splendid bay is what looks like a town but is really a camp for Palestinian refugees, nine thousand in all. For twenty years such camps have been the new homeland of our people.

Crowded wasn't the word for it. But still, we were luckier than the others living in tents. During the winter storms my friends wouldn't come to school because their tents had been blown down. The small brother of one of my friends was washed away by a flood which tore through the camp.

The only regular cash coming in was a monthly payment of £100 Lebanese [$31.20] by my mother's uncle—which doesn't go far with fourteen people.

Also we had to register as refugees with the UN. We received rations from the UN Relief and Works Agency (UNRWA). But UNRWA itself says that it can't afford anything more than a bare subsistence diet of fifteen hundred calories a day.

But hunger one can learn to bear; what was unbearable was the humiliation of having to stand in line with our cans and sacks to collect our rations as "bakhshish." We had become beggars, just beggars, with our begging bowls in our hands, except that the alms came from the UN and not from individuals. In the photos UNRWA has of ration distribution you will see few adults in the queues. They can't bear to go, so they send the children, as was the case with us. When my sisters began working as school teachers in 1957, UNRWA cut our rations, which was a blow, but we felt happier for being less dependent.

The best thing UNRWA has done for the Palestinians is to provide them with education. I liked school very much, I think we all did, because it was the only place where we could show that we were still human beings and not just a number on a ration roll. I first went to an Anglican school in Tyre and then to an American missionary school in the neighboring town of Sidon on an UNRWA scholarship.

I won another scholarship to the American University of Beirut where I planned to become a pharmacist, which is a good progression for a girl in this part of the world. The scholarship was not sufficient to cover all the costs of living in Beirut and my family couldn't help. So I could only stay a year at the University, and having to leave was the biggest disappointment I've faced so far.

I took a job as a teacher of English in Kuwait and did this for six years. I don't particularly like teaching but I had to start earning in order to help the family. One of my brothers got his degree in engineering and is working in Abu Dhabi in the Arabian Gulf, and another brother, who graduated in business administration, is working in a bank, also in Abu Dhabi.

With all our contributions the family is comfortable once again. We can now afford to send one of my younger sisters to the university but—how ironical this is!—she's more interested in becoming a *fedayee* (a Palestinian resistance fighter). One of my brothers and I are full-time *fedayeen*.

Many of our Lebanese friends ask my mother, "Do you really want to go back to Haifa after all these years?" And my mother answers, "Yes, I'd go tomorrow. It's true we have had a hard time and now things have become easy: we have a pleasant apartment, enough to eat, funds for the children's education and extras like TV. What is more, I'm a Lebanese from Tyre. So I'm not a stranger, but I'm at home. Lebanon is my country but it is not my place; my place is Haifa."

And my friends ask me whether I want to return to a

country I barely know, since I left Palestine as a small child. And my answer is, "Yes," because I too have learned that while I am never a stranger in any Arab country, I can never feel at home.

I learned that I was something called a "refugee" when I was six or seven years old; I was quarreling with a neighbor's child and she said to me, "You are a refugee so you shouldn't shout at me." How could I escape being aware of the Palestine problem? My parents talked of their former life in Haifa, my friends lived in the unnatural conditions of the camp and we learned about Palestine in school.

By the time I was sixteen I was secretly a member of the Arab Nationalist Movement, believing in a liberated Palestine within a unified, socialist Arab world. My elder brothers and sisters had joined this party before me. We planned, we dreamed, we argued. I visited the West Bank, what was left of Palestine, and traveled all over it to get to know my country.

(17:25 hours. Compass bearing 070 degrees.)

It took June 1967, and the loss of all Palestine and the expulsion of another quarter million Palestinians to make me decide that I had to do something positive for the cause of liberation. This is the biggest defeat that the Israelis have brought on themselves by their military victories. They brought a whole new generation of Palestinians into the battle who believe only in the armed struggle against Israel.

And so I joined the Popular Front for the Liberation of Palestine. Last summer I did full commando training with the PFLP, after which I was selected and trained for this mission.

17:28 hours. Compass bearing 118 degrees.

The Israeli Mirages stayed with us until we crossed the Lebanese-Syrian frontier. I spoke to the new Damascus airport tower in Arabic and told them we were going to land there—I didn't ask permission. He replied that we could land on the right runway but I told him we were going to land on the nearer left runway because we were very short of fuel.

On the intercom I told the cabin crew to evacuate the passengers by the emergency exits as soon as the plane landed because it was going to be blown up. I asked the captain to switch off the engines as soon as we touched down, otherwise we would taxi too near the airport building. "I can't do it," he said. "Then I can do it," I replied. I also told him to apply the brakes slowly, otherwise I might fall and the hand grenade would go off. In fact, he made a very good landing.

17:35 hours. Touchdown at Damascus.

As soon as we stopped rolling, I looked into the passenger cabin and called out, "Evacuate immediately." At this moment the crew seemed alarmed and dashed past us into the plane. They were in their shirt sleeves and my friend shouted to them, "Take your jackets." But they didn't stop. I also called, "Thank you for your cooperation."

"You're most welcome," came from the co-pilot.

In two minutes the plane was empty. I only saw the last four or five persons diving through the emergency exits and I told them, "Slowly, go slowly." But they didn't know who I was and didn't listen.

I went down the length of the plane to make sure it was empty. My friend then placed his bombs in the cockpit. He dashed out and stood with me near an emergency exit and I threw two grenades into the first-class compartment. As soon as we threw them, we slid down the emergency chute. My friend landed on my head with a terrific bump and I felt as if my legs were broken. We picked ourselves up and ran for twenty meters and waited for the explosion. Nothing. It was agony to think that the job would only be half done.

Then my friend rushed back to the plane to reset the explosions. Because he is very tall he was able to pull himself up through another chute. I ran after him towards the plane. After a long minute in the plane, he slid out again and we ran back once more.

Still no explosion. Only two minutes later was there a big bang and the nose of the plane crumpled. My friend fired many shots into the wing of the plane to set the fuel tanks on fire but there was so little in them that they didn't ignite.

So it was all over. "Thank God," I said to myself. I felt very relaxed and very relieved and glad that no one had been hurt.

We started walking towards the airport building when a bus came along and picked up the passengers and us. We remained in the bus for half an hour while the Syrians cleared the airport building. I noticed my Greek friend and told him, "My friend and I did this." He burst into tears, and to comfort him I told him I would ask the Syrian authorities to cable his mother so that she needn't worry unnecessarily. We offered the passengers cigarettes and my friend gave the children sweets which they took cheerfully.

Since we had to wait, I said a few more things to the passengers to explain why we had hijacked the plane: "You may think we are criminals, but we are not. We are freedom fighters. The United States has supported Israel with Phantom planes and napalm and we have to make our protest felt by the American government. We were driven out twenty years ago and in 1967 Israel took the rest of our country and our homes. Tell others not to come to Israel as tourists. We are not against Jews, but only against Zionists."

After I had finished speaking, a lady, who said she was from California, asked me whether I had learned my English "in America or in England." "In my country," I said. "We are not as ignorant as the Zionists say we are."

I would have liked to have seen the pilot again to ask him whether we had done a good job on the flight, to talk to him about Palestine and to invite him to visit us in Jordan. But this wasn't allowed. I only saw one of the pursers, who told me that one lady had been injured getting out. I asked him to give her our apologies.

I got engaged four months ago to another resistance fighter, but who knows when we will be able to get married.

One question remains: will I have to hijack another plane to see my home town again . . . ?

Interviewer: G. H. Jansen

2. Diary of a Resistance Fighter

This unusual document is the battlefield diary of a PFLP resistance fighter, covering roughly the period from King Hussein's declaration of martial law (September 17) to the cease-fire negotiated between the government and the guerrillas on September 25. It describes the battle in the area of Hussein refugee camp, on the northern edge of Amman, where sixty thousand people live in a tangle of alleyways and small tin-roofed shacks. The worst casualties in the fighting were in the camps, where thirst and starvation exacted an equal toll to napalm. The identity and fate of the diarist (known only by his code-name, "Bassem") are unknown. The journal was first published in al-Hadaf, *the Popular Front newspaper, then released on November 12 by Liberation News Service through its Amman correspondents, George Cavalletto and Sheila Ryan, who provided the notes.*

Wednesday, September 16

Everybody is expecting the onslaught of the storm.

I heard most of the Arab radio stations saying that the silence in Amman is the tense quiet before the storm. But I have been telling my friends all day that I am not expecting anything.

The tension in the streets, the tension among the people, is only superficial. In fact I think the tension among the people is increasing because the radio keeps saying that this is the tension before the storm.

Anyway, I don't think that anything is going to happen soon. The king still needs time. Many days still lie ahead of us. The city was very normal this morning after the king established the Daoud military government.* But since noon,

---

* On the morning of September 16, King Hussein appointed a new military government, nominally headed by Brigadier Mahmoud Daoud, the prime minister, but actually run by Hussein himself and Field Marshal Harbes Majali, whom Hussein made commander-in-chief of the army and military governor of Jordan. (Several days later, when Daoud was sent to Cairo to represent the king at the Arab summit conference, he resigned, denounced Hussein's attempt to liquidate the commandos and asked for political asylum in Libya.)

Hussein had been preparing this new attempt to crush the Palestinian resistance since August, when he agreed to the "peace plan" put forward by U.S. Secretary of State Rogers.

In the last weeks of August, Hussein pulled his army away from the border with Israeli-occupied Palestine, concentrating the troops around Amman. In the first two weeks of September the Jordanian army destroyed a number of guerrilla bases in southern Jordan, attacked bases in the north and engaged in almost nightly firefights with commandos and militia in Amman.

In the first two weeks of September the king's strategy emerged: Hussein's forces were clearing the commandos out of certain areas (especially in the south), forcing the commandos to expend valuable ammunition and trying to erode the morale of the fighters and the population in general.

The final phase in Hussein's strategy began to unfold early Wednesday, September 18, when his new military government declared martial law and ordered the *fedayeen* militia, the part-time fighters who make up most of the resistance's armed men, to turn in their weapons to the commando offices.

The commandos responded by placing all their fighters under a unified command, and called for a general strike to begin the next day and to continue until Hussein's "fascist military government" was toppled.

tension has been rising without a real, direct cause.

I noticed this when I was near the Philadelphia Hotel, so I went to ask about it at the office of the Popular Front nearby, at the edge of the Jaufa district. Z. was there. He also thought that nothing would happen, but he believes that everyone should act as if the battle is going to break out in a minute.

Comrade A. told me that a lot of tanks have been seen gathering at many points around the city since morning. According to him, tanks were coming from Madaba in the south toward the capital. Comrade A. thinks that the hours of the night are going to be critical, that then the explosion will happen and the battle will begin. But he didn't convince me, and he couldn't explain to me why he thought as he did. Laughing, he told me that my problem is that I use logic to analyze people's illogical behavior.

When I was leaving the Jaufa office I heard the Haj, who was in his fatigues, saying to the young men, "Oil your Klashnis, men."

And suddenly the city was rudely silent and empty, as if something had happened while I was in the office.

I couldn't find a car, so I walked to Hussein mountain. The whole time I was thinking about what might happen. I am sure that this is muscle-flexing, no more. No one really knows why this military government was established just now, but someone told me that the king had discovered a plot among some of his officers which was scheduled to go into action Saturday. This story makes me even more certain that what we see is only muscle-flexing.

Note: a few minutes ago, Comrade A. came. He says that the Popular Front has put him on alert, and that he is supposed to sleep in my room here in Hussein refugee camp. He said that people are saying that a lot of officers were put in jail.

SIMPLIFIED MAP OF AREA OF AMMAN DISCUSSED IN DIARY

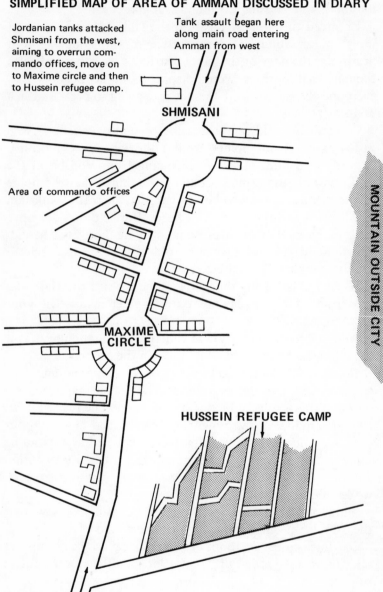

Jordanian tanks attacked Shmisani from the west, aiming to overrun commando offices, move on to Maxime circle and then to Hussein refugee camp.

Tank assault began here along main road entering Amman from west

SHMISANI

Area of commando offices

MOUNTAIN OUTSIDE CITY

MAXIME CIRCLE

HUSSEIN REFUGEE CAMP

Road leading to business and market district

Thursday, September 17*

For the first time, writing in this book has become very difficult: it is different now—like carving a tombstone or composing a will.

Today was terrifying. We were angry. We were tense. We quarreled with each other. I think this was because of the continuous explosions. But our young men fought bravely.

I was in the streets all day. When I came back a few minutes ago, I was looking around and it seemed to me that yesterday was a very distant day in someone else's imagination.

The men of the Popular Front are everywhere. Morale is excellent. Everyone is awaiting two alternatives; they feel it every instant. Either to die or to win.

I met Comrade A. when I was coming home. He was moving a lot of ammunition. "You know," he said, "I believe more than ever that our people are going to win. Do you know Abu Hussein? His house was destroyed and his wife and daughter were killed. He wrapped his wife and daughter in a blanket, and he took up his gun. He is standing over there; you can see him."

---

* At approximately five in the morning on Thursday, September 17, King Hussein's artillery, positioned on the hills surrounding the city, launched a merciless attack on Amman. Soon tank columns tried to enter the city at strategic points, one being the main road from Suwelih, west of the city; this road enters the city in the Shmisani district, where many commando groups had offices. (The army's objectives in this area were to overrun the commando offices, move on in the large traffic circle known as Maxime, and then to the nearby Hussein refugee camp.)

King Hussein later admitted that when he ordered his army's attack he thought he could crush the resistance movement in one day. Captured Jordanian soldiers told commandos that their officers had said they would eliminate full-time commandos in four to six hours, and that it would take them almost no effort to crush the *fedayeen* militia.

Many people died today. The shooting cannot possibly stop tomorrow.

I was on alert all night and I went out with a reconnaissance patrol.

At about five o'clock in the morning, Comrade Abu Ali told us that tanks were coming along the Ainrazel road and from Suwelih, and have concentrated before the hills of Sports City. Shelling started before he finished speaking.

It seems that the cannons of the tanks were aimed directly at the offices of the commando organizations. Immediately our men went down and started machine-gunning the tanks from a distance. I saw heavy firing from our anti-tank guns and RBJ bazookas.

Our friends reported that about fifty trucks full of infantry were driving behind forty Centurion and Patton tanks and around thirty armored half-tracks. Then the men of Fateh started using their mortars. The tanks stopped shelling for fifteen minutes.

At about six o'clock the infantry charged under the cover of fire from the tanks and started moving on our offices in Shmisani.

The offices of the organizations are all near each other: the headquarters of the Popular Liberation Forces, the Palestine Armed Struggle Command, the Arab Liberation Front, the Popular Front for the Liberation of Palestine, the Popular Liberation Army, and the Democratic Front. The attack was against all of them, completely simultaneously.

Suddenly we all got together. All the barriers between organizations disappeared. We met together in a trench, behind a wall, on the sites of the ruins of the offices. All of us from different groups were working together without hesitation.

We waited until the infantry approached us. I don't remember that any of us shot. Then all at once we opened up with our machine guns. After two minutes the army men started running away. We watched them run under the light of shells and artillery until they reached their tanks and hid.

At seven o'clock in the morning the guards in the Popular Forces headquarters at Shmisani were fighting bravely. I had never seen people fighting that way. Their office had been nearly completely demolished, and the tanks had gotten very near. We saw no one leave the battle until they all left, the officers last.

By about eight o'clock all the ammunition had been used up for the B-10 anti-tank rocket launcher in the Arab Liberation Front office. It was very clear that a gap had opened in our lines. Then the Popular Liberation Forces started using their mortars, and for the first time we used our Grinoff and the Fateh men used their Deutschka [anti-armor machine guns].

The tanks stopped suddenly. We didn't understand why until the artillery on the hills started firing at us again.

It seems that the Arab Liberation Front lost many heavy machine guns in this shelling, and that they ran out of Haun ammunition.

It is very clear that the Jordanian artillery tried to concentrate on the Palestine Armed Struggle Command office, but shells landed on the Arab Liberation Front office, which is close to the PASC headquarters.

I was with two men from Fateh and one comrade from the Popular Front and one from the Democratic Front when the tanks moved, like iron hills. We had never seen such intense fire. The heavy machine gun of the Democratic Front was silent because there was no ammunition for it. If we had more ammunition we would have used it effectively to hunt down the soldiers hiding among the low hills.

At 8:40 the army's rockets and tanks totally destroyed our office. We continued to hide in the ruins until the tanks reached the square in front of the Ministry of the Interior. They stopped firing and began to shell.

At 9:15 the tanks stopped firing. They began to use heavy machine guns until new tanks came to complete the circle around the offices. Only then did we retreat.

I think among all the commandos we lost twenty killed and thirty wounded during the fighting up to ten o'clock in the morning. We said to each other, now the battle has started. The tanks had taken one line of no real value. But now if the tanks want to advance, they must fight with us for every square inch.

We were everywhere. We went up very near to the blind tanks and when they drove forward we fought them at close range.

Then something unexpected happened. The cannons of the tanks shelled the houses in a totally unnecessary way, savagely, without even differentiating between homes and commando offices.

It was really frightening. We were paralyzed, seeing the houses collapsing and suddenly seeing in the unexpected rubble many of the small private things of people, the warm small things of people, torn, sometimes bloody. In the midst of that hell we heard people crying out: "Comrades, please rescue me." "Comrades, I am wounded." "Comrades, I am dying. The army killed me."

It was a horrible shock. Like blind steel beasts, tanks rolled toward Maxime circle. All the commando organizations evacuated their offices and retreated. Men were running from the tanks as if the surprise had really worked, as if everybody really didn't know what to do.

Something really strange happened. Abu Ammar [Yasser Arafat] came down to Hussein Street. He asked the fighters who were retreating to stop running away and to plant mines and build barricades of cars, gas cans, any kind of metal.

He brought his own car himself, and with some other men, pushed it into the middle of the street. Immediately high morale filled the area and men started to come back.

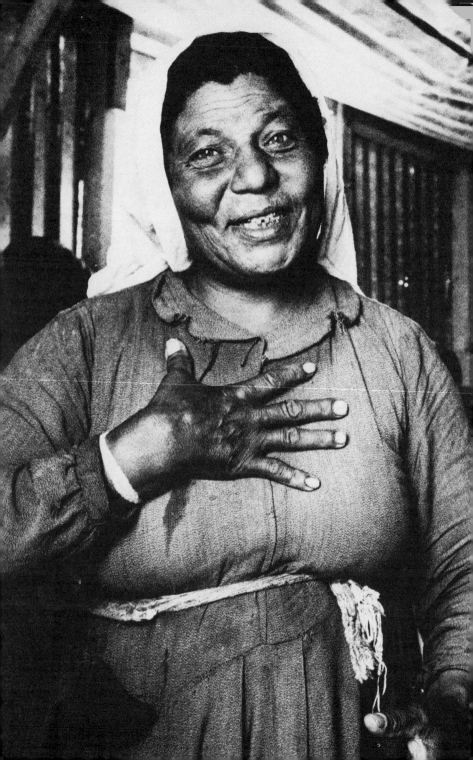

Abu Ammar shouted, with his Egyptian accent, "Two hours, my comrades, and by God, we are going to give them a lesson they'll never forget."

From between the houses, men came back with the RBJ bazookas to Maxime circle. Suddenly Maxime circle turned into an unimaginable hell. The tanks began to pull back very rapidly. The tanks were so large that when they were retreating they looked, in a way, comical. They went back on the road as far as their morning position, where they had been before the battle, and from there started shelling the houses around Maxime again.

As I went back with my group I saw Abu Ammar, Abu Maher, Abu Eyad, Naef Hawatmeh, Dr. Monef El Razaz and Farouk El Kadoumi leave the office of the Popular Front–General Command.* Everybody went off alone.

Abu Maher and Dr. Razaz were walking together, and when Abu Maher saw me, he laughed and called. "I hope you are feeling good. The bastards ran away."

At one o'clock in the afternoon, the tanks tried again to take Maxime circle. This time they didn't come by the main road, but by the smaller streets between the houses. Four tanks parked beside the office of the Popular Front–General Command for nearly fifteen minutes without moving. Then two RBJs fired from a short distance away and hit them; two tanks erupted into flames and explosions, while the other two retreated and shot wildly.

We knew that the soldiers in the tanks had been shocked but that the shock would pass and they would return to search the area. So we pulled back from the positions where we had ambushed the tanks.

---

* Leaders of different resistance groups, who sit on the Central Committee of the Palestine Liberation Organization. Abu Maher, who speaks to "Bassem" in the next paragraph, is a leader of the Popular Front. Members of the Central Committee met at least once a day in Amman throughout the war to coordinate the fighting.

The tanks returned then, the two of them, and rocketed the houses. They destroyed one completely and hit the others. The owner of one house lay dead under the rubble; his three children were still miraculously alive. They were sitting alone in the ruins. It was very sad to see them.

We could see them but we were unable to approach them. The tanks kept coming and demolished the Arab Palestine Organization office. Like an animal with a nervous breakdown, a tank clambered all over the cars parked nearby.

The two tanks turned around and went back to the place where the other two tanks were still burning. The three children were still sitting in the ruins, as if they were immobilized by sadness.

Suddenly Abu Hussein appeared behind the ruins of the house, exactly behind the children. He called to them, but they didn't look at him. He crawled up until he reached them and pulled one of them toward him. He took the small hands of the other children, and they all disappeared.

We waited a few minutes and again we shot our RBJ bazookas. Another tank caught fire with a tremendous roar. Everybody started shooting from everywhere, while the other tank moved about and shot madly at the houses around it. Then, when it was far enough away, it fired ten rockets and hit many houses.

A new column of tanks approached Maxime circle, but again we forced them back. The tanks gathered in a special formation and rocketed and shelled Hussein Street methodically, inch by inch, as if they wanted to destroy the barricades and detonate the mines we had planted.

Fire was everywhere. Shells were exploding all over the street, but we held our position. We heard people crying from many places.

At that moment I received a message to return to the refugee camp. We were expecting the war to come to every house in the camp.

They shelled the outskirts of the camp as I reached it, then artillery began hitting the camp like a rain of fire. All at once, death lost its meaning. One could think that the people lying there were sleeping, resting on the side of the road. Death, ruins, gunpowder, dried blood looking like red mud, the pale faces, fear—in a few hours all this can become a sort of habit which a person can really coexist with.

We formed special teams and moved most of the dead and injured to houses, schools and UNWRA centers.

I really needed the order which came to me at five o'clock from the headquarters of the Popular Front: "Go home and sleep well. We'll need you all day tomorrow."

Tomorrow, who knows?

Friday, September 18

Again we forced them to retreat. The day ended with us still keeping them from Maxime circle, which by then was like a garage full of burned steel.

The shelling was frightening today. Artillery shells rained on the streets and the refugee camp, which cannot defend itself from that death falling from the sky.

The most important thing that happened today is that the army called on loudspeakers for the commandos to surrender. We shot at those loudspeakers and silenced them.

When the tanks moved on us at noon, with the soldiers hiding behind them, we forced them to pull back again.

I had a feeling that this would be a very long, long battle. Comrade Z. told me today that we have enough ammunition to fight three months. There is enough food for now, but he asked me to think about a way to get more if we need it.

Comrade Q. was afraid today. I felt rather sad when I saw him feeling shy after we discovered him spending the day hiding. I began to think about the meaning of courage and the meaning of cowardice. One day I think I'll write about these magnificent words which actually mean nothing. They are words we use to describe our feelings in a certain situation, but we use them only when we are no longer in that situation.

I am very tired today. I don't know what is happening in Amman and the rest of the cities. I don't know what is happening to our comrades.

And now I am looking at my fingers as they write, and at the gasoline lamp, and I ask myself how many things the human being can learn. These fingers which are writing now were pulling the trigger all day and counting bullets, moving the dead bodies, digging graves and patting the shoulders of frightened children.

A while ago we dug a grave for many martyrs, and we buried them. Now they are embracing one another beneath the earth, in limitless love, completely united. And this, I think, is the fate of poor oppressed people, fighting for their share in this world.

Saturday, September 19

If things are relative in this world, even concerning human death, I could say that today was better than yesterday. Today we got more people from the Popular Liberation Forces and Fateh, and the Popular Front sent us more ammunition and people.

A volunteer from Aleppo—I don't know how we found him among us—said that he wanted to fight. We spent the entire day planting mines in the streets of Hussein refugee camp. I can truly say that we built our own hell under the hell of their tanks.

When their tanks reached our area this morning, they had to retreat. They started shelling and again death started.

At noon, the man from Aleppo, as we call him, remarked to me, "These Arab regimes are still silent. I am afraid all of them are cooking up something against us." I felt a little scared, as if a hand had caught my neck in the darkness.

Monday, September 21

I couldn't write yesterday. But the tanks are still outside our lines and today for the first time we were asking ourselves about the end of all this.

We are now in the fifth day. A lot of stories are being told about the capture of a few leaders of Fateh. Tanks are now able to enter some areas of the refugee camp, but they cannot remain. They rocketed the area between Hussein camp and the nearby mountain. Long ago the Democratic Front had an *ashbal* camp for young boys there; today it wasn't there any more.

Abu Eyad's letter broadcast on Amman radio today left a kind of sadness in all the comrades.*

They have destroyed all the commando offices outside the refugee camps. We have less and less anti-tank ammunition. They rocketed the Hussein and Nuzha refugee camps and Hadadi Valley more than ever today. In fact now no one cares about burying the dead.

In the evening the loudspeakers again called us to surrender. They are calling to the commandos and to all the young men. All the young men—this is a fantastic equality. But it shows that they are planning a genocide, a genocide

---

* Abu Eyad, a leader of Fateh, was captured by the Jordanian army. Subsequently, Amman radio broadcast what purported to be a letter from Abu Eyad to King Hussein, asking for an end to the bloodbath and requesting a cease-fire under terms unfavorable to the commandos. The Central Committee of the PLO rejected the cease-fire arrangements, saying that Abu Eyad did not know the real situation of the fighting and that no agreements could be made by leaders who were prisoners of the army.

that neither bothers to disguise itself nor is ashamed. They have threatened to level all the refugee camps.

So now they are making no distinctions between commandos and young men, between resistance and refugee camps. Is there some significance in this? Yes, of course. Our friends are still holding fast.

The men of the Popular Front are everywhere. Their faces look alike, exhausted, covered with grime, determined.

Today in a moment many things were equated—things I thought would never be equated: a glass of water and bullets and a piece of bread, sleeping and death, comrades and the camp.

Tuesday, September 22

I am afraid that here at least everything is coming to an end. I can see only that people prefer to die resisting.

Today resistance was weak on the nearby mountain, but very heroic and brave in this refugee camp. I wanted to think our gunfire is faltering because we haven't enough ammunition, not because our men are being killed. But the facts are frightening. Many friends have been killed. Many bullets are gone.

We don't have enough food and we haven't slept sufficiently. Now all day long the loudspeakers are asking the refugee camp to surrender. No one really understands the meaning of these words. How can a refugee camp surrender, and to whom? Is there a surrender greater than that of the life of the camp?

My comrade told me that a young man went to a woman's home and asked her to give him refuge. She refused, and said to him, "You are no better than my son, and my son fought until he was killed. So why shouldn't you fight to the last drop of blood?" Sometimes heroism takes on a harsh voice, but it seems necessary.

Death is in every square inch of the Hussein refugee camp. Also thirst and hunger. The cruelest thing is for death to look into the eyes of a scared child.

Wednesday, September 23

The king's infantry entered the refugee camp. They concentrated their power behind the ruins, while the tanks shelled incessantly. We didn't have a real supply of ammunition left in the camp. We fought from house to house. They paid a very steep price for every yard they advanced.

They killed many young men, a number I can't count. A certain weeping spreads throughout the camp, like the weeping of one woman, like the weeping of the mother of the camp—weeping for the hungry, thirsty, fearful, those waiting for the unknown, weeping for a person dying alone under a hammering he cannot resist.

These people gave a real lesson to those who are watching.

My comrades and I gave what was left of the food to women and children. Now our men fight starvation in the first line as they face the tanks.

The headquarters of the Popular Front asked me to give my position over to our woman comrade, S., and to try to reach the Wahdat refugee camp.*

Wahdat is said to be in a stronger position, but the road to Wahdat is death. Wahdat camp is death, exactly as Hussein camp is death. And I don't know if I will be able to reach there.

---

* Wahdat refugee camp is on the southern edge of Amman. Slightly larger than Hussein camp, Wahdat houses seventy-five thousand people who were forced out of Palestine in 1948. For eight days Wahdat was severely shelled, and phosphorus bombs were freely used against it by the army. A quarter of the houses at Wahdat camp were completely destroyed, according to a survey by the Red Cross.

3. Black September: An Organized Retreat
Interview with Yasser Arafat

The implications of the September events in Jordan are a subject of heated debate. Fateh's optimistic view is presented here through an interview with Yasser Arafat published in its official English language organ, Fateh, *on March 23, 1971.*

Fateh: What is your evaluation of the Eighth National Assembly held in Cairo in early March?

Arafat: The Eighth National Assembly was not expected to be historic—particularly since a number of "time bombs" and "mines" had been planted for us there. It was part of the plot being waged against the Palestinian revolution for these time bombs and mines to explode during the Assembly meeting.

What we succeeded in doing was to prevent this from happening.

We prevented the explosion of any crisis.

What actually took place in the Assembly was totally different from what was carried by the news agencies.

The Eighth National Assembly was more positive than any of the previous assemblies for the following reasons:

1. It was the first assembly to ratify a formula for Palestinian (national) unity through ratification of a comprehensive political plank. The political plank was discussed for four hours in the Unity Commission and was subsequently approved by the National Assembly. The Assembly also approved the Organizational Skeleton—with the exception of two points dealing with the manner in which the Executive Committee would be elected—by the Political Bureau or the National Assembly at large.

2. A genuine, democratic atmosphere prevailed throughout the deliberations and allowed all points of view on the Palestinian scene to be expressed. This, in itself, is one of the most genuinely democratic expressions in the Arab homeland.

3. For the first time, the Palestinian National Assembly endorsed Fateh's slogan calling for the establishment of a democratic state in Palestine. Although previous assemblies had discussed this objective, they had not endorsed it. This is an unprecedented, great achievement. It is a cultural event.

4. Another positive aspect of the National Assembly is that it convened the enlarged Popular Congress which was attended, among others, by some one hundred ten Jordanian nationalist leaders. The significance of this is important. It reflects the ability of the Palestinian revolution to attract such leadership while being subjected to an extermination war by the Jordanian regime. The Popular Congress, in other words, was a slap in the face to those who claim that the revolution is losing ground in Jordan.

Fateh: What is the Palestinian revolution's answer to the political solution or so-called Rogers peace plan?

Arafat: The answer lies in the survival of the revolution as a basic and determining element on the scene. Israel will never accept any peace formula as long as the Palestinian revolution remains an effective factor because in such a case Israel would not have achieved its basic objective: security.

The Palestinian people have the only and final say in their historic, cultural, settler and property rights. World Zionism and imperialism realize fully what this implies.

Fateh: The Palestinian revolution celebrates this week the third anniversary of the battle of al-Karameh which took place on March 21, 1968. Would you comment on that?

Arafat: The revolution which was able to restore *al-Karameh* (i.e., dignity) at the Battle of al-Karameh despite all the adverse conditions which confronted it at the time is capable of plowing its way despite all plots and "mines" and of achieving victory.

Fateh: Addressing Palestinian Youth in Amman on January 30, 1970, you said: "Nineteen hundred sixty-nine was the year of Arab plots and 1970 will be that of international conspiracies." This was reported in the English edition of *Fateh* dated February 6, 1970 (vol. II, no. 3). Time proved that your revolutionary flair was correct. What does the year 1971 have in store for the Palestinian revolution?

Arafat: The year 1971 will be that of epics. In its course, the fate of the whole Arab nation, and not only that of our Palestinian people, will be decided—and for generations to come.

Fateh: What exactly took place last September in Jordan and how did this affect the revolution?

Arafat: What took place in Black September was not simply an attack by the Jordanian military regime against the revolution but an attempt at genocide against the Palestinian population as a whole. The attempt was written, produced and directed by the Central Intelligence Agency. Delivering his "state of the world" message to the U.S. Congress in late February, Nixon confessed that the gravest threat to peace in the world since he took office in 1968 were the September events in Jordan. This reveals the forces which the revolution confronted and defeated last September. Nixon's confession is six months late. He was six months late in substantiating our charge of U.S. involvement when we seized in Ashrafieh Hospital in Amman the identification card of a U.S. Marine corporal (Mark Lanners England of the U.S. Marine Corps, service number 2356949).

The Palestinian revolution was not defeated last September—neither militarily nor politically.

The confrontation showed that the Jordanian Army could not destroy the resistance despite its use of the equivalent of 120,000 tons of TNT.

This quantity of ammunition could not have been used by the Jordanian Army against the Palestinian revolution had it not been for unlimited U.S. supplies.

The Palestinian revolution forces inflicted about seven thousand casualties on the Jordanian Army. In other words, 18 percent of the whole Jordanian armed forces were felled by the Palestinian revolution in September. King Hussein himself admitted two thousand serious injuries in the ranks of his army. In Amman alone, the Jordanian Army lost ninety-one tanks, mostly of the Patton type: thirty-eight were destroyed completely and fifty-three were damaged.

These figures were confirmed by U.S. replenishments. The U.S. has replenished the Jordanian Army with forty-five Patton tanks and fifty tank engines. The army also lost one hundred twenty other vehicles.

Had it not been for emergency shipments of ammunition from the U.S., including unprecedented and uninterrupted airlifts, the Jordanian Army could not have been able to bear the brunt of the fighting.

The burdens borne by the revolution in Black September were also heavy.

The revolution took it upon itself to care for the families of over 3,400 killed and to treat some 10,800 injured.

It undertook to rebuild the (refugee) camps which were shelled with artillery, such as the Wahdat Camp in Amman, where destruction was about 80 percent complete.

It shouldered the responsibility of twenty thousand Palestinians who were detained from one to six months and that of their families.

It took it upon itself to look after the people who fled from Zarqa, Irbid, Amman and Ramtha as a result of the barbaric assault.

The Palestinian revolution's material losses amounted to £ 10.5 million sterling. Only part of this loss was compensated for through Arab contributions—mainly from Algeria and Libya. The Arab Relief Committee, on the other hand, started its work with a four-month delay.

Meanwhile, military and financial aid is being pumped to the Jordanian regime. The Jordanian regime has received— since September—the equivalent of $105 million in military and financial aid. This excludes the value of ammunition stocks delivered in September.

Fateh: Do the figures of 3,400 killed and 10,800 injured refer to casualties in the ranks of the revolution's military cadres?

Arafat: No. Most of the casualties involved civilians. To give you an idea, our fatal military losses included nine hundred and ten fighters. Of these, eight hundred and twenty-six came from Fateh.

Fateh: Why did the Palestinian revolution agree to end the fighting in Jordan and to conclude an agreement with the Jordanian regime in Cairo September 27?

Arafat: As I told you, the September assault was not only directed against us as Palestinian revolutionaries but it was an attempt at genocide against the Palestinian population as a whole.

When they shelled the camps with artillery fire their intent was to exterminate our people, our women and children.

We had to prevent the genocide and to avoid the creation of "two Yemens." And it is a characteristic ability of a revolution to retreat one step in order to advance two. The important thing is that the retreat should be organized and calculated.

Moreover, it goes without saying that the regime cannot coexist with us as the events have proved and that a revolution of the people can never be defeated.

Fateh: How would you comment on claims that the Palestinian revolution has ended, or at least been brought to its knees?

Arafat: The assault on the Palestinian revolution has many facets. Besides the military assault, there is a financial, informational and psychological assault aimed at leading the people to believe that the revolution has ended, or that it has completed its role, or is unable to fulfill the hopes pinned on it.

But six months have elapsed since September and the revolution is here to stay with all its leadership and struggling cadres.

Of course, there are those who mourn the revolution.

The so-called peace plan cannot be implemented as long as the people adhere to the revolution. So it is part of the plot to lead the people to believe that the revolution has ended.

The forces of the revolution have increased in number since September. To cite just one example: we lost nine hundred and ten fighters in September but four thousand five hundred fighters have since deserted the Jordanian Army and joined the ranks of the Palestinian revolution. This is over and above the graduates of our military training camps.

On February 11-12, five months after Black September, the Palestinian revolution proved it was staying put and defying. This is what took place in Mt. Hamalan (in Amman), after it was claimed that the Palestinian revolution had relinquished the arms of the militia. At 5:30 A.M. that day, about two thousand troops sneaked into Hamalan to lay their hands on arms stores of the militia. They discovered that we could not have been deceived into giving up our arms. We counterattacked. We struck with rockets and heavy artillery. We closed down Amman airport for forty-eight hours and hit three planes. Our losses were thirteen killed. Theirs were seventy killed and many injured.

In other words, the revolution which was begun in the late 1950s and launched in 1965 when the people were still sleeping; the revolution which continued in 1967 when people were still stunned; and the revolution which was able last September to withdraw its head from under the guillotine—this revolution will never end or be brought to its knees.

4. PFLP and the September Attack
Interview with Ghassan Kannafani

The Marxist parties view the future evolution of the Palestinian struggle rather differently from Fateh. Ghassan Kannafani, a novelist and founding editor of the PFLP weekly al-Hadaf, *sets out the vision of the Popular Front five months after Black September. In this interview with the* New Left Review, *published in May-June 1971, Kannafani answers criticisms of the hijackings, highlights the dilemmas faced by the resistance in the summer of 1970, and analyzes the present stage of the Palestinian revolution.*

NLR: The Popular Front is best known in the non-Arab world for its hijackings in September 1970. A lot of criticisms of the hijackings have been made. Some of these are bourgeois criticisms. But there are two others which I would like to pose here. The first criticism has been made both by people within the Palestinian resistance, such as the Central Committee spokesman Kamel Radouan, and by people outside: it is that the hijackings gave Hussein an excuse to attack the resistance at a time when he would not otherwise have done so. The second criticsm is made mainly by people outside the resistance movement. This is that the hijackings gave an illusory sense of power and confidence to the Palestinian masses which was far in advance of their real organizational and military strength. The hijackings were thereby a substitute for organizing the masses, and were a theatrical event that encouraged fantasy. This is not to deny that the hijackings had the positive effect of giving you a world audience on television to whom you could explain the purpose of the Palestinian resistance. This point is not in question. But do you now defend the hijackings?

Kannafani: First of all, I appreciate the fact that you reject bourgeois moralism and obedience to international law. These have been the cause of our tragedy. Now, I would like to answer your questions. I want to talk in general about this kind of operation. I have always said that we don't hijack planes because we love Boeing 707s. We do it for specific reasons, at a specific time and against a specific enemy. It would be ridiculous to hijack planes at the present moment and land them in Cairo, for example, or in Jordan. It would have no meaning now. But you have to analyze the political situation in which we carried out these operations, and the aims we wanted to achieve. Let us recall the situation. On July 23 Nasser accepted the Rogers plan, and a week later the Jordanian government did so too. Once again the Palestinians were put on the shelf. If you read the Arab and international press between July 23 and September 6, 1970, you will see that the Palestinian people were again being treated exactly as they were between 1948 and 1967. The Arab papers started writing about how "heroic" the Palestinians are, but also how "paralyzed" they were, and how there was no hope for these "brave heroes." The morale of our people in Jordan, the West Bank and Gaza was extremely low. On top of that a delegation from the leadership of the Palestinian resistance movement, the PLO Central Committee, went to Cairo to negotiate with Nasser and his government; they spent days and days discussing whether they would allow us to restart broadcasts from Egypt again, after the closing down of our radio in mid-August. The delegation then complained to the Arab League and tried to get them to discuss the question. Before July 23 the Palestinian resistance was pictured in the Arab press as the great hope of the Palestinian people; at the same time all Arabs consider the Arab League to represent the *lowest* form of politics, the most paralyzed political body, in the Arab world. Now we had the highest form of politics approaching the "dirty shelter" of the Arab League. This showed that the revolution was threatened with liquidation, whether Hussein smashed it physically or not. Everyone—including those who criticized the PFLP operation—was convinced that the destruction of the resistance was an essential part of the Rogers plan.

NLR: You agree that Nasser and the Egyptian regime supported this?

Kannafani: The Egyptian regime was one step removed from direct participation in this liquidation, since it had no direct contact with the Palestinians; it was in a safer position. The only way the Egyptian regime could help Hussein was by keeping silent: and that it did, to the extent that it could resist the pressure of the Arab masses. For the first three days of the fighting in September the Egyptian government, and all the other Arab governments, were silent, because they thought that the resistance movement could not survive for more than three days. Then they were forced to move, because the people in the streets of Egypt, Syria and Lebanon were angry at the massacre; but the first five thousand Palestinian victims fell in Amman in silence, and no one complained.

The Rogers plan presupposed the liquidation of our movement, and this was now approaching in an atmosphere of Palestinian submissiveness. Therefore, something had to be done: first of all, to tell the world that we were not going to be put on the shelf for the second time, and secondly to tell the world that the days when the USA and reactionary

Arabs could dictate to our people were over. Moreover, there was the question of the morale, the fighting ability, of our own people. We could not let things remain like that when a massacre was on the way, even if we had sat down quietly on the steps of His Majesty's palace, and kissed his hand.

NLR: So you don't accept the notion that Hussein himself was unsure of what to do, but that the army forced him to move.

Kannafani: Absolutely not. This is complete rubbish. It is true that there are still parts of the resistance movement who think it is possible to "neutralize" the Jordanian regime; but this is nonsense. As for the argument that the hijackings provoked and accelerated Hussein's attack, the short answer to this is that the Jordanian regime had already stopped guerrilla actions south of the Dead Sea, blocked forces moving towards Eliat, and prevented our units attacking the Naharin dam in the north of the West Bank. At the same time the Jordanian army put mines at most of the points where guerrillas crossed the Jordan river, and forced the guerrillas to go through certain specific corridors; these corridors were ambushes. They were sending us to be killed anyway. This was all happening *before* the September massacre; it was a massacre in another form.

Thus the real clash was taking place all the time: they were forbidding us to practice our *raison d'être*. They were preventing us making raids against Israel, and suppressing our political activities in the cities. So our own actions, including the planes, were not provocations; they were the movement of a revolution trying to escape from a circle in which it was trapped.

NLR: How was your action going to do that?

Kannafani: All our activities were an attempt to get out of our situation. For example, we held demonstrations in Amman shouting "Down with Nasser" and "Down with

Egypt"; perhaps they were a mistake, but they were one of the many ways in which we tried to break out of the circle.

NLR: It was obvious that Hussein was going to attack the resistance once he had accepted the Rogers plan. You then had a choice: either you waited for him to attack you, or you could attack him first. Yet in either case, it seems that you never intended to overthrow Hussein, and never imagined that you could. Wasn't your aim essentially to preserve the organizational position of the resistance, and wasn't this the idea behind the hijackings?

Kannafani: You musn't isolate the hijackings from the total political context. For example, Fateh sent rocket-launchers to Ghor-Safi below the Dead Sea, and blew up the potassium factories. We were all trying to break out, to give the Palestinian masses more hope, and to say that the battle was going on. We wanted to put pressure on the Jordanian government to postpone its attack on us. Our relationship with the Jordanian government is not based on common convictions, only on pressure; we have no common ground with them. It was a question of balance of power. All our actions, from the great error of going to the Arab League, to the hijackings themselves (which were the highest form of pressure), were forms of pressure. Some of them were miscalculated negatively, and some positively. On the other hand, there certainly were individuals and organizations within the resistance who did believe there was a possibility of overthrowing the king. They were in error.

NLR: You didn't even then believe that you could overthrow the king, by waiting for him to attack you? It was thought that the people would be united by the initial adoption of a defensive position.

Kannafani: That was our dilemma, and we were in crisis. The resistance, and all the Arab military governments, were in a crisis, which was the price of the Rogers plan. If we had decided to fight Hussein, we should have chosen the time and the place. But as Hussein attacked us, we had no choice; we had to fight at a time and place of his choosing.

Thus the hijackings were part of an extremely dangerous mosaic that made up the Arab and Palestinian map from July 1970 until now. There were a lot of other factors too. We *were* in a corner, and we had two possible ways of getting out. Either we could defend ourselves till victory, against Hussein, or we could "lose the battle by winning it" if we attacked Hussein. But the outcome was not decided only by us, it was also decided by the other side; they had more plans than we did. You should remember that Hussein had to prove to the Americans that they did not need to create a Palestinian state. The Americans were wondering whether to bring in a Suharto-type officer to replace King Hussein with a coup in Amman, which would usher in a Palestinian state there. The Israelis were also discussing this. Hussein wanted to win back his prestige, and this he did; Nixon has now changed his mind, and the Americans once again believe that Hussein is capable of handling the situation.

As for the hijackings, their psychological importance was much greater than their military importance, at this stage of the revolution. Now, if we had been at the final stage of the revolution, or even at the advanced first stages of the revolution and we had hijacked planes, I would have been the first to denounce it. But in the preparatory phase of the revolution, military operations have their psychological importance.

NLR: You still think you were correct to carry out the hijackings therefore?

Kannafani: I think that, generally speaking, these operations were correct. Maybe we made some tactical mistakes. Perhaps we should have made the whole Palestinian resistance share much more in responsibility for them, and then if they had decided two hours later to release the planes, perhaps we should have released them. Maybe we should not have been so stubborn. But you can't imagine what this all meant to the people at that time. You raised the question of whether the hijackings created an atmosphere among the Palestinian masses which the resistance movement was unable to absorb and organize. This may have been the case. But even if it is true, we fought for twelve days in September, and we obliged the Jordanian army to fight the longest war in its history because of what we had done.

NLR: In September, many commentators believed that the Palestinian resistance could only win, either if the Jordanian army itself split and a section of it went over to the resistance, or if an outside Arab regime—Syria or Iraq— intervened and helped. Did you expect either of these eventualities to occur?

Kannafani: I don't think either of these would have given the resistance a victory. In a guerrilla war conditions are different, and what is important is the *aim* of a particular action. The aim of the Jordanian regime was to finish the resistance completely. But the aim of the Palestinian resistance was not to overthrow the Jordanian regime, but merely to put pressure on it. Neither of these two aims succeeded, so nobody really won. Of course, to some extent, we had to surrender certain points and go underground. But the battle is still going on; the retreat to underground activity or to the mountains is only a tactical aspect of regulating the balance of power.

NLR: You don't deny that both the possibility of operations against Israel from Jordan and the politico-military room for manuever of the resistance within Jordan have been massively reduced by the September events? Isn't the Hashemite monarchy continuing to try to disarm the militia in Amman and to win direct control of your refugee camps, and other strong positions?

Kannafani: I know. I don't deny that the Jordanian regime has won some ground, and forced us to retreat. But I would like to point out two things, to put the September events in their context. The Jordanian regime had nearly succeeded in preventing us from making any raids against Israel *before* September; this was not a result of September, but one of the factors that led to September. We had to tell our people we were doing something; we couldn't sit in Amman and do nothing. Now we are in the mountains, in a preparatory stage, and the revolution has taken a more realistic form than it did when people thought it was at a very advanced stage. I am against saying that we are defeated, because in the past, our real strength was exaggerated and we now have a size proportionate to our strength. We never had room for maneuvering in front of our own people and world public opinion, and some leaders had no such room even in front of their own militants. It will take a long time to restore the previous balance of power with the Jordanian government and we will continue to retreat until we have a correct understanding of our own strength. There are plenty of examples in history of people with rifles living in the mountains, ambushing a truck and shooting the odd soldier, and achieving nothing else. This is our problem, and there is a debate going on within the resistance about it; indeed the PFLP is being accused of not wanting to surrender the militia's arms. In fact, I don't believe that a Fateh fighter would surrender his arms.

NLR: To what extent has the Popular Front changed its strategy since September? George Habash was reported in January to be saying that the time had come to overthrow the Hashemite monarchy. Is this true?

Kannafani: The Popular Front has always insisted that we have four equal enemies: Israel, world Zionism, world imperialism led by the United States, and Arab reaction. The overthrow of these reactionary Arab regimes is part of our strategy, part of liberating Palestine. The overthrow of the Jordanian regime must be a part of the program for a

Palestinian FLN. We have to do it, but not necessarily tomorrow. We have always insisted on the need to do this, but it must form part of a general strategic line.

NLR: It is now five months since the events of September. What, in your opinion, have been the effects on the Palestinian people?

Kannafani: It is normal for some to leave during periods of hard fighting. Advanced periods of struggle are attractive to people, who join because there is no price for joining the revolution. They stay at home, they continue going to their jobs; if someone is studying at Damascus University, for example, he can take a year off and work with the resistance. On the other hand, shocks like September crystallize the strength of the revolution, because they have forced it into the mountains. There are now commandos living in the Ajloun forests of north Jordan; they are living in caves, with limited water and food, and little ammunition. In this situation, we can't expect that the thousands who went around Amman in khaki carrying their Klashnikovs will live this kind of life. In the cities, organization and recruitment are different. We used to have a known office, and we could recruit and train people openly in the camps. Now we have a different relationship with the masses: we are not wearing khaki and walking down the street, and we are not making speeches in the camps. We have to operate in a different way, and that is exactly where a *party* is necessary. Although it is difficult in the mountains, the situation is even more difficult in the cities. A lot of people had a bourgeois sense of haste, but we are now in a stage of retreat. Militarily and politically, this is not a mistake, and it is not dangerous. But it does pose psychological problems, because of the need to keep the people with us. Some elements on the West Bank are now calling for a Palestinian state. We knew that they were discussing this plan in private among each other for three years after the June war and that they were in contact with

the Israelis, with the Arab reactionaries and with the impe-
rialists. It is only since the resistance movement was forced
backwards that they have dared to raise this project openly.
At the same time, the events in September made the masses
on the West Bank aware of what it would mean to have
Hussein back again, and the resulting reaction of a people
under occupation and without a proper organization is to
say: "Anything, except Hussein again." For the West Bank a
Palestinian state would be better than having King Hussein's
regime again. This is a very temporary reaction, resulting
from a psychological shock.

Gaza is another story altogether. The resistance was on the
defensive on the West Bank and on the East Bank, but it
escalated suddenly in Gaza in a remarkable way. The Popular
Front has the strongest influence in Gaza, so we acted. Let
me mention one specific case, that of Youssef el-Khatib Abu
Dhumman. He was the head of Popular Front military
operation in Gaza, and he was killed at the beginning of
December. For six days there were continuous strikes and
mass demonstrations in Gaza; so everyone knew that men
were still fighting. This raised the level of action in Gaza,
although it made our casualties higher than they had ever
been before.

NLR: What has created the greater militancy in Gaza?

Kannafani: The population of Gaza is 360,000; the majority are Palestinian refugees. In Gaza people are familiar with
arms. They were trained by the PLA under the Egyptian
administration, unlike the West Bank. Another factor is that
the Arab Nationalist Movement was suppressed in Gaza by
the Egyptians, but never to the extent that it was in the West
Bank. When Gaza was occupied the ANM had its cells there;
whereas Hussein handed the West Bank to the Israelis in a
"clean" state, as he has put it himself—there was not a single
ANM cell there. So we had the minimum base to start with in
Gaza. There is also a psychological factor: Gaza is surrounded

on the west by the sea, on the south by Sinai, on the east by the Negev, and on the north by the Israeli state. The Palestinians there are psychologically besieged, and used to difficulty. On the West Bank contacts were much easier in the first months of occupation; it was simpler to send money, men and weapons into the area. The people on the West Bank got used to easier methods, and they weren't able to resist Israeli counter-measures. In Gaza they were tougher and more professional. Another factor was that the Jordanian regime in Amman kept on paying the salaries of teachers, detectives, state employees and the like; this is the only way a reactionary regime can keep the loyalty of these people. The Israelis also paid salaries to these people. It is not true that most of them were *against* the resistance, but they were certainly not in a hurry; in the Gaza strip people were under greater pressure.

I would now like to make some more general comments. In every revolution there is an initial wave of enthusiasm which peters out after a time, because it is not deeply rooted. I think that our first wave reached its peak at Karameh, in March 1968; after that, we started to decline, because we were returning to our real proportions. In such periods of relapse, there are always divisions, exaggerations, romanticizations, tendencies to individualism and to turning the revolution into a myth and so on. These are the illnesses of the underdeveloped world, and they express themselves in a period when one is not engaged in real revolutionary work, but one is nevertheless regarded as making a revolution. If the revolution doesn't develop out of this, if it doesn't do something like Mao's long march, or acquire more force from outside through the liberation of an Arab state, then defeats will have a dangerous effect on the morale of the masses. The period of decline did not begin in September, it began after Karameh.

NLR: Can we now come to the question of Israel itself?

Do you think there is such a thing as an Israeli nation? The Matzpen group and others inside Israel have argued that there may not originally have been a Jewish nation, but the Jewish immigrants who have come to Palestine have established there a new community which can be called the Israeli nation.

Kannafani: That is the Maxime Rodinson solution. It is a fantastic intellectual compromise; it means that any group of colonialists who occupy an area and stay there for a while can justify their existence by saying they are developing into a nation.

NLR: So you don't think the Israelis are a nation?

Kannafani: No, I don't. It is a colonialist situation. What you have is a group of people, brought for several reasons, justified and unjustified, to a particular area of the world. Together, they all participate in a colonialist situation, while between them there are also relations of exploitation. I agree that Israeli workers are exploited. But this is not the first time this has happened. The Arabs in Spain were in the same position. There were classes among the Arabs in Spain, but the main contradiction was between the Arabs in Spain as a whole and the Spanish people.

NLR: So you do see contradictions within the Israeli population which can divide them in the future, and provide the Palestinian resistance with allies within Israeli society?

Kannafani: Of course. But this will not happen easily. First of all, we must escalate the revolution to the stage where it poses an alternative to them, because up to now it has not been so. It is nonsense to start talking about a "Democratic Palestine" at this stage; theoretically speaking it establishes a good basis for future debates, but this debate can only occur when the Palestinian resistance is a realistic alternative.

NLR: You mean it must be able to provide a practical alternative for the Israeli proletariat?

Kannafani: Yes. But at the moment it is very difficult to get the Israeli working class to listen to the voice of the Palestinian resistance, and there are several obstacles to this. These include the Israeli ruling class and the Arab ruling classes. The Arab ruling classes do not present either Israelis or Arabs with a prospect of democracy. One might well ask: where is there a democracy in the Arab world? The Israeli ruling class is obviously an obstacle as well. But there is a third obstacle, which is the real, if small, benefit that the Israeli proletariat derives from its colonialist status within Israel. For not only is the situation of Israeli workers a colonialist one, but they gain from the fact that Israel as a whole has been recruited to play a specific role in alliance with imperialism. Two kinds of movement are required to break down these barriers, in order for there to be future contact between an anti-Zionist Israeli proletariat and the Arab resistance movement. These will be the resistance movement on the one hand and an opposition movement within Israel itself; but there is no real sign of such a convergence yet, since, although Matzpen exists, what would be necessary is a mass proletarian movement.

Interviewer: Fred Halliday

5. The Resistance After September: An Appraisal

Robert Elias Abu Shanab

Professor R. E. A. Shanab, who teaches philosophy at Florida State University, takes a hard and skeptical look at the state of the Palestinian movement since the September events. His balance sheet is more negative than those of the previous two interviews, but it is too concrete to be easily dismissed.

Though the guerrillas demonstrated their willingness and determination to protect their basic right to struggle for national liberation, the outcome of the September civil war was detrimental to the Palestinian resistance movement. Admittedly the resistance movement attained some positive results; the negative results, however, outweighed the positive ones. In what follows I shall confine myself to some of the negative points that stood out following the civil war.

1. Prior to the civil war the Palestinian resistance movement enjoyed full freedom throughout the Arab world, especially in Jordan where the guerrillas created a "state" within a state. Previous attempts to restrict its freedom failed—owing primarily to the overall political-military strategy that was operative, subsequent to the June 1967 war, between the concerned Arab states and Israel. However, following the cease-fire proposal of August 1970, the overall

political perspective shifted from its primary concentration on Israel to the harassment of the guerrillas. Thus at present the guerrillas do not enjoy the freedom of movement they did prior to the cease-fire. As a matter of fact, the Jordanian army, in its recent encounter with the Palestinian guerrillas, was able to expel them from Jordan. Most of the guerrillas are stationed now in Syria and southern Lebanon. It should be pointed out, however, that both Syria and Lebanon, notwithstanding their rhetoric, are fully cognizant of the problems that developed in Jordan as a result of the encounter between the guerrillas and the Jordanian army. Thus both Syria and Lebanon are keeping the guerrillas under close surveillance.

2. There seems to be somewhat of a disarray in the Palestinian organizations. Some Arab papers reported that the Palestinian guerrillas are "in total disarray after having been the center of attraction and hope of the Arab masses and the peg for the overall Arab revolution."* Some sources also reported that a serious leadership crisis was on the verge of occurring. For example, some Fateh leaders were dissatisfied with the behavior of Yasser Arafat, Central Committee Chairman of PLO, concerning his frequent absences from Jordan. Some Fateh leaders maintained that the undertaking of foreign trips by Arafat is not as imperative as the restructuring of the Palestinian organization.† There are also other reports emanating from the Arab countries, to which the guerrillas concede, that the Arab masses, especially the Palestinians on whom the guerrillas relied, are withdrawing their moral and material support. A significant number of Palestinians are disillusioned with the movement, and there

---

* Quoted in "The Palestinian Commando Movement," by Mark Ethridge, Jr. Reprinted in *Tallahassee Democrat*, December 6, 1970.
† *See* "Clashes Mar Arab Guerrilla 'Time-out' " by John K. Cooley, *Christian Science Monitor*, December 5, 1970, p. 2.

appeared, for the first time since the June war of 1967, strong criticisms and skepticism of the effectiveness of the movement. As one Palestinian intellectual put it:

> We've backed the *fedayeen* for three years with all the money and affection we could muster, and what did they accomplish. They picked fights with the Lebanese and Jordanian armies instead of enlisting their help. They brought death and destruction to Arab cities, but they never established a single base on the occupied West Bank. Their military effectiveness against Israel has been negligible and their Arab politics abominable.*

The loss of support of a significant number of the Palestinian masses has indeed been so far the most detrimental outcome of the civil war. Without this mass support, the Palestinian revolution is doomed to failure.

3. The flow of funds to the Palestinian organizations from rich conservative countries such as Saudi Arabia and Kuwait has been curtailed. The Saudi Arabian government, which prior to the civil war was one of the largest sources of financial support to the guerrillas, discontinued its support. Equally significant has been the change in attitude of some other Arab governments such as Egypt, Syria and Libya. The commandos had in the past depended for their successes on these governments in providing them with moral and some financial support. Syria's Premier Assad had withdrawn all help to al-Sa'iqah, a Syrian-based Palestinian guerrilla group with an estimated seven thousand followers. Egypt, Libya and Sudan provided nothing more to the Palestinians than verbal support. This lack of support from the Arab countries has meant that the guerrillas had to operate without a reliable rear base. Clearly this loss of tactical support and the discontinuation of funds have affected the resistance movement.

---

* Quoted in *Newsweek,* December 21, 1970, p. 43.

4. Another salient feature about the outcome of the civil war is the curtailment of action against Israel, as is evidenced by lack of guerrilla activities either inside Israel or the occupied areas, excepting of course the Gaza Strip. Prior to the civil war the Palestinian guerrillas were successful in disrupting the normal lives of the Israelis. Due to constant guerrilla activities both inside and outside Israel's border, the Israelis were faced for the first time since the establishment of the state with an intolerable situation. Domestically the guerrillas' activities had depressed the Israeli morale. As one Israeli analyzed and explained it: "Things have reached such a point that people have to be continually injected with morale boosters in order to preserve their confidence in our military strength and to prevent them from losing it altogether."* Indeed, precautionary measures, prior to the civil war, were to be seen everywhere in Israel. In addition to this, the guerrillas' activities have affected Israel economically. As an Israeli columnist explained it:

> The terror hurts Israel in terms of defense expenditure. Added to the huge burden of maintaining its out-of-proportion Army, Air Force and Navy, Israelis now are forced to spend millions of dollars on the fortifications and fences built all along the cease-fire lines, and on a variety of preventive measures inside the country. Israel's defense budget comes to almost $1 billion, 35 percent of the government budget and 20 percent of its gross national product.†

Whereas prior to the civil war the Palestinian guerrillas' activities were maintained at a maximum, they are now practically nonexistent. For the main concern of the Palestinian movement at present is to secure and establish a firm base in the

* Quoted in H. Sharabi, *Palestine Guerrillas* (Washington, D.C.: Center for Strategic and International Studies, 1970), pp. 8–9.
† *See* " 'Damn Everybody' Sums Up the Angry Mood of Israel" by Amnon Rubenstein, *The New York Times Magazine*, February 9, 1969.

Arab states, especially in Jordan. With the virtual elimination of commando activities inside Israel, and the acceptance of the cease-fire, the daily routine in Israel has returned to normalcy; precautionary measures have been lifted; tourism in the occupied areas is thriving; economic life has also been restored to normal; a general relaxed mood prevails among the Israelis. Alarmed by such signs of relaxation, Golda Meir told her parliament: "What has happend to us in the past year? We are behaving as if there is not danger ahead of us—as if we have achieved the peace we long for."*

The period following the civil war required a critical appraisal of the Palestinian organization; it became evident that a more efficient organization is needed to avert the further crippling of the resistance movement in the Arab world. But no substantial change has occurred within the Palestinian organization. Instead of working sincerely toward a unification of all groups, each organization engaged in holding each other responsible for the massacre of the Palestinian masses. Indeed the Palestinian resistance was more divided after the civil war than prior to it.

In March 1971, the Palestinian National Congress again achieved nothing substantial. In the open forum of the Congress, profound disagreements between Fateh and the more radical groups—such as PFLP and DPFLP—arose over the questions of national unity and the restructuring of the organization. For example, DPFLP and PFLP, unlike Fateh, wanted to dissolve the Central Committee of the PLO; instead they proposed to form a new executive committee in charge of selecting members for the new National Council. With respect to the question of a Palestinian national unity, DPFLP, for example, proposed the establishment of a new relationship among all the organizations that comprise a United Front whose fundamental objectives would be: "(1)

---

* Quoted in *Time,* August 16, 1971, p. 28.

the political and formalized independence of each component force; and (2) the adoption of adequate measures to prevent the Palestinian people from accepting any political solution."* Fateh, on the other hand, proposed that all organizations work within the PLO, and abide by the decisions of the new general command—proposed by Fateh—which will assume the responsibility of directing the affairs of the Palestinian revolution. The inability of the Palestinian revolution to solve the problem of national unity within a workable scheme has increased the counterrevolutionary elements in the Arab world. There is much discussion at present for the creation of a Palestinian state in the recently occupied part of Palestine. Such a move has even found support from the Palestinian masses. Unless a sincere effort is made by the various Palestinian commando movements to organize themselves in order to deal effectively with the counterrevolutionary elements in the Arab world, their chance of survival is slim.

* *See* "Interview with Hawatmeh" in *Resistance in the Middle East*, Spring 1971, no. 2, p. 7.

6. An End

Khalil al Hindi

Khalil Hindi left the Democratic Popular Front for the Liberation of Palestine around September 1970, after serving on its central committee. His critique of the resistance is taken from the original draft of his contribution to the PLO study of the September conflict, which is appearing in Arabic under the title "The Palestine Resistance and the Jordanian Regime." The PLO has authorized its inclusion here.

It is natural that the strategy of the resistance is based in general on the abolition of the Zionist state. But that doesn't solve the problem. The resistance does not enjoy any superiority over the enemy. Even if it could mobilize all the Palestinian forces in the future, the resistance will not be able to achieve numerical superiority over the enemy—which is the condition for a successful popular war. The resistance, moreover, is confronting Israeli society from outside; the prevailing circumstances force it to act from outside the occupied territories—and from outside the area occupied in 1948 even in the best of circumstances. Thus the resistance is confronted with two problems which it must solve: (1) mobilization of enough forces to confront the technical and military

superiority of the enemy with the qualitative and quantita-
tive superiority of the struggling masses; and (2) providing
the necessary conditions for the free movement of the resistance in Arab lands. Thus the basic problem becomes a quite
simple question: Shall all the efforts be concentrated on
changing the Arab regimes, or on the struggle against Israel?

In fact, this problem is not new. It did not originate with
the appearance of the resistance, although it has appeared
more clearly since then. Even before the establishment of the
state of Israel, the Palestinians faced two enemies—Zionism
and British imperialism—and had to choose which to fight
first. Since 1948, the Palestinians have been faced with the
problem of which comes first, unity or liberation? Today, if
we say that efforts should be concentrated on changing the
Arab regimes (i.e., postponing the anti-Zionist struggle for
the sake of the anti-imperialist struggle), that would mean
leaving the Zionist danger diffuse; it would expose the Arab
liberation movement to the constant threat of that danger
and deprive the anti-imperialist struggle of the explosive
element which infuses the social contradictions in the region.
But on the other hand, concentrating on the Zionist enemy
means, effectively, confronting Zionism under the conditions
which most favor it—Arab weakness and backwardness, plus
the ability of the reactionary Arab regimes to conspire
against the mass movement and attack it from behind. These
problems do not involve the Palestinian people alone, but all
the Arab people. To solve them, we need a general Arab
strategy.

The Strategic Gap and the Political Paralysis

In the summer of 1970, when Egypt and Jordan accepted
the Rogers peace plan, it became obvious that the resistance
was suffering from political paralysis. Its reaction was
chaotic: official delegations to Arab states, demonstrations

and publicity campaigns against the Rogers plan and those who accepted it, splits inside the resistance, and escape from confronting the actual problem by hijacking planes under the pretext of attacking imperialist interests in the region and frustrating the peaceful settlement.

The resistance acted as though it could avoid the coming explosion in Jordan. It started to talk about a "mysterious third party" which is stirring up trouble and creating misunderstandings between the resistance and the regime. It denounced "agent elements who have falsely convinced the king that the resistance aims to overthrow the regime." Meanwhile, the resistance intensified its publicity campaign against the regime and accumulated its forces inside the cities in order to restrain the regime and force it to withdraw from the clash for which, it was clear, the regime was planning and preparing its forces.

The Political Dilemma Creates a Military Dilemma

The resistance assumed a purely defensive posture. It waited for the regime to act, in order to react. Even when it was sure that the army was going to attack, the resistance did not resort to military operations. In Zarqa, for example, the resistance leadership acquired information on the night of September 16 indicating that the army would move to occupy the city the next day. The information was so accurate that it even pinpointed the moment of attack. The command at Zarqa thought it advisable to attack the assembled forces of the regime before they moved and spread. Contact was established between the command at Zarqa and the general command of the resistance in Amman, but the reply from headquarters was, "Control yourselves. Don't start the attack. Be alert." But after the clash had begun, it was too late for the resistance to seize the military initiative.

It adopted the tactic of stationary defense, which allowed the attacking forces the maximum freedom of movement. Initiating a few limited assaults and dispatching a few fighting patrols didn't change the overall picture.

The dilemma in which the resistance put itself becomes more and more obvious when we see that it had no defense plans, only a security plan; the difference between the two is great. To make the difference clear, imagine that we want a defense plan for a particular house. This would entail fortifying the outlets, digging trenches and patrolling the area around the house. A security plan, by contrast, would mean no more than blocking the doors and windows. Confining the plans of the resistance to security measures means that while the resistance had concentrated its forces in the cities (especially in Amman), it had not formulated a plan guaranteeing an effective role for these forces, either defensively or offensively. Hence, the concentration of forces in the cities was only a shifting of the struggle between the regime and the resistance to a higher level of acuteness. The concentration of forces aimed at restraining the regime from undertaking the liquidation campaign. This could only work if the balance of power had swayed in our direction, or at least if there were an equilibrium where generalized action from our side would threaten the regime. But in this case, the balance was on the side of the regime; concentrating our forces virtually provoked the regime to start the confrontation and at the same time limited the ability of the resistance to maneuver or move swiftly.

The lack of an offensive (or even a defensive) plan meant that the resistance was fighting blindly. The resistance forces in general fought as individuals or as separate groups without a common network, like a sectional operations room linked to a principal command. Even if such operations rooms were present, their effect was limited, for they could not control and direct the forces because they lacked an organized means of communications and because of the multiplicity of resistance battalions.

Regardless, the absence of a general and sectional plan forced the resistance to follow a method it had developed in its previous battles with the regime. This was based on dividing every city into sections, and every section into radii of action. Each radius was defended by groups belonging to one or more organizations. Naturally, such a system lacks tactical elasticity, and the radial defense lines were smashed under the weight of heavy collisions with the Army. The combat was reduced to a fight waged by individuals and separate groups. Another factor which encouraged this futile tactic is simply guerrilla training. Commandos are trained to form small groups to execute accurately planned and precise operations after submitting these operations to intensive and careful study. This style of combat was totally unsuited to the new circumstances.

The Disintegration of the Resistance Forces

The greatest defect of September was the disintegration of the resistance forces and the need for the unification of the command. The resistance used to come out of every crisis with a "unification" formula more developed than its predecessor. But all these formulas were confined to political coordination between the organizations at the level of summits and high-level cadres; real unification at the base was never achieved—and perhaps was not even sought. The last formula was for a central committee of the resistance, as well as central committees of cities and different districts. But this formula was unable to control things even in times of relative quiet. The committees did not have any commanding authority. There was no accepted leadership to guarantee those committees the power to execute their decisions or to examine the objective situation on the battlefield, so that decisions could be based on direct, visual knowledge of past mistakes. Instead, these committees had to reach their decisions on the basis of reports and information submitted by representatives of every organization—without having any means of verifying these reports. The committees charged all the organizations with the responsibility for executing their decisions through the intermediaries of their representatives on the committees. In brief, these committees had no independent existence.

Practically speaking, this situation led to an exaggeration of the resistance forces, because of the competitive relations ruling the various groups. Every battalion knew well that its political weight directly reflected its military weight—its human power and mobilization ability. Therefore, all organizations tended to exaggerate about their cadres and arms. The sum of all these exaggerations was very far from the real number.

The multiplicity of groups also had harmful effects on the political stands of the resistance. Many of these were not decided by the different organizations on the basis of precisely determined objectives and an actual study of the possibilities, but on the basis of competition. The political stand and conduct of a revolutionary organization should reflect the revolutionary trends among the masses, but they should also be more progressive. They should not be a direct reflection of the masses' temperament. But rivalry made each organization try to win the masses to its side by taking stands that coincided with the masses' temperament. Independent leadership was sacrificed. The standard of the revolutionary movement was lowered to that of the most backward sections of the masses. Moreover, the general stand of the resistance was not always determined by that of the most effective and largest forces. Several times, the stand was determined according to the attitudes of the marginal forces which moved the dominant forces due to factors of rivalry.

The problem of the multiplicity of groups is central, but it has not been understood completely in the resistance, which attributes it to the attempts of the different Arab regimes to encircle the resistance by creating battalions directly linked to them. But this interpretation evades the problem of what permits the regimes to succeed in establishing their own organizations. This problem cannot be isolated from the effect of the dispersal of the Palestinian people. Depriving the Palestinian people of an independent, united social structure and distributing them throughout the Arab world where some are relatively incorporated in the social structures of the "host" countries made the Palestinian people vulnerable to the effects of the ideological trends prevailing in the Arab world. The financial aid offered by the Arab regimes to their satellite organizations constitutes only a secondary factor.

It is of interest to note that most Arab political forces are represented in the resistance on the ideological level. There are representatives of the Arab nationalist movement, the Syrian Baath, the Iraqi Baath, the new left, Nasserism, and the Arab Communist parties. Every organization in the Palestinian field reflects the status, strength, and capabilities of the Arab force it represents. The Palestinian new left, for example, reflects the weakness of the Arab new left, which is still in the beginning of its formation. We find also that Nasserism, from the ideological point of view, occupies a dominant position in the resistance, embracing more than one organization. This is merely an expression of the supremacy of the ideological trend of Nasserism in the region.

The resistance organizations that represent the Nasserite trend are not necessarily tied to the Nasserite regime, but they bear the features of the Nasserite ideology—the theory of social coexistence, enmity with imperialism (without pushing this enmity to its logical end), participation in the game of Arab coexistence, pragmatism.

The formation of a large national front, embracing all the resistance forces, was impossible without a solid axis which could subordinate other forces to its policies and programs. Fateh, the greatest force, could not impose its dominance completely because it is tied to the balance of the Arab states. Fateh was unable to take a firm political position distinct from many of the other forces, because that would mean clashes with the Arab regimes which stood behind these forces. Add to this the fact that objective circumstances allowed the marginal organizations to stay alive and attract some support, while not allowing the greatest force to distinguish itself at the level of effectiveness. The resistance is tied, in the minds of the masses, to military operations against the Zionist enemy. But these are limited by circumstances: having to start operations from outside the occupied territories, geographical barriers (the river), the difficulty of organizing Arab residents of the occupied territories (who then become a human obstacle between the resistance and the Israelis), etc. Military operations are basically limited to the ambush and raids through the river. The small and the large organizations were equally capable of performing such operations, but even the largest could do nothing more.

Independence from the Arab regimes is a basic condition for solving the problem of multiplicity, but the period subsequent to September has shown only a further loss of independence. Some organizations have tried to exploit the contradiction between Jordan and the other Arab powers (in the first instance, Egypt and Syria), which value the resistance as a pressure urging Israel toward a peaceful settlement. Other organizations have drawn nearer the other Arab axis, Iraq and Algeria, in an attempt to obstruct the closeness between the first organizations and the states of the union. This will make the organizations lose part of their independence, because it binds together, for the first time, organizations that have never before united with certain Arab regimes, while in the past holding relations with all the Arab regimes allowed a range of maneuver and independence.

Ironically, this situation only threatens to disperse the resistance forces further. Before September, the resistance was the result of the balance of Arab states; now it risks becoming a direct extension of the Arab axis, participating in the game of Arab struggles and disputes. But only through independence does the resistance have a future. And this can only come with a sound political program and strategy, built upon the complementarity of the Palestinian and Arab struggles.

PHOTOGRAPHS BY JEFFREY BLANKFORT

Cover   *PLO women's militia training*
22-23   *Women waiting for water at Schneller camp/
        near Amman, August 1970*
114-15 *Fateh graduation/Amman, August 1970*
121   *Fateh militia graduation/Amman, August 1970*
122-23 *Fateh ashbal training/Bakaah camp (Jordan),
        August 1970*
124   *Fateh ashbal training/Bakaah camp (Jordan),
        August 1970*
179   *PLO women's militia*
180-81 *DPFLP women's militia training/Amman,
        July 1970*
182   *Women's militia at rally/Amman, July 1970*
209   *Cholera immunization by Association of
        Palestinian-Jordanian women, project of
        DPFLP/Bakaah camp, August 1970*
210   *Meeting of Association of Palestinian-Jordanian
        women, project of DPFLP/Amman, July 1970*
215   *Office wall at al-Hadaf (organ of PFLP)/Beirut*
220-21 *Palestinian militia/Amman, July 1970*
249   *Yasser Arafat at Fateh graduation/Amman,
        August 1970*
250   *Agricultural worker from Ghor Valley/Bakaah
        camp (Jordan), August 1970*
285   *PLO women's militia training near Schneller
        camp/Amman, August 1970*
286   *Fateh ashbal training/Telesata camp (Lebanon),
        July 1970*